Reason
and
Passion

Reason and Passion

Justice Brennan's Enduring Influence

EDITED BY *E. Joshua Rosenkranz*

AND *Bernard Schwartz*

A Project of the Brennan Center for Justice at NYU School of Law

W · W · NORTON & COMPANY · NEW YORK · LONDON

The text and display of this book are composed in Adobe Garamond.
Composition and manufacturing by the Haddon Craftsmen, Inc.
Book design by Jack Meserole.

Library of Congress Cataloging-in-Publication Data

Reason and passion : Justice Brennan's enduring influence / edited
by E. Joshua Rosenkranz and Bernard Schwartz.
p.   cm.
ISBN 0-393-04110-7
1. Brennan, William J. (William Joseph), 1906–   .   2. United
States—Constitutional law—Interpretation and construction.
3. Political questions and judicial power—United States. 4. Civil
rights—United States.   I. Rosenkranz, E. Joshua.   II. Schwartz,
Bernard, 1923–   .
KF8745.B68R43   1997
347.73'2634—dc20
[B]
[347.3073534]
[B]   96-43133
CIP

W. W. Norton & Company, Inc., 500 Fifth Avenue, New York, N.Y. 10110
http://www.wwnorton.com

W. W. Norton & Company Ltd., 10 Coptic Street, London WC1A 1PU

2 3 4 5 6 7 8 9 0

Contents

Criminal Justice

Equality

Government

Contents

Perspectives

Preface

The Supreme Court of the United States is far more than the usual court. The Court is primarily a political institution, in whose keeping lies the destiny of a mighty nation. Its decrees mark the boundaries between the great branches of government; it allocates power between the federal government and the states; and it regulates the relationship between government and the individual. A judge on such a tribunal has an opportunity to leave an imprint on the life of the nation that no mere master of common law possibly could. To be a judge, endowed with all the omnipotence of justice, is certainly among life's noblest callings; but the mere common-law judge, even in a preeminently legal polity such as that in Britain, cannot begin to compare in power and prestige with a justice of our Supreme Court. A judge who is regent over what is done in the legislative and executive branches—the *deus ex machina* who has the final word in the constitutional system—has attained one of the ultimate summits of human authority.

Only a handful of men in all our history have made so manifest a mark on their own age and on ages still to come as Justice William J. Brennan, Jr. History will rank him with Justice Oliver Wendell Holmes and Chief Justice John Marshall in his impact upon both the law and society, and second to none as the Supreme Court's most beloved member.

Many think of Justice Brennan simply as an ardent defender of the press or opponent of the death penalty. The truth is that the Brennan reach was far broader. In his thirty-four years on the Court, he reshaped entire fields of the law that affect us all—civil liberties, race relations, family, privacy, crime, religion, race, poverty, politics, and much more.

In so doing, Justice Brennan crafted an intricate and sweeping legacy, based largely on his premise that constitutional interpretation demands equal parts of "reason and passion"—a command of law and logic coupled with a comprehension of the often unintended manner in which laws can affect real people with their own hopes and aspirations. Only when infused with these two ingredients, he believed, could the Constitution fulfill its primary purpose of protecting the dignity of the individual.

Justice Brennan's legacy, though embattled, has largely withstood two decades of withering attack from the changing membership of the Court, as well as from Congress and presidents. This book is both a tribute to Justice Brennan and a survey of his enduring influence on American law and life. The authors are well-known writers, journalists, judges, lawyers, scholars, and others. They show how pervasive Justice Brennan's role has been in transforming the law to meet what Holmes called "felt necessities of the times."

"The history of the United States," says Charles Warren at the outset of his now-classic history of the Supreme Court, "has been written not merely in the halls of Congress, in the Executive offices and on the battle field, but to a great extent in the chambers of the Supreme Court of the United States." Justice Brennan's vital role in the history of the nation is amply demonstrated by this book.

EJR
BS

Foreword

William H. Rehnquist

It is a great pleasure to write this foreword for *Reason and Passion,* which so eloquently captures the profound influence of Justice William J. Brennan, Jr.

I well remember my first meeting with Bill Brennan; Lewis Powell and I were newly appointed to the Court, and Chief Justice Burger had invited us to join the other members for lunch on a day shortly before we were to be sworn in. I had the natural awe of any lawyer with respect to the members of the Supreme Court, and wondered just what kind of an occasion it would be. But the lunch could not have been more cordial and friendly, and the warmest and most cordial of all was Bill Brennan.

From that day in early 1972 until he retired in the summer of 1990, I had the pleasure of serving with him as a colleague on the Court. I was one of three chief justices and twenty associate justices who shared this experience. Each of us was the beneficiary of his legendary warmth and charm, and of his strongly held and incisively presented views on important constitutional questions.

At times I am sure that Bill Brennan felt I did not benefit enough from the views he expressed, since he and I often ended up on opposite sides of significant decisions of the Court. But not only those who agree with a position that is ably expounded benefit from the exposition; so do those who end up disagreeing with the position. By this process of elucidation through criticism and disagreement, the first draft of a prevailing opinion may be refined and revised by the input of others to make a better product than any solo writing would have been.

Bill Brennan's near record-breaking tenure on the Court spanned a time of fundamental disagreements among the justices about questions of constitutional law. But these disputes were by no means confined to

The author is chief justice of the United States. He served with Justice Brennan for eighteen years.

the time in which he served; they have been going on at least since the beginning of this century. During other periods in the Court's history, these sorts of disputes had seriously affected the personal relations between justices on various sides of the questions. But to his great credit, Bill Brennan never allowed even profound disagreement over important questions of constitutional law to affect the civility and friendship which he extended to every one of his colleagues. His colleagues, responding to his feeling for them, reciprocated with feelings of friendship and admiration for him. Bill Brennan was the intellectual leader of those espousing his views during my time of service with him, and that position should earn him a high place in the annals of our Court. His determination not to allow disputes over the law to become a basis for personal disparagement or dislike should earn him an equally high one.

PILLARS OF JUSTICE

BRENNAN OPINIONS

1956-1990

©1990 HERBLOCK

Setting
the
Stage

My Life on the Court

WILLIAM J. BRENNAN, JR.

I can scarcely admit to myself that forty years have passed since President Eisenhower appointed me to the Supreme Court of the United States, and six have passed since I retired. Some authors in this book have observed that my thirty-four years on the Court nearly broke the record, but those exhilarating years passed in a twinkle of an eye. I was startled when others pointed out that I served with 22 of the 108 justices who ever served on the Court. I never considered them en masse; I counted each, individually, as a cherished friend who taught me about law and life.

When you get to be ninety, you learn to stay away from numbers. But I cannot resist a comment on what my dear, dear friend David Souter calls "the gravitational pull of the Brennan total."

David tallies up "the sheer number, the mass of opinions" that bear my name. Gazing up from my desk at the forty-odd shelf feet of my judicial opinions all bound neatly in red, I must reluctantly acknowledge that "mass" is apt description. The 461 majority opinions. The 425 dissents and 474 other opinions. Yet each opinion must also be viewed independently. For each was shaped by the heroic efforts of litigants and judges, the profound insights of scholars, countless hours of impassioned debate among my colleagues on the bench and my law clerks in chambers, and, I admit, quite a bit of hand-wringing on my own.

This last point underscores what I will, at the risk of sounding ungracious, declare to be the fundamental flaw of this book. I am inexpressibly grateful to all the authors who contributed to this volume. I am deeply, deeply touched. Each essay is more eloquent, more flattering, than the next. I would love to believe the authors are writing about me when they write collectively about "Justice Brennan's Enduring Influence." But the truth is they are not. The truth, which I cannot stress strongly enough, is that I served on a court of nine. The strides we made on the Court during my tenure we made as a team. The majority opinions that bear my name could not have existed without my colleagues' input and votes. I was never alone, except occasionally in dissent. And there is no "Brennan legacy" that can be teased out and considered on its own merits.

I am often asked to identify my favorite opinion from those red volumes. I have steadfastly refused, for that would be almost as impossible as picking a favorite child. I will, however, say that high on the list of the Court's accomplishments during my tenure were a panoply of opinions protecting and promoting individual rights and human dignity.

As I have said many times and in many ways, our Constitution is a charter of human rights and human dignity. It is a bold commitment by a people to the ideal of dignity protected through law. The vision is deeply moving. It inspires our own citizens and countless millions abroad—from figures as august as Brian Walsh on the Supreme Court of Ireland and the European Court of Human Rights to David Halberstam's anonymous Romanian who exults, "We are going to have . . . the same freedoms you have in the West!"

Just as notions of dignity have changed with time, so too has our charter. Some disagree with my perspective, but I approached my responsibility to interpret the Constitution in the only way I could—as a twentieth-century American concerned about what the Constitution and the Bill of Rights mean to us in our time. The genius of the Constitution rests not in any static meaning it may have had in a world that is dead and gone, but in the adaptability of its great principles to cope with current problems and present needs. As Justice Benjamin Cardozo expressed it in his classic book *The Nature of the Judicial Process,* "a *constitution* states or ought to state not rules for the passing hour, but principles for an expanding future." To be "true to its function," he continued, it must never lose "its power of adaptation, its suppleness, its play."

Only from this perspective was the Court able to erect some of liberty's most enduring monuments, such as the classic decision, shortly before I took the bench, that a public school cannot slam its doors on pupils based on their skin color. Thanks to the evolving understanding of the Constitution, no future child is likely to confront the same first view of the Supreme Court that Bob Carter poignantly describes—a view of a justice, quite literally, "turning [his] back on black people and manifesting indifference to their needs and aspirations."

In my time, it was the "living" Constitution, infused with a vision of human dignity, that prohibited local police from ransacking a home without a warrant (in 1961) and forbade state prosecutors to compel an accused to convict himself with his own words (in 1964). Only the freedom to reinterpret constitutional language enabled us to make the leap described by Lani Guinier and Pam Karlan, ruling (in 1962 and 1964) that each American should have an equal vote. Only with the faith in a malleable Constitution could Ruth Ginsburg and Wendy Williams have conceived of developing the string of test cases (beginning in the 1970s) in which we ruled that laws could not treat men and women differently. The same essential vision girded our enduring ruling, described so eloquently by Tony Lewis, that the press must have protection to report on matters of public concern (in 1964). It was the Constitution's "suppleness" that allowed us to conclude (in 1970) that the government may not cut a welfare recipient's lifeline without first holding a hearing, a ruling so rich that Steve Breyer, Tony Mauro, and Jeff Toobin could see in it three different meanings.

The essays in this book depict how these rulings emerged out of everyday human dramas. Consider the picture of the Cleveland police breaking down Dollree Mapp's door, ransacking her home, and then violently twisting her arm and handcuffing her because she dared to examine their phony warrant. Or think of Esther Lett and her four nieces, who were rushed to the emergency room after eating putrid food out of garbage cans—all because the welfare agency cut off their benefits before they had a chance to prove the agency had made a grievous mistake. Imagine Sharron Frontiero, who worked just as hard as her male counterparts in the air force, but received inferior benefits. Or what about Charles Baker and thousands of other citizens of Tennessee cities who seethed about having twenty-four times less voting power than their rural neighbors. At the heart of each drama was a person who cried out for nothing more than common human dignity. In each case, our Constitution intervened to provide the cloak of dignity.

If this book describes a coherent legacy, it belongs not to me but to these courageous Americans who dared to fight so others would not have to.

That is not to say that this string of cases achieved a comprehensive definition of the constitutional ideal of human dignity. We do not yet have justice for all who do not partake in the abundance of American life. We are still striving toward that goal, and doubtless it will be an eternal quest.

One area of Supreme Court law more than any other besmirches the constitutional vision of human dignity. My old friend and colleague Harry Blackmun called it the "machinery of death": It is the death penalty.

Although the Court was unmoved by the evidence presented to it in 1987, it was then, and it remains today, an uncontroverted fact that the races of a capital defendant and the victim are among the most powerful predictors of whether the defendant lives or dies. The statistics, some of which I reviewed in my dissent, paint a chilling portrait of racial discrimination. Yet racial disparity is but one of a host of inequalities that inhere in the death penalty. Another is the stunning lack of counsel adequately equipped to afford capital defendants a fair opportunity to defend their lives in the courtroom, and the puzzling move to defund the most effective defenders. Equally disconcerting is the growing pressure to dispense with independent judicial review of death sentences, even though, by conservative estimates, the reversal rate of capital convictions and sentences is 45 percent.

Yet the ultimate problem is more fundamental. I have long believed that the death penalty is in all circumstances a barbaric and inhuman punishment that violates our Constitution. Even the most vile murderer does not release the state from its constitutional obligation to respect human dignity, for the state does not honor the victim by emulating the murderer who took his life. The fatal infirmity of capital punishment is that it treats members of the human race as nonhumans, as objects to be toyed with and discarded.

The machinery chugs on unabated, belching out its dehumanizing product. It is distressing. But I refuse to despair. I know, one day, the Supreme Court will outlaw the death penalty. Permanently. I hope I will live to celebrate the day, but I am supremely confident the day *will* come.

If our free society is to endure, and I know it will, those who govern must recognize that the Framers of the Constitution limited their power in order to preserve human dignity and the air of freedom which is our proudest heritage. The task of protecting these principles does not rest solely with nine Supreme Court justices, or even with the cadre of state and federal judges. We all share the burden.

As David Souter observes, it is too early to know how history will judge what we tried to do while I served on the Court. But we must not await history's verdict. Too much work remains. Too many injustices persist. Too many wrongs cry out to be righted. These are obligations we cannot ignore and dare not neglect.

Perhaps my ultimate reflection is unremarkable: Continuous hard work is needed if we are to realize the true potential of our Constitution and its Bill of Rights. To paraphrase Thomas Jefferson, eternal vigilance is the price of liberty and dignity—two of the true measures of freedom.

If I have drawn one lesson in my ninety years it is this: To strike another blow for freedom allows a man to walk a little taller and raise his head a little higher. And while he can, he must.

The Common Man as Uncommon Man

David Halberstam

The beginning was not exactly auspicious. When the appointment was announced it was clear that he was, as far as the knowledgeable world of Supreme Court insiders was concerned, the anonymous man. Which meant in addition, it appeared, that he was the undeserving man as well, since if he was deserving they all would have known of him. Not surprisingly, the news of William J. Brennan's appointment to the Supreme Court of the United States of America was greeted primarily by expressions of doubt. Indeed, the more knowledgeable the source, it can safely be said, the greater the doubts about Brennan's capacity to serve on so august a tribunal. He was hardly one of the legendary names of the legal profession. He was not one of those men (and now women) who are marked for their brilliance early on, and who, even as they are finishing law school, are spoken about with an unnatural (and often undeserved) reverence as future Supreme Court justices, and whose names as they reach their forties are inevitably on the short list of potential justices put forth whenever there is a vacancy on the Court.

By contrast, William J. Brennan was a relatively minor figure on a state supreme court, hardly the most luminescent figure even there. He seemed to exist in those days very much in the shadow of the seemingly far more brilliant and better connected Arthur Vanderbilt. Of Bill Brennan it appeared that the best that could be said early on was that he was something of a workhorse. Even worse, those who did not approve said, his appointment was quite possibly *political.* For it was the fall of 1956, and there was a presidential election on. Dwight Eisenhower was running against Adlai Stevenson. Sherman Minton had just resigned from the Court for reasons of health. There had already been some pressure

The author has written numerous books, including a highly praised trilogy on power in America. He has won every major journalistic award, including the Pulitzer Prize.

for Ike to appoint a Catholic to the Court (particularly, pressure from Cardinal Francis Spellman, reminding us once again to be careful of what we ask for since we may well get it).

By chance Herb Brownell, Ike's attorney general, had attended a conference earlier that year devoted to the issue of modernizing all court procedures. What could be more harmless and less controversial? Everyone, after all, is for better, more expeditious, and more modern judicial procedures. Brennan had spoken there and made a good impression on Brownell, one of Ike's top political advisers. Ironically, Brennan had filled in at the last minute for the scheduled speaker, the far better known—and far more accomplished—Vanderbilt. A bona fide Republican, who was the true architect of the modernization of New Jersey's court system, Vanderbilt hoped passionately, now that a Republican was finally in the White House, to gain his rightful place on the Supreme Court. But Vanderbilt had become ill at the last minute. After that Brownell had started thinking of Brennan as a potential Court appointee. He seemed able, reasonably young, moderate—his principal work had been corporate—and he was a Catholic from a swing industrial state that Ike would need to carry. If he was a Democrat, he did not appear to be a particularly liberal or offensive one; why, a man as solid as Arthur Vanderbilt had apparently vouched for him by putting him on the New Jersey Supreme Court; and it was not the worst thing in those days to pick a centrist Catholic Democrat, a potential means of inviting other Catholics to Ike's cause that November.

Checking out a potential Supreme Court nominee in those pre-fax, pre-Nexis, pre–e-mail days was a great deal simpler. The ferocious politicization of the process, as the Court became ever more the central instrument of an increasingly bitter cultural debate, had not yet begun. The process was almost quaint and somewhat antiquated. Only the mildest scrutiny of Brennan took place. Nothing very damaging was turned up. Joseph McCarthy did not appear to like him very much and seemed to take offense from two of his speeches against witch hunting, but this was 1956, two years after the Senate had turned against McCarthy, and with a Republican president installed, McCarthy had already been cast aside by his own party and was in the final stages of his alcohol-driven decline. To the Eisenhower people Brennan appeared to be a political centrist who would probably go along with the administration's general vision, whatever in fact that was, for Ike was alternately quite liberal in some of his attitudes and then, in other areas, even more conservative than Bob Taft.

The towering figures at Harvard Law School who were supposed to know who Bill Brennan was—he had after all gone to Harvard Law— and who naturally expected to give the imprimatur of their clan to any Supreme Court nominee, were most demonstrably not impressed by the appointment. Paul Freund, one of the law school's most cerebral figures, a principal Felix Frankfurter protégé, and a man who, like Arthur Vanderbilt, was to endure a lifetime on the short list for the Court but never to be nominated, wrote to Frankfurter of his doubts about the choice of this anonymous law school classmate. The most critical evidence that Brennan was probably mundane—since brilliant students always recognize other brilliant students very early on—was that neither Freund nor his friend Milton Katz, another star in that class, even remembered Brennan. "I am chagrined to say that I don't remember him as a classmate," Freund wrote Frankfurter.

Frankfurter replied in kind, having checked Brennan out through the Harvard network and found that he had not even taken his course in constitutional law. That was another strike against him. "Maybe he gave himself the pleasure of listening in," Frankfurter wrote archly. More typical was the comment of Fred Rodell, the liberal Yale professor, who wrote his friend Justice William O. Douglas of his own doubts about Brennan, because he was "chosen for all the wrong reasons." Perhaps even Bill Brennan shared that vision of himself as the unlikeliest of nominees. He was, he said at the moment he joined the Court, the mule at the Kentucky Derby. "I don't expect to distinguish myself but I do expect to benefit by the associations," he added.

How then, as we come to the end of this century and the end of a singular era in American life which saw the dramatic expansion of the mandate of the Court, particularly in the area of personal liberty, do we come to accept the fact that it was more than just the Warren Court that so profoundly changed American life? How did this quiet, self-effacing man of surpassing humanity and modesty, and with an intellect defter and more forceful than almost anyone realized, become quite likely the dominating figure of the Court over more than a third of a century, and equally likely the most influential political figure in America in the postwar years? Or, as federal Judge John J. Gibbons noted, Brennan was "more humane than Holmes, broader in outlook than Brandeis, more practical and flexible than Black, a finer scholar than Warren, more eloquent than Hughes, more painstaking than any of them. He appears, in other words, to be the most outstanding justice in our century."

Part of the answer, I think, is in the almost unique nature of the man himself: He has been in our lifetime, perhaps more than anyone else I can think of, including his friend and colleague Earl Warren, the common man as uncommon man. No one who has ever met him can be other than moved by the powerful and enduring quality of his humanity. He is a man defined by his own innate decency and kindness. His constant courtesy and sweetness are no small things. They are a central part of him, and they were as important to him when he was at the height of his power on the Court as they were when he began his professional journey. He has always been unaffected by position, and he remains incapable of posturing. With others all too often in the rise to a position of power, personal humanity calcifies, and humility evaporates. If truth is the first casualty of warfare, then modesty is the first casualty of judicial empowerment. But Bill Brennan has never forgotten the most elemental truth of social relations—in order to gain dignity it is important to bestow it on others. He has always treated everyone he meets, regardless of station, with a human grace that is absolute. He is always more curious about you and what you think, it sometimes seems, than you are about him.

Once, some fifteen years ago, I took a young friend of mine named Gerry Krovatin to visit the Justice in Nantucket at the small cottage Brennan rented every summer (until, to the bitter disappointment of a number of us, the proprietor raised the rent so spectacularly that he was not able to afford it and did not return to our island). Gerry was then in his mid-twenties, just starting out as a litigator in Newark. He was a great Brennan aficionado, and this day happened to be his birthday, so the visit had been arranged as a birthday present. He was slotted for thirty minutes with the Justice. I came along, later very glad that I did, for I watched one of the most graceful human performances I have ever seen in my life. The session did not last thirty minutes. It lasted two hours. And while my young friend was able to ask Brennan a few questions about certain cases, the morning was far more about Krovatin than it was about Brennan. The Justice peppered him with questions, about Newark, about lawyers and judges they both knew, about what my young friend wanted to do with his life. It was a marvelous morning. The distance between them, so great at the beginning, had narrowed completely at the end; instead of being Supreme Court justice and young apprentice lawyer, they could as easily have been two young law school classmates who had not seen each other in a few years. Bill Brennan not only managed to pick up a very great deal of information that morning, but he cast his special grace upon Gerry Krovatin, making him feel intelligent and valuable, and Bill Brennan managed as well, I suspect, to make himself feel just a bit younger.

Looking back now it is easy to have some sympathy for someone as cerebral and admirable as Paul Freund for not understanding Brennan's uncommon qualities earlier on. For Brennan was the classic late bloomer, not unlike Warren, and not unlike the president himself who appointed (and later disparaged) both. Brennan was a man whose intelligence was practical rather than abstract, driven not so much by theory as by a simplicity of humanity. The more he was exposed to, the more that was demanded of him, the more he grew in both stature and intellect, and the more he expanded his own personal vision of American life. His was the triumph of common sense and innate human empathy over pure theoretical intellectual firepower, the kind of firepower which tends to demonstrate itself early on, but often atrophies because an individual's humanity is not worthy of his intellect. With Bill Brennan the miracle was that the two were always in sync. He was always able to see the best in others around him.

The talents and beliefs of his colleagues and even his adversaries almost never bothered him and certainly never threatened him. As he became more and more influential, he did not, like so many before him, change and become a prisoner of his ego. He never lost his empathy for those who were different. These qualities—they are, for lack of a more sophisticated phrase, the qualities of goodness—do not necessarily sound so uncommon, but they are uncommon among the powerful. In addition, they became in time a very valuable professional tool, for they helped make him an uncommonly effective member of the Court, with a rare ability to bring others of seemingly differing views to a consensus that a less graceful and generous-spirited man might not have been able to do.

The other quality which sets him apart is that he is in the rarest sense a witness to the two very different Americas which have existed in this century and which in very different form still exist today. He came to the Court a little more than a decade after the end of World War II, as this country was surging into what became known as the American Century, but he has roots in the simpler, poorer, far more austere America which existed earlier in the century, an America economically and socially far crueler, where only a small percentage of people enjoyed the affluence and dignity of middle-class life. If he eventually became, out of his own hard work and good fortune, and out of the general rising level of affluence in America, part of the class which takes the fairness of the law for granted, he started out in a class far less favored and in an era where there was a powerful sense that the law belonged to the rich and powerful.

Nothing less than an economic revolution took place in his lifetime. If the benefits were obvious in the years after World War II, then the revolution itself had begun with the coming of Henry Ford's assembly line and the discovery of cheap oil in the Southwest of the United States at the beginning of the century. The combination was to usher in the most dramatic change imaginable in the quality of life in the United States for ordinary people. The oil culture of the twentieth century, as Naohiro Amaya, a brilliant Japanese intellectual, called the era, replaced the coal culture of the nineteenth century. A significantly more benign, more just capitalism succeeded the harsher, less generous one of the previous age, one in which workers were doomed to live in perpetual economic serfdom. Workers became for the first time the beneficiaries of their labor and received as well the dignity which came with middle-class life. The supremely affluent and powerful America which came together after World War II was produced by that age—and by the devastation which was wrought by two world wars elsewhere. We were rich in a poor world. Not only was America rich, but, perhaps equally important, never before had the wealth of a nation been shared so equitably by so many ordinary people.

If that prosperous, ever more confident country was the America which Bill Brennan served in his historic tour on the Court, then he knew all too well the harsher, more austere America which had preceded it. Like Earl Warren, some fifteen years older, his family's knowledge of that more wretched era was all too real. It was one of the many bonds he and Warren enjoyed; both their fathers had been union men in an age when the essential fabric of American capitalism was bitterly and violently and more often than not successfully anti-union. If anything, the Warren home had it worse. Matt Warren, a railroad car repairman, had been severely punished for his union activities. His had been a particularly bitter life, and Earl Warren in later years would tell friends that when he eventually read Dickens's *Oliver Twist* he thought of his own father's life.

The life of Bill Brennan's parents was not that cruel, but it was hard enough. They were, the son liked to point out, a bit luckier than most of their neighbors. William Brennan, Sr., like his wife, had come from County Roscommon in Ireland to escape the relentless, crushing poverty there; the senior Brennan had arrived here in 1892 when he was twenty, and he worked, fittingly enough, since this was still the coal age, as a coal stoker in Trenton before moving on to shovel coal into the giant furnace at the Ballantine Brewery in Newark. This was a time when the Irish were still the out Americans, and when signs warned "No Irish Need Apply" and "No Dogs or Irish Allowed."

If Bill Brennan, Sr., eventually became something of a prominent political figure in the Newark area, he nonetheless had started his life with nothing going for him but his ambition and his willingness to work hard. The work of a coal stoker was brutally hard, long unsparing twelve-hour days of labor under the most dangerous and unpleasant conditions imaginable, with virtually no benefits or protection. There was in the Brennan family no shortage of firsthand knowledge of men who had been maimed and crippled by their work, and of families left destitute by the cruelty of the fates of the workplace. The senior Brennan was unusually ambitious and independent, and trusted by his peers; in time he became an officer in the union which represented the coal workers. Then he served as a reform politician in Newark. Because of his success, his family became neither poor nor rich.

Those years shaped the son profoundly. Though he eventually became the beneficiary of a good education at both Penn and Harvard Law and though America itself was a far more affluent society with more protection given to working people, as a grown man Bill Brennan could look at working people and see his own father and his fellow coal stokers. When he looked at families without social benefits, he could remember the devastation caused around him as a boy, by accidents and lay-offs. And when he heard older and more established Americans voice ethnic prejudice in the most casual way against the newer and more uncertain and less rooted ones, he could remember that the same things were said about the Irish, his own people.

Bill Brennan eventually went from outsider to insider, from the son of the Ballantine coal stoker to a seat on the Supreme Court, but he never forgot where he came from, and he never forgot the fragility of the lives of ordinary people. Nor did he forget the aspirations of his poor Irish-American neighbors, people often scorned in those days by others more senior in residence here, who saw only the lesser marginalized quality of the lives of these newcomers, not their hopes and their dreams. He did not, and this was crucial, lose his faith in the hopes and possibilities of ordinary people. One of his favorite quotes, one he liked to pass on to journalists and law clerks alike throughout the years, came from the Yeats play *Cathleen Ni Hoolihan.* In it an old woman leaves a house. "Did you see an old woman going down the path?" asks Bridget, one of the characters in the play. "No, I did not," says Patrick, who had just arrived after the old woman left, "but I saw a young girl and she had the walk of a queen."

In those postwar years as America became richer and more affluent it also became involuntarily more confident as a society. Inevitably in this raw new confidence it turned to issues of social and economic justice. No one was more clearly an architect of this new era than the man who had once described himself as a mule at the Kentucky Derby. Bill Brennan and his colleagues on the Court ended up pushing the rest of the society forward to face what were often unwanted issues about personal levels of freedom. They embarked on a historic journey, doing nothing less than setting the outer limits on the concept of freedom for their fellow citizens. That his greatest contribution is an expanded vision of personal liberty is no small thing to say about any man, and particularly a man so seemingly ordinary. For that we all owe more gratitude than we realize.

This process is often difficult and painful, and it often makes us contrary and irritable with each other. When the pain seems too great, we should try and remember that it is this very experiment, this determination to become a just and free society, which sets us apart from so many other nations, particularly from those we claim to abhor the most. For the process of extending freedom to everyone—including people who are often not very likable—is not an easy one. We tend to forget that our greatest export to the rest of the world is not our automobiles, or our new modern high-tech software, or our medical devices, or even our movies and our popular music. The truth is that our greatest export may very simply be our concept of freedom for all citizens, and our belief that it is both a worthy and an attainable goal. What we take for granted, others see as the most precious thing America has to offer.

I was reminded of this some seven years ago when Soviet communism was collapsing; even Romania, the most Stalinist of states, it appeared, was likely to enjoy some measure of freedom. One night I was watching ABC News. An ABC reporter had managed to interview an ordinary Romanian citizen who spoke half in tears and half in joy: "We are going to have freedom of speech! A free press! A free mass media! A political system which is pluralistic!" For a moment the man seemed to be so overcome by his emotions that he was unable to talk. And then he spoke again: "The same freedoms you have in the West we are going to have. We are going to be free! Free!" I think Bill Brennan would know exactly what he was talking about.

How Justice Brennan
Changed America

BERNARD SCHWARTZ

If we look at justices in terms of their role in the decision process, William J. Brennan, Jr., was actually the most influential associate justice in Supreme Court history. Indeed, according to a recent biography, "more than any justice in United States history, Brennan would change the way Americans live."

To understand the Brennan impact, we should go back to 1956, the year the Justice was appointed. The America of that day was very different from America today. Perhaps, on the surface, the country was mirrored by Norman Rockwell and *Ozzie and Harriet*. Underneath, however, it was a far different place. America was still the home of Jim Crow, the third degree and the chain gang, the rotten borough, the poorhouse, and self-devouring individualism. True, with its 1954 *Brown* desegregation decision, the Supreme Court had just begun to ensure that equal protection was more than a hortatory slogan for racial minorities. For years after it was decided, however, *Brown* was more an *ought* than an *is*—a constitutional desideratum that did not square with the dual school system and pervasive segregation that remained untouched by the decision.

Justice Brennan did not, of course, personally change all this. But he did play a crucial role in the Court that transformed America—the Warren Court—and its successor under Chief Justice Burger, which, despite expectations to the contrary, confirmed and, in places, even extended the Warren revolution. What Brennan did was to serve as the catalyst for some of the most significant decisions during his tenure. He was the leader of the Court's liberal wing under Chief Justices Warren, Burger, and Rehnquist. More important, the Brennan jurisprudence set

The author is Chapman Distinguished Professor of Law at the University of Tulsa College of Law.

the pattern for much of American legal thought toward the end of this century. So pervasive was the Brennan influence that the English periodical *The Economist* headed its story on his retirement *A lawgiver goes.*

Before his 1956 appointment, Brennan had been a judge in New Jersey, rising from the state trial court to its highest bench. "One of the things," Justice Felix Frankfurter once said, "that laymen, even lawyers, do not always understand is indicated by the question you hear so often: 'Does a man become any different when he puts on a gown?' I say, 'If he is any good, he does.' " Certainly Justice Brennan on the Supreme Court proved a complete surprise to those who saw him as a middle-of-the-road judge. He quickly became a firm adherent of the activist philosophy and a principal architect of the Warren Court's jurisprudence. Brennan had been Frankfurter's student at Harvard Law School; yet if Frankfurter expected the new justice to continue his pupilage, he was soon disillusioned. Justice Brennan himself told the story of how, after Brennan had joined the Warren Court's activist wing, Frankfurter quipped, "I always encourage my students to think for themselves, but Brennan goes too far!"

On the Warren Court, Brennan soon became the Chief Justice's closest colleague. The two were completely dissimilar in appearance. Brennan is small and feisty, almost leprechaun-like in appearance, yet he has a hearty bluffness and an ability to put people at ease. Brennan's unassuming appearance and manner masked a keen intelligence. He was perhaps the hardest worker on the Court. Unlike many justices with strong views, Brennan was always willing to mold his language to meet his colleagues' objections, a talent that would become his hallmark on the Court. Thus, it was he who suggested the compromise approach in the landmark *Bakke* decision, as well as the intermediate standard of review that now governs in gender discrimination cases.

ACTIVISM VERSUS RESTRAINT

Roscoe Pound tells us that there is an antinomy inherent in every legal system: The law must be stable and yet it cannot stand still. It is the task of the judge to reconcile these two conflicting elements. In doing so, jurists tend to stress one principle or the other. Stability and change may be the twin sisters of the law, but few judges can keep an equipoise between the two.

Justice Brennan never pretended to try to maintain the balance. He was firmly on the side of change, leading the Supreme Court's effort to enable the law to cope with rapid societal transformation. Before Brennan's appointment, the Court had been divided between two antagonistic judicial philosophies that differed sharply over the proper role of the judge. In simplified terms, the division was between judicial activism and judicial self-restraint. The rule of restraint had been the handiwork of that seminal figure of modern American law, Justice Holmes.

"The pace of change," Toynbee tells us, "has been accelerating constantly." That has been particularly true in recent years. In the society of the second half of this century, the issues confronting the courts have also begun to change. Judges like Brennan came to believe that even the Holmes canon could not suffice as the bedrock of judicial review. Brennan was willing to follow the rule of restraint in the economic area. It was, indeed, an opinion that Brennan wrote, although it was unsigned (*New Orleans v. Dukes* [1976]), that confirmed the Burger Court's deferential approach in cases involving economic regulation.

Notwithstanding this judicial deference in the economic realm, Brennan believed that the Bill of Rights provisions protecting personal liberties imposed more active obligations on the judges. When a law infringed upon the personal rights the Bill of Rights guaranteed, Brennan refused to defer to the legislative judgment that the law was necessary. Brennan rejected judicial restraint because he believed that it thwarted effective performance of the Court's constitutional role. Judicial abnegation, in the Brennan view, meant all too often judicial abdication of the duty to enforce constitutional guarantees.

JURISPRUDENCE

A judge's jurisprudence is revealed in his decisions and opinions. The Brennan concept of law is derived primarily from his important opinions. These will be summarized here.

Apportionment. Chief Justice Warren wrote in his *Memoirs* that *Baker v. Carr* (1962) "was the most important case of my tenure on the Court." It ruled the federal courts competent to entertain an action challenging legislative apportionments. Before *Baker*, the Court had held that legislative apportionment presented a "political question" beyond judicial competence. In *Baker*, the Brennan opinion overruled the earlier cases and held that attacks on legislative apportionments could be heard and decided by the federal courts. The *Baker* opinion was the foundation for the principle that the Constitution lays down an "equal population" principle for legislative apportionment. Under this principle, substantially equal representation is demanded for all citizens.

Brennan's *Baker* opinion worked an electoral reform comparable to that achieved by Parliament when it translated the English Reform Movement's program into the statute book. The result has been a virtual transformation of the political landscape, with voting power shifted from rural areas to the urban and suburban concentrations in which most Americans have come to live.

First Amendment.   In *New York Times v. Sullivan* (1964), Brennan gave a new perspective to freedom of expression by ruling that the Constitution confined governmental power to fix the bounds of libelous speech. A public official had recovered substantial libel damages against a newspaper. The Brennan opinion reversed, holding that the publication was protected by the First Amendment, which required a "rule that prohibits a public official from recovering damages for a defamatory falsehood relating to his official conduct unless he proves that the statement was made with 'actual malice'—that is, with knowledge that it was false or reckless disregard of whether it was false or not."

New York Times limits the power to award damages for libel in actions by public officials against those who criticize their official conduct. The Brennan opinion was based upon the "general proposition that freedom of expression upon public questions is secured by the First Amendment." It gave effect, Brennan said, to the "profound national commitment to the principle that debate on public issues should be uninhibited, robust, and wide-open, and that it may well include vehement, caustic, and sometimes unpleasantly sharp attacks on government and public officials."

Desegregation.   *Brown* may have sounded the legal tocsin for Jim Crow. But the decision remained a virtual dead letter for years. By that time, as Justice Black put it, "The original plaintiffs have doubtless all passed high school age," but they were still not able to attend white high schools. It was the Brennan opinion in *Green v. County School Board* (1968) that corrected the situation fourteen years after *Brown.* The Brennan declaration that the time for "deliberate speed" had run out was the strongest statement since *Brown* itself. *Green* required elimination of the "dual [school] system, part 'white' and part 'Negro.' " It was not enough for school boards merely to remove the legal prohibitions against black attendance in white schools. Instead, school boards "were . . . clearly charged with the affirmative duty to take whatever steps might be necessary to convert to a unitary system in which racial discrimination would be eliminated root and branch."

Brennan's opinion imposed the affirmative duty to immediately dismantle all dual school systems—a duty that required school authorities to "come forward with a plan that . . . promises realistically to work *now.*" If they did not come forward with such a plan, the courts could do so. From the *Brown* invalidation of segregation, the Court had moved to the *Green* affirmative duty to provide a fully integrated school system. Warren's note to Brennan upon joining the *Green* opinion says it all: "When this opinion is handed down, the traffic light will have changed from *Brown* to *Green.* Amen!"

Strict Scrutiny Review. In legal impact, no Brennan opinion was more far-reaching than *Shapiro v. Thompson* (1969). The justices originally voted to uphold a state law requiring a year's residence for welfare assistance on the ground that it had a rational basis in the state's use of its resources for its own residents. Brennan persuaded a majority to reject this approach and strike down the residence requirement. Brennan's opinion ruled that since the requirement restricted the fundamental right to travel, it had to be supported by a *compelling* governmental interest. None was present here.

Under Brennan's *Shapiro* opinion, the test of mere rationality gives way, in cases involving fundamental rights, to one of strict scrutiny under which a challenged law will be ruled invalid unless justified by a "compelling" governmental interest. Under *Shapiro,* judicial review takes place within a two-tier framework: strict scrutiny and mere rationality. The tier in which legislation is placed all but determines the outcome of constitutional challenges. Legislation is virtually always upheld under the rationality test, since a law is almost never passed without any rational basis. The converse is true under the compelling-interest test: If a statute is subject to strict scrutiny, it is nearly always struck down.

Brennan's *Shapiro* approach has become established doctrine. It has been applied to a wide range of rights deemed fundamental: the rights guaranteed by the First Amendment, the right to vote, the right to marry, and the right of women to control their own bodies, including the right to terminate pregnancies.

Roe v. Wade (1973) was based directly upon the *Shapiro* approach. In striking down abortion laws, the Court applied the compelling-interest test. "Where certain 'fundamental rights' are involved," states *Roe,* "regulation limiting these rights may be justified only by a compelling state interest." The state's determination to recognize prenatal life was not a compelling state interest, at least during the first trimester of pregnancy.

Roe v. Wade would probably not have been decided this way if Brennan's *Shapiro* opinion had not laid the doctrinal foundation. Had *Shapiro* confirmed the rational-basis test as the review standard even in cases involving fundamental rights, *Roe v. Wade* would have been deprived of its juristic base. One of the most controversial decisions might never have been made.

Sex Discrimination. In 1971, the Court reviewed a sexual classification under the rational-basis test. Had the Court continued to follow that approach, it would have aborted the substantial development in sex discrimination law that has occurred. That that did not happen was largely the result of two Brennan opinions.

In *Frontiero v. Richardson* (1973), Brennan felt, as he wrote in a memorandum to the justices, "that this case would provide an appropriate vehicle for us to recognize sex as a 'suspect criterion.' " Accordingly, he wrote an opinion that provided for strict scrutiny in sexual classification cases. It agreed with the contention "that classifications based upon sex, like classifications based upon race, alienage, and national origin, are inherently suspect and must therefore be subjected to close judicial scrutiny." The *Frontiero* statute was ruled invalid, not under the rational-basis test, but under the strict-scrutiny requirement of compelling interest.

Brennan could, however, secure only three other votes for his *Frontiero* opinion. To obtain a majority, he compromised in the next sex discrimination case, *Craig v. Boren* (1976). Brennan realized there that he could not secure five votes for a *Frontiero*-type opinion that treated sex as a suspect classification subject to the compelling-interest requirement. "To withstand constitutional challenge," states Brennan's *Craig* opinion, "classifications by gender must serve important governmental objectives and must be substantially related to attainment of those objectives." This test has enabled the Court to apply a stricter standard of review in sex equality cases than would have been permitted under the narrow rational-basis standard. Under it, the Court has invalidated a number of laws that treat men and women differently and that would have been upheld had the rational-basis test been the governing review standard.

***Griswold* and *Bakke*.**   The Brennan influence extends far beyond his own opinions. His forte was his ability to lead the justices to the decisions he favored, even at the cost of compromising his own position, as in the adoption of the intermediate review standard in sex discrimination cases. More than any justice, Brennan was the strategist behind Supreme Court jurisprudence—the most active lobbyist (in the non-pejorative sense) in the Court, always willing to take the lead to mold a majority for the decisions that he favored.

His was the behind-the-scenes influence in securing constitutional recognition for the right of privacy in *Griswold v. Connecticut* (1965). The original draft opinion of Justice Douglas was based upon a different ground, but Brennan wrote to Douglas urging that a right of privacy could be inferred from the Bill of Rights' specific guarantees. Douglas followed the Brennan suggestion and the final *Griswold* opinion ruled that there is a constitutionally protected right of privacy.

It was also Brennan who was responsible for the upholding of affirmative-action programs in *Regents v. Bakke* (1978), the leading case on the subject. Justice Powell, whose vote provided the 5–4 majority, had decided to vote against affirmative-action programs. Brennan persuaded him to rule in his crucial opinion that while the quota provisions in the medical school admissions program before the Court were invalid, race could be considered as a factor in determining what students to admit. This enabled almost all affirmative-action programs to continue in operation.

HEART VERSUS HEAD

In many ways, the case that best exemplifies the Brennan approach is *Goldberg v. Kelly* (1970). That case does not rank with the landmarks of jurisprudence; it remains largely unknown except to specialists. Yet, in its own field, it ranks as a leading case which Brennan himself has said was "the opening shot in [the] modern 'due process revolution' " that has transformed our administrative law. Before *Goldberg v. Kelly*, it was settled law that the right to notice and hearing guaranteed by due process applied only in cases where personal or property "rights" were adversely affected by administrative action. If the individual was being given something by government to which he had no preexisting "right," he was being given a mere "privilege." Such a privilege, said a 1944 case, "may be withdrawn at will and is not entitled to protection under the due process clause."

This privilege concept was applied to licenses to sell liquor, to operate billiard parlors, and to engage in other occupations deemed of little social value. But its broadest application was in the burgeoning field of social welfare. During this century, government has become a gigantic fount that pours out largesse on which an ever-increasing number of people depend. Under the traditional approach, all this public largesse involved mere privileges. In consequence, an ever-larger area of administrative power was being insulated from the safeguards of due process. The joyless reaches of the welfare state were littered with dependents outside the pale of constitutional protection.

All this was changed by *Goldberg v. Kelly*. As recently summarized by Brennan, it held that, under due process, "a hearing was required before a welfare recipient's benefits could be terminated." In his opinion, Brennan enunciated a rationale rejecting the privilege concept that had previously barred welfare recipients from constitutional protection. Brennan stated that the recipient's claim could not be answered by the argument that "public assistance benefits are a 'privilege' and not a 'right.' " The opinion characterized welfare benefits as a "matter of statutory entitlement" and added that it "may be realistic today to regard welfare entitlements as more like 'property' than a 'gratuity.' "

Some commentators, a Brennan lecture tells us, "have characterized *Goldberg* as an effort to make the welfare system more rational." To the Justice himself, however, "the decision can be seen as an expression of the importance of passion in governmental conduct, in the sense of attention to the concrete human realities at stake. From this perspective, *Goldberg* can be seen as injecting passion into a system whose abstract rationality had led it astray."

This was a most unusual way for a judge to explain his decision. Brennan has, however, pointed out that, since the welfare procedure in *Goldberg* provided for a post-termination hearing, "one could say that

New York's welfare termination procedure provided considerable protection against arbitrary decisions." That was not enough because, to the Justice, the "significant issue . . . was whether progress in the rationality of government always means progress in the law of due process."

Brennan gave a negative answer because "the state's procedures lacked one vital element: appreciation of the drastic consequences of terminating a recipient's only means of subsistence." Procedure "only *after* benefits were terminated was profoundly inappropriate for a person dependent upon the government for the very resources with which to live."

To reinforce this conclusion Brennan quoted from accounts in the brief of four named welfare recipients who suffered what even a *Goldberg* critic calls "unspeakable personal tragedies from the erroneous cutoff of welfare benefits." According to Brennan, in these accounts the brief "told the human stories that the state's administrative regime seemed unable to hear."

To Brennan, then, law as "a product of formal reason" is not enough. The *Goldberg* procedure may have been "in many respects . . . a model of rationality." But, says the Justice, it "did not comport with due process. It did not do so because it lacked that dimension of passion, of empathy, necessary for a full understanding of the human beings affected by those procedures."

Goldberg demonstrates, Brennan himself points out, that the law "is not simply the blueprint for an empire of reason." Sterile rationality is not enough to determine whether the law "treats its citizens with dignity." That "is a question whose answer must lie in the intricate texture of daily life." In a case such as *Goldberg,* according to Brennan, "Neither a judge nor an administrator who operates on the basis of reason alone can fully grasp that answer, for each is cut off from the wellspring from which concepts such as dignity, decency, and fairness flow." Law based upon reason alone would have been "blind to the brute fact of dependence." Instead, Brennan states, "In the bureaucratic welfare state of the late twentieth century, it may be that what we need most acutely is the passion that understands the pulse of life beneath the official version of events." Otherwise, the law may have its reasons, but they will too "often seem remote from the human beings who must live with their consequences."

In the Brennan conception, "the progress of the law depends on a dialogue between heart and head." His jurisprudence is based upon "the important role that qualities other than reason must play in the judicial process." Brennan writes that he "refer[s] to these qualities under the rubric of 'passion'. . . . By 'passion' I mean the range of emotional and intuitive responses to a given set of facts or arguments, responses which often speed into our consciousness far ahead of the lumbering syllogisms of reason." These are "the responses of the heart rather than the head."

As Brennan sums it up, "Only by remaining open to the entreaties of reason and passion, of logic and of experience, can a judge come to understand the complex human meaning of a rich term such as 'liberty,' and only with such understanding can courts fulfill their constitutional responsibility to protect that value."

LIVING LAW

The Brennan approach to law has been called "instrumental rationality." Under it the judge reflects upon the values and ideals underlying the legal system, seeks to understand what those ideals require in the practical world, and molds his decision to accomplish the desired result. The end is to ensure that the proper values prevail and that the decision adopts the best means for attaining that goal. In achieving the goal, the judge is not to be deterred by logic or even a mass of precedent the other way. The Brennan jurisprudence was in large part based upon rejection of the formal logic and case law that stood in the way of giving effect to the Justice's scale of values. Once Brennan determined what the desired end should be, he never had difficulty in fashioning the legal means to achieve that end.

The Brennan influence has been pervasive, helping to make both the law and the society what they are today. It was the Justice who helped make activism the dominant legal approach—in both the forum and the academy—during his judicial tenure. With the retirement of Chief Justice Warren, many expected the Court to tilt away from its activist posture. If the Warren Court had made a legal revolution, a counter-revolution was seemingly at hand. It did not, however, turn out that way. If anything, the intended counterrevolution served only as a confirmation of most of the Warren Court jurisprudence. Indeed, the entire record of the Court since Brennan's appointment is one of activism. As Anthony Lewis summed it up, "We are all activists now."

In the end, the underlying question comes down to how we resolve the antinomy in the Pound aphorism: The law must be stable and yet it cannot stand still.

During his confirmation hearings, Chief Justice William H. Rehnquist was asked, "How can you not acknowledge that the Constitution is a living, breathing document . . . ?" The question put to the Chief Justice is a crucial one. Justice Brennan never had any doubt about the proper answer. A legal system created in an age of knee breeches and three-cornered hats can serve the needs of an entirely different day only because our law has recognized that it could hardly have endured through the ages if its provisions were fixed as irrevocably as the laws of the Medes and Persians. The constantly evolving nature of jurisprudence has alone enabled our system to make the transition to the twentieth century.

Brennan is the outstanding example of a judge who has not taken stability as his legal polestar. He has been the leading opponent of the view that constitutional construction must be governed only by the original intention of the Framers. As explained by Brennan himself, "This view demands that Justices discern exactly what the Framers thought about the question under consideration and simply follow their intention in resolving the case before them." Throughout his tenure, Brennan rejected this "original-intention" jurisprudence. To him the meaning of the Constitution is to be found in today's needs, not in a search for what was intended by its eighteenth-century draftsmen.

To Justice Brennan, then, the outstanding feature of the Constitution is its plastic nature. The same is true of his general conception of law. Its rules and doctrines are all malleable and must be construed to meet the changing needs of different periods. That he has succeeded in elevating his view to the level of accepted doctrine is shown by the opinions already discussed. They bear ample witness to his success in giving effect to the concept of a flexible law which is constantly being adapted to meet contemporary needs. Above all, the Brennan jurisprudence was based upon what he termed "the constitutional ideal of human dignity." This is what led him to his constant battle against the death penalty, which he considered a violation of the ban against cruel and unusual punishment. The battle to outlaw capital punishment was a losing one for the Justice but it was the only major one he did lose in his effort to ensure what he said was "the ceaseless pursuit of the constitutional ideal." The ultimate Brennan legacy was that no important decision of the Warren Court was overruled while the Justice sat on the Burger and Rehnquist Courts.

I cannot conclude this account of Justice Brennan without touching upon the Justice as a human being. Even his ideological foes stressed, as one put it upon his retirement, that "you cannot dislike this man on a personal level." No justice enjoyed more respect and affection among his colleagues. He had warm relations with everyone on the Court and always had a friendly word for everyone, from the chief justice to the maintenance staff.

What struck those who met Brennan was that he remained unceremonious and unassuming, despite his reputation as the most influential justice during the past half century. He once related to me with awe how, at a charity auction, someone bid several thousand dollars to have lunch with him and Mrs. Brennan.

Civil
Liberties

Speech: Uninhibited, Robust, and Wide-Open

TOM WICKER

If Gregory Lee Johnson had never burned an American flag during the 1984 Republican national convention in Dallas, Justice William J. Brennan, Jr., still would rank among the great judicial protectors of American liberties—particularly freedom of speech, perhaps first among those liberties.

Johnson *did* burn that flag, however, as an expression of his criticisms of government and the Republican convention's policies. He *was* convicted of violating a Texas statute prohibiting any person from desecrating the American flag in a way that would "seriously offend" others—as his act certainly did.

Johnson's appeal went all the way to the Supreme Court—with consequences that included history's first demand by a president for a restriction on the First Amendment, and the brilliant assertion by Justice Brennan—perhaps his most celebrated judicial act—of the true meaning of the amendment and the flag.

That President George Bush would seriously seek to limit First Amendment protections through a change in the Constitution may have been surprising. That William Brennan rose so powerfully to their defense was not. He already had established himself as a staunch proponent of free expression and as a significant intellectual theorist and historical interpreter of the First Amendment's often-disputed meaning and application.

Brennan's thirty-four-year tenure on the Supreme Court ended in 1990. That span covered more than half the brief period in which First Amendment issues had been serious concerns for the Court. The justice himself, in a lecture at Brown University in 1965, suggested why this was so:

The author was a columnist for the *New York Times*. He has published nine novels and five books of nonfiction, including a recently released account of race relations in America, *Tragic Failure*.

[I]n our frontier days not so much problems of individual liberty as problems of the respective domains of federal and state power incident to territorial expansion and economic growth came to the surface. Issues of individual liberty and the relationship of the citizen to his government waited in the wings pending the events of this century that brought them to the fore.

"Events of this century"—various Communist-subversive scares, the civil rights movement, numerous obscenity and religious disputes, for instance—did focus attention at last on what Brennan called in his lecture at Brown "the cherished rights of mind and spirit—the freedoms of speech, press, religion, assembly, association and petition for redress of grievances." All, of course, fall under the protections of the First Amendment; but how far do those protections reach? Do they apply to the states as well as to the federal government? Are other values superior to them? In the period when such questions have been at issue, no one has had greater or more beneficial effect on their resolution—on the preservation and advancement of First Amendment freedoms—than William J. Brennan, Jr., an architect of American liberty as it is enjoyed (and sometimes denounced) today.

By the year of his retirement, he had participated in 252 decisions affecting free speech, and by the count of Geoffrey Stone in the *University of Pennsylvania Law Review* he had "accepted the free speech claim" in 221 of these cases, though the Court's majority did so in only 148. Thus, Brennan's remarkable First Amendment influence was exerted not only in majority decisions but in eloquent dissents that often were vindicated by time and evolving Court attitudes. (As he has observed, "Radical shifts in judicial doctrine are rare. They usually occur over long periods step-by-step.")

The "flag-burning" case, however, and Brennan's ruling (for a 5–4 Court majority) that the Texas law Johnson had violated was invalid as an infringement on free speech, is probably what Americans remember most vividly of Brennan's long, distinguished service on the Court. Many still angrily denounce the ruling, and Congress still tries to undo it.

Actually, not one case was involved, but two. In the original *Johnson* case, Brennan's decision dismissed the state's supposed interest in preventing breaches of the peace (the government may "not assume that every expression of a provocative idea will incite a riot"), downgraded the offense claimed to have been given to others by the burning of the flag ("no reasonable onlooker" would have taken Johnson's act as "a direct personal insult or an invitation to exchange fisticuffs"), and—most important—roundly asserted that "government may not prohibit expression simply because it disagrees with its message."

The Court majority, Brennan went on to say, *not* the Texas legislature, was reaffirming "the principles of freedom and inclusiveness that the flag best reflects, and . . . the conviction that our toleration of criticism such as Johnson's is a sign and source of our strength." He concluded ringingly, in a definition of American intellectual freedom that might well be inscribed on his tombstone: "If there is a bedrock principle underlying the First Amendment, it is that the government may not prohibit the expression of an idea simply because society finds the idea itself offensive or disagreeable."

Logical and reflective of proclaimed values as the flag-burning decision was, however, it could not quiet the simplistic patriotism and the national outrage Johnson had aroused by burning the flag—a response that demagogic politicians had encouraged. At the time, so vociferous was the criticism of Brennan and the Court ruling that it might have been thought that flag burning was the most threatening problem faced by the republic, and that the Court had rendered the nation incapable of defending itself against a rampant epidemic of torched flags.

President Bush actually called for a constitutional amendment to nullify the Court decision and allow legislatures to make a criminal act of flag burning—even if the burning was a calculated political act, and despite the language of the First Amendment protecting such speech. Congress would not go as far as Bush demanded, but it did enact legislation called the "Flag Protection Act of 1989," designed to avoid the defects of the invalidated Texas statute.

The "flag protection" legislation promptly, expectably, and purposely was violated, and in *United States v. Eichman* (1990), the Supreme Court was called upon to decide its constitutionality. In some ways, this might have been a more difficult decision than the one involving the Texas law. After all, Congress had excluded from its act any specific "content-based limitation" on speech, meaning that flag burning was prohibited regardless of the intended message; President Bush defended the legislation and contended that, unlike a mere state law, the flag protection act represented a national consensus, and such a consensus, measured by public outrage, did seem to confront a Supreme Court supposed to be well aware of the "election returns."

Justice Brennan, writing for the same 5–4 majority, cut through the uproar to the central point. The congressional act, though different from the Texas statute, suffered the same flaw: "It suppresses expression out of concern" for the message expressed. Why? Because "the government's desire to preserve the flag as a symbol for certain national ideals is implicated 'only when a person's treatment of the flag communicates [a] message' to others that is inconsistent with those ideals."

Brennan's opinions in these cases often had been foreshadowed, not only by his soundly based general hospitality to free speech claims, but specifically in numerous opinions and dissents. In the years of the active civil rights movement, for example, several southern states sought by legislation squarely aimed at the NAACP to prohibit its attempt to gain federal court support for the protection of blacks' constitutional rights.

Virginia's legislation to this effect was invalidated by the Supreme Court—in an opinion by William Brennan—holding that NAACP-assisted litigation was not aimed at settling private differences but was "a means for achieving . . . equality of treatment" for the black community. Thus, it was "a form of political expression" and perhaps "the most effective form of political association"—both clearly protected by the First Amendment.

As indicative of his free speech views, though usually stated in dissent, was Brennan's consistently expansive view of the citizen's right to a public forum. It's the prevailing judicial view that, even where government has no power to *prevent* protected expression, it may have some power to *regulate* the means of expression; hence, the questions of how, where, and when offensive but protected speech may be uttered are vital to the protection of the right itself. Few would contend, for instance, that even protected speech could legitimately issue from a loudspeaker for hours on end in a residential neighborhood between midnight and morning; the forum, not the speech itself, would be the issue.

Brennan, however, dissented from a majority ruling that a military base could exclude all political activity in its public areas; he wrote that base officials might exclude civilian traffic entirely but "could not choose freely to admit all such traffic *save for the traffic in ideas.*"

He dissented again from a holding that a state fair could prohibit political and religious groups from distributing their literature anywhere but in assigned, rented booths—an unconstitutional restriction, he thought, because it "sharply limited" the number of persons the groups could reach. He dissented, too, from a majority that upheld a city's right to prohibit the posting of signs on public property—a ban that "sweeps so broadly and trenches so completely on the use of an important medium of political expression that it must be struck down as violative of the First Amendment."

Through such dissents, Brennan consistently demonstrated his understanding that if truly free expression were to be extended even to unorthodox and unpopular ideas, such ideas need access to a broad range of means of communications, particularly for individuals and groups with limited funds.

Over the years of his service, too, Brennan's view of obscenity had evolved toward a larger freedom for its expression. Originally, he had believed obscenity was not protected speech; but that view only raised the problem of deciding what *was* obscenity—a conclusion the Court could never agree upon. After years in which he and his colleagues had groped ineffectually for an acceptable definition of obscenity, Brennan shifted his focus—in a typically eloquent dissent—to the state's grounds, if any, for suppressing obscenity.

Here, too, he found only "essentially unfocused and ill defined" reasons "predicated on unprovable . . . assumptions about human behavior, morality, sex and religion." These loose assumptions, he concluded, "cannot validate a statute that substantially undermines the guarantees of the First Amendment." Hence, "in the absence of distribution to juveniles or obtrusive exposure to unconsenting adults," government has no power "wholly to suppress sexually oriented materials on the basis of their allegedly 'obscene' contents."

It was only to be expected, therefore, that it would be argued from the same sensibility that even burning a flag was a form of speech deserving of protection. And the same developing ideas of free speech also underlay Justice Brennan's decision in *New York Times v. Sullivan* (1964), which was acclaimed—though also deplored, as are all groundbreaking ideas.

This Brennan opinion, ranking in public fame with his rulings in the flag-burning cases, bluntly stated the premise from which, it may be assumed, his convictions about the free expression of ideas had arisen: "We consider this case against the background of a profound national commitment to the principle that debate on public issues should be uninhibited, robust, and wide-open."

There surely are those who do not concede that "profound national commitment" to such a principle. After *New York Times,* however, there can be none who fail to recognize Justice Brennan's own dedication to it, and his ability to articulate, defend, and advance it.

The *Times* case primarily concerns freedom of the press, since it upheld publication of an advertisement that was critical of public officials in Birmingham, Alabama. (In 1960, while this case was pending in the Supreme Court, I traveled to Birmingham as a *Times* reporter on a campaign trip with Richard Nixon, who was then running for president. Nervous company lawyers counseled me not to identify myself, while in that city, as a representative of the *Times.* They feared I might somehow be seized by its authorities—none of whom, in the event, evinced any interest whatever in my presence.)

The *Times* case as a landmark of First Amendment jurisprudence had important effect beyond press issues. It widened the latitude of free speech because, as Brennan put it in his opinion, "erroneous statement is inevitable in free debate" and therefore even false statements must be protected. Otherwise, "a rule compelling the critic of official conduct to guarantee the truth of all of his factual assertions would lead to intolerable 'self-censorship.' "

That is, a critic might withhold his criticisms for fear that he could not prove them in court, or could not bear the expense of a court proceeding, thus "dampen[ing] the vigor and limit[ing] the variety of public debate." This reasoning is as true for vocal debate—freedom of speech—as for published criticism—freedom of the press.

The *Times* case did not, however, grant license to calculated falsehood. While Brennan's decision held that an official could not recover damages owing to a merely inaccurate charge against him, the ruling made clear that the critic would be liable if he had made such a charge *knowing* that it was false or with "reckless disregard" of whether or not it was false.

As was stated in a later court decision applying the *New York Times* standard, "although honest utterance, even if inaccurate, may further the fruitful exercise of the right of free speech, it does not follow that *the lie, knowingly and deliberately published* about a public official, should enjoy" protection. Using a "known lie as a tool is at once at odds with the premises of democratic government and with the orderly manner in which economic, social, or political change is to be affected." (Political candidates relying on so-called negative advertising, take note.)

Despite this useful caveat, by freeing public debate from the "chilling effect" of a critic having to prove his every charge, perhaps in court and at great expense, the *Times* case not only revolutionized the law of libel, it assured a vigorous assertion of free speech even in criticism of governmental authority.

In his 1965 lecture at Brown University (honoring Alexander Meiklejohn), Justice Brennan noted that *New York Times* was not based on the usual tests of "clear and present danger" or "redeeming social values" or a "balance" of conflicting values; it rested, instead, on a historical analysis of "the central meaning of the First Amendment."

The Court had discovered that meaning, Brennan said, in a statement to Congress by James Madison—sometimes called "the father of the Constitution"—that "the censorial power is in the people over the government and not in the government over the people." One may reasonably conclude that Brennan's description of how "the Court" discovered historical meaning actually refers to William J. Brennan, Jr., the author of the *Times* ruling.

It follows that Brennan was able—though laymen know little of the procedures and techniques by which Supreme Court justices persuade or fail to persuade one another—to convince four other members of the Court of that "central meaning," and of its application to the *New York Times* case: specifically that citizens may freely criticize the government they themselves have empowered and over which they retain sovereignty; in legal and historical terms, "seditious libel" cannot be made an offense. As Brennan's decision had proclaimed: "The right of free public discussion of the stewardship of public officials was thus, in Madison's view, a fundamental principle of the American form of government." (In Brennan's view, too, obviously, and thus in that of the Supreme Court majority he was able to persuade.)

"Free public discussion," moreover, refers not only to publications in the press but to speech in barrooms, barber shops, public forums, discussion groups—anywhere, in fact, that citizens may gather to talk about their government and its policies or anywhere that a lone eccentric or group of nonconformists voices his or her or their opinions—even opinions offensive to the general view, like the burning of an American flag in protest of government policies.

Before *New York Times,* the Supreme Court in *Barr v. Matteo* (1959) had created an absolute privilege barring libel suits against high-ranking government officials for statements, even if defamatory, made in their official capacity—just as members of Congress may not be questioned "in any other place" for statements made on the House or Senate floor. The threat of such suits, it was reasoned, would inhibit—or "chill"— the member of Congress or the official in the performance of his or her duty.

New York Times applied this logic in the other direction; the threat of a libel suit would not be allowed to deter or chill a citizen in the performance of his—equally important—duty to evaluate the policies of the government over which, in America, the citizen is sovereign.

That is the essential principle—the sovereignty of the citizen, not the government—that the First Amendment jurisprudence of William J. Brennan, Jr., has retrieved from effective disuse. The remarkable body of Brennan's opinions and dissents—his *thought*—was assembled, painstakingly, studiously, open-mindedly, as time and events made necessary. It is not too much to say that before Brennan entered the picture, that great principle was honored mostly in lip service, and was even openly disregarded.

From Madison to Brennan is a leap of more than a century, during which—no doubt primarily for the reasons Justice Brennan voiced in his Brown lecture—the intrinsic relation of citizen to government, government to citizen, was largely overlooked. The overpowering need for development of a continent, a nation, an economy took precedence. In that time, even into the late twentieth century—with its strictures on supposed subversion, its penalties on those who followed an unorthodox political course, its resistance to elementary ideas of equality—the principle of citizen sovereignty, however honored in oratory, was largely ignored in practice.

Many, including some who may lie in unhonored graves, are to be thanked for the redemption of that principle. But no one was more instrumental in its reassertion, no one gave it more persuasive voice, than Justice William J. Brennan, Jr., who found not just the law but the language to prevail in that robust "marketplace of ideas" that surely will be his monument.

The Press: Free but Not Exceptional

ANTHONY LEWIS

If the American press became more probing and irreverent of government in the last third of the twentieth century—and it did—Justice Brennan played a crucial part in the transformation. His 1964 opinion for the Supreme Court in *New York Times v. Sullivan* was received by reporters and editors as a charter of freedom. In holding that public officials could not win libel damages for honest mistakes in comments about them, he encouraged the press to look beneath official views: a role it soon fulfilled in its coverage of Vietnam and Watergate. In the *Sullivan* case and many others he was a powerful influence for freedom of the press.

But it is important to understand that Justice Brennan never subscribed to the notion of press exceptionalism, the idea that the press has different and special rights under the Constitution. Indeed, he did not hesitate to warn the press against a narrow, self-regarding attitude. Instead, he saw the press clause of the First Amendment ("Congress shall make no law . . . abridging the freedom . . . of the press") as one strand in a web of freedom that protects citizens as it does journalists in their right to speak out and participate in the democratic process.

THE ACTUAL-MALICE STANDARD

Times v. Sullivan was one of the few Supreme Court decisions that deserves the overused description "constitutional landmark." It transformed the American law of libel. It had a profound impact on the civil rights movement in the South. And it introduced sophisticated legal thinking into the work of journalists—for good and ill, some would say.

The case is so well known that a brief summary suffices. On March

The author is a columnist for the *New York Times* and author of *Make No Law: The Sullivan Case and the First Amendment* and *Gideon's Trumpet*. He covered the Supreme Court for the *Times* from 1957 through 1964, and has received two Pulitzer Prizes for national reporting.

29, 1960, the *New York Times* printed a full-page advertisement in support of Dr. Martin Luther King, Jr., and the movement to end racial segregation in the South. The ad spoke of brutal efforts to suppress the movement; naming no names, it blamed "Southern violators" of the Constitution. But Lester Bruce Sullivan, a city commissioner of Montgomery, Alabama, sued for libel, claiming that the ad referred to him inferentially in describing some events in Montgomery—and falsified those events. Under Alabama law (as under the common law of England and most American states) the publisher had the burden of proving challenged statements true in all material particulars, and the *Times* admitted that there were some errors in the advertisement. For example, the ad said that protesting black students had sung "My Country, 'Tis of Thee" when they had actually sung "The Star-Spangled Banner," and it said wrongly that the protesters had been locked out of their dining hall. The judge therefore instructed the jury that the advertisement was false. The jury found that it did refer to Commissioner Sullivan, and it awarded him the damages he sought, $500,000—at the time the largest libel award in Alabama history.

The judgment for Commissioner Sullivan was extremely menacing to the civil rights movement. Dr. King's strategy was to appeal to the conscience of the country; he believed that most Americans were unaware of the cruelty of southern racism and would condemn it if they knew. But that depended on newspaper, magazine, and broadcast coverage of the marches and sit-ins and other efforts to dramatize racism. Libel cases like Sullivan's—and others that followed—were designed to scare the national press out of covering the story.

In distant hindsight, it looks easy for the *New York Times* to invoke the First Amendment and upset Commissioner Sullivan's damage award on appeal. But at the time it looked impossible. Libel had always been regarded as outside the scope of the First Amendment. Libel law was a state matter; no libel judgment, no matter how outlandish, had ever been upset as a violation of the Constitution.

That was the situation until March 9, 1964, when the Supreme Court decided the *Sullivan* case. It reversed the $500,000 award. But the larger meaning of the decision lay in the way Justice Brennan analyzed the problem. His opinion enlarged the freedom not of the press alone but of all who speak or write about the work of government.

"The central meaning of the First Amendment," Justice Brennan said, is the right to criticize government. If anyone who criticizes officials has to prove the truth of his every statement when challenged, people will be afraid to speak out. "Would-be critics of official conduct may be deterred from voicing their criticism, even though it is believed to be true, because of doubt whether it can be proved in court or fear of the expense of having to do so."

To prevent the chilling of would-be critics, he said, the First Amendment allowed officials to recover libel damages only if they proved "actual malice"—that a false statement about them had been published deliberately or recklessly. He gave no protection to intentional lies, for as he said later the "calculated falsehood" is a dangerous weapon in the hands of the unscrupulous.

A special quality of the *Sullivan* opinion was its focus on the practical impact of things like the burden of proving truth. In that respect it grew out of earlier Brennan opinions on other subjects. In *Speiser v. Randall* in 1958 he held unconstitutional a California law giving tax exemptions to veterans if they took an oath not to advocate overthrow of the government; it would, he said, discourage people from making statements "close to the line." The actual working "of the method by which speech is sought to be restrained must be subject to close analysis and critical judgment in light of the particular circumstances to which it is applied."

A similar theme was there, as Professor Robert C. Post of the University of California at Berkeley has noted, in the 1959 decision in *Smith v. California*. A Los Angeles ordinance made it a crime for a bookseller to have anything obscene in his shop. The law violated the Constitution, Justice Brennan said for the Court, because it did not require proof that the bookseller knew something in his stock was obscene. Without that limitation, he wrote, the bookshop owner "will tend to restrict the books he sells to those he has inspected; and thus the State will have imposed a restriction upon the distribution of constitutionally protected as well as obscene literature."

The earlier cases show that Justice Brennan was concerned with freedom of expression generally, not just with freedom of the press. And that is in fact evident in the *Sullivan* opinion itself, despite its place in the hearts of journalists as their victory. In the very first sentence Justice Brennan described the case as one about "the constitutional protections for speech and press." And in what may be the crux of the opinion, he drew an analogy to cases holding that the public official is immune from libel suits over his official comments so he will not fear to speak vigorously. "Analogous considerations support the privilege for the citizen-critic of government," Justice Brennan wrote. "It is as much his duty to criticize as it is the official's duty to administer." The citizen-critic, not just the press.

Justice Brennan produced the *Sullivan* opinion with remarkable speed, just two months and three days from argument to announcement. Significantly, he managed to hold a majority behind the opinion's reasoning despite what we now know were waverings by two of his colleagues. It was a fine example of what Professor Post called "his uncanny knack for creating crucial court majorities from the splinters of disparate perspectives." In the end only Justices Hugo L. Black, William O. Douglas, and Arthur Goldberg declined to join, urging instead in concurring opinions that officials be barred altogether from suing for libel, even when they have been damaged by calculated falsehoods. The advantage of Justice Brennan's more discreet formula is evident, as a practical matter, if we consider how absolute protection for defamatory comments might have aggravated tendencies toward arrogance in the press—and public dislike of press pretensions.

Ten months after the decision in *Sullivan,* Justice Brennan applied its reasoning to protect derogatory statements by an eccentric public official: Jim Garrison, the New Orleans district attorney, best known for his abuse of power in pursuing nonexistent conspiracies in the assassination of President Kennedy. In this case Garrison had called eight local judges inefficient and lazy. He was prosecuted for criminal libel, under a Louisiana law that allowed conviction for false statements if they were made with enmity or ill will. The Supreme Court reversed Garrison's conviction. Even if criticism of public officials was motivated by hatred, Justice Brennan said, the critic who believed what he said was true was protected from libel suits. His analysis rested, again, on the nature of our political system. "Speech concerning public affairs," he said, "is more than self-expression; it is the essence of self-government."

Press versus Privacy

One Brennan opinion that did favor the press over other interests was in *Time, Inc. v. Hill,* decided in 1967. It was an unusual case in its facts and in its handling by the Court. James J. Hill, his wife Elizabeth, and their five children were held hostage in their home outside Philadelphia by three escaped convicts. The Hills were not physically harmed, but they were distressed by sensational stories about the incident in the press. They moved to Connecticut to put the episode behind them. Three years later *Life* magazine did a picture story on a new play about a family held hostage by escaped convicts. The play was not based specifically on the Hills' experience, and it portrayed the convicts as far more brutal. But *Life* photographed the actors in the Hills' former Philadelphia home and presented scenes from the play as if they had actually happened to the Hill family. The family, disturbed, sued Time, Inc., publisher of *Life,* for invasion of privacy. Mr. Hill won modest damages in the New York courts, $30,000. Then the Supreme Court agreed to decide whether that award violated the publisher's First Amendment rights.

At first a majority of the justices voted to sustain Mr. Hill's judgment. Justice Abe Fortas circulated an opinion that bitterly criticized *Life*'s behavior. He wrote: "Needless, heedless, wanton and deliberate injury of the sort inflicted by *Life*'s picture story is not an essential instrument of responsible journalism. Magazine writers and editors are not, by reason of their high office, relieved of the common obligation to avoid deliberately inflicting wanton and unnecessary injury." But Justice Fortas lost his majority. The case was reargued in the next term. (Richard M. Nixon argued both times for Mr. Hill.) By a vote of 5 to 4 the Court now reversed the judgment. Justice Brennan, writing for the majority, said Mr. Hill could not win damages for invasion of his privacy unless he proved that *Life* had published its story "with knowledge of its falsity or in reckless disregard of the truth": the *Sullivan* formula.

The difficult and profound question raised by the *Hill* case is why a test devised to protect criticism of government should be applied to protect a magazine's false picture of a private family. Justice Brennan said:

> The guarantees for speech and press are not the preserve of political expression or comment upon public affairs, essential as these are to healthy government. One need only pick up any newspaper or magazine to comprehend the vast range of published matter which exposes persons to public view, both private citizens and public officials. Exposure of the self to others in varying degrees is a concomitant of life in a civilized community. The risk of this exposure is an essential incident of life in a society which places a primary value on freedom of speech and of press. . . . We create a grave risk of serious impairment of the indispensable service of a free press in a free society if we saddle the press with the impossible burden of verifying to a certainty the facts associated in news articles with a person's name, picture, or portrait.

But a legal system could have more regard for private victims of prurient journalism, like the Hills, without demanding that the press verify what it prints about them "to a certainty." Justice John Marshall Harlan, dissenting in the *Hill* case, said the press should be subject to damages in such a case if it were merely negligent, a lower standard than the "recklessness" of *Times v. Sullivan*—for example, if it failed to make a "reasonable investigation."

The case of *Time, Inc. v. Hill* was reckoned a victory for the press. But if it encouraged too-easy invasions of privacy, it may have been a Pyrrhic victory. Justice Harlan warned: "A constitutional doctrine which relieves the press of even this minimal responsibility . . . in cases of this sort seems to me unnecessary and ultimately harmful to the permanent good health of the press itself." As Justice Brennan had demonstrated in *Sullivan,* he understood the need to balance freedom against other important interests such as reputation. In the *Hill* case, however, a fear that the press might face oppressive lawsuits for inadvertent mistakes in dramatizing stories evidently overrode Justice Brennan's usual concern for the countervailing interest there, the value of privacy. His dismissal of that value was surely too easy. In a world that has known Orwell's Big Brother, and that now lives with electronic networks tracking our lives, many would resist the proposition that "exposure of the self to others" is a necessary part of living "in a civilized community."

The Public-Private Question

The question of how far the First Amendment should reach from the public to the private sphere in protecting speech and press occupied the Supreme Court for years in the libel field. Justice Brennan took the position, in the 1971 case of *Rosenbloom v. Metromedia,* that critical comment should be protected by the rule of *New York Times v. Sullivan* so long as it dealt with an issue of public concern. "If a matter is of public or general interest," he said, "it cannot suddenly become less so because a private individual is involved, or because in some sense the individual did not 'voluntarily' choose to become involved. The public's primary interest is in the event." His view, again, would have been highly protective of the press; but only two other members of the Court joined him. There was no majority for any one doctrine in the *Rosenbloom* case.

The public-private question was finally settled, or so it seemed, in 1974. A bare majority of five held, in *Gertz v. Welch,* that the decisive element was not the subject matter under discussion but the characteristics of the person who was the target of the challenged comment. If the target was a "public figure," then he or she could recover libel damages only by proving knowing or reckless falsehood: the *Sullivan* test. An ordinary private person had to prove only that the defendant had published a false statement "negligently," the difference being that failure to check a story before publishing it was negligent but not reckless.

But what was a "public figure"? Justice Lewis F. Powell, Jr., writing for the Court, said there were two kinds: someone generally famous, like a movie star, and someone who had thrust himself into a particular public controversy. Justice Brennan dissented, sticking to his *Rosenbloom* view that the answer should turn on the subject matter, not the person. Yet in a way, *Gertz* was a triumph for the process he started in *New York Times v. Sullivan*. For the Court, in holding that even the purely private person must at least prove negligent publication, extended the First Amendment into all but the farthest corners of the libel field. For 173 years, before 1964, libel was entirely a matter of state and local law, untouched by the First Amendment. Now virtually all libel cases were governed by rules that the Supreme Court had applied under the federal Constitution.

Another important step in the constitutionalizing of libel law came when a 5–4 majority of the Court in 1986 held that a private person who brings a suit over a matter of public concern must prove that the statement he or she challenges was false. That reversed the common-law rule that the libel defendant has the burden of proving truth: a change of great benefit to the press because truth is often hard to prove. Justice Brennan wrote no opinion in the case but played a part in its decision. The justices were at first divided 5–4 *against* changing the burden of proof, with Justice Brennan in dissent. Chief Justice William Rehnquist assigned the Court's opinion to Justice Sandra Day O'Connor. As she worked on it, and got her colleagues' views, she changed her mind. The opinion then had to be reassigned, and that duty fell to the senior associate justice in the new majority, Justice Brennan. He gave it to Justice O'Connor.

PRIOR RESTRAINTS

The single most stressful test for freedom of the press while Justice Brennan served on the Court was the *Pentagon Papers* case in 1971, and there again he played a vigorous part on the side of freedom. The *New York Times* and then the *Washington Post* published excerpts from a top-secret official history of the origins of the Vietnam War. The government, claiming that continued publication would endanger the war effort, sought "prior restraints"—court orders prohibiting the newspapers from publishing any more of the papers. The Supreme Court held, 6–3, that no injunction was justified and the papers were free to publish. An unsigned opinion said the government had not overcome the presumption against prior restraints, and each of the nine justices wrote a separate concurring or dissenting opinion.

Justice Brennan, along with Justices Black, Douglas, and Thurgood Marshall, had voted to set aside a lower-court injunction against the *Times* without even hearing argument. In his opinion, Justice Brennan said the vice in the case lay in the granting of any temporary restraining orders or stays at all. A lower court had stopped publication on the theory that it "might," Justice Brennan said, "prejudice the national interest in various ways. But the First Amendment tolerates absolutely no prior judicial restraints of the press predicated upon surmise or conjecture." Reflecting on the *Pentagon Papers* case in future years, press lawyers found the phenomenon addressed by Justice Brennan its most disturbing feature: that judges, faced with a huge mass of material, tended to yield to government arguments that something in there might be dangerous—and would issue temporary restraints.

The issue of prior restraints arose again when a number of judges around the country imposed what the press called gag orders to keep newspapers from publishing alleged confessions and other material about criminal defendants before their trials. In *Nebraska Press Association v. Stuart* in 1976, the Supreme Court held that such an order, granted in a sensational Nebraska murder case, was unconstitutional. The opinion of the Court, by Chief Justice Warren E. Burger, rested on the facts of the particular case. Justice Brennan, concurring, said he would hold that judges may never use prior restraints as a way to assure fair trials. "Discussion of public affairs in a free society," he said, "cannot depend on the preliminary grace of judicial censors."

THE STRUCTURAL MODEL

Before *Times v. Sullivan* there was virtually no constitutional law of the press. Afterward, hardly a Supreme Court term passed without a press case. From time to time the press side of a case lost, and then Justice Brennan would be found among the dissenters. That was so when the Court in 1972 rejected a claim that journalists are entitled to a First Amendment privilege not to testify when they are called before a grand jury investigating a crime of which they have knowledge. He dissented in part when the Court held in *Herbert v. Lando* in 1979 that a libel plaintiff, who must prove that the defendant published a falsehood knowingly or recklessly, is entitled to question the defendant in pretrial discovery about what he knew when he published.

But if Justice Brennan disagreed when a majority of the Court rejected positions advanced by the press, he did not think that those decisions spelled doom for freedom of the press. In an address at the dedication of the Samuel I. Newhouse Law Center at Rutgers University in 1979 he chided the press for crying doom. He quoted newspaper editors as calling the decision in *Herbert v. Lando* "Orwellian" and saying it had the "potential of totally inhibiting the press to a degree seldom seen outside a dictatorial or fascist country." He had dissented, Justice Brennan said, but the decision "deserved a more considered response on the part of the press." The injury "was simply not of the magnitude to justify the resulting firestorm of acrimonious criticism." The Court had not in any way restricted the press's right to publish what it would, he said, or trimmed its constitutional protections against libel suits. The majority had made a nice judgment, and a practical one, between the press's desire for decisional privacy and an offended libel plaintiff's right to learn what he had to show in his suit. The press, he said, must also address questions of degree rather than engage in extravagant denunciations if it wanted to affect the thinking of judges. "This may involve a certain loss of innocence," he added pointedly, "a certain recognition that the press, like other institutions, must accommodate a variety of important social interests."

In his Rutgers lecture Justice Brennan offered a new analysis of the way the First Amendment protects freedom of expression. First, he said, the amendment "more or less absolutely" forbids government to stop the individual from speaking out or the press from publishing what it knows. The clear example is the rule virtually forbidding prior restraints. But second, Justice Brennan said, there was what he called the "structural model." This protects speech and press in their roles as part of the democratic system. It is the role that James Madison had in mind for the press and the citizen, and that Justice Brennan celebrated in *New*

York Times v. Sullivan. Under the structural model, he said, "the press is not only shielded when it speaks out, but when it performs all the myriad tasks necessary for it to gather and disseminate the news." But the stretch of that protection, he said, was "theoretically endless." So freedom of the structural kind always had to be weighed against other social interests. And the press had to understand that.

Justice Brennan soon had the opportunity to bring his idea of the "structural model" into an actual case. In *Richmond Newspapers v. Virginia* in 1980 the Supreme Court dealt with a judge's closing of his courtroom to the public and the press during a murder trial. By a vote of 7 to 1, the justices found that the closing violated the First Amendment, but there was no majority opinion. Justice Brennan, writing separately, said this was not a traditional First Amendment case of government interference with expression. It involved the amendment, rather, in its "structural role . . . in securing and fostering our republican system of government." Giving the public and the press *access* to governmental institutions and information plainly served to inform the citizenry, but that could not be an absolute right. It depended on the tradition of openness in a particular area, and on the importance of public access. Both those considerations argued for open courtrooms.

The *Richmond Newspapers* decision was the first time the Supreme Court had applied the First Amendment to require public or press access to government proceedings. It was in that sense a revolutionary decision, though the Court did its best to mute the significance of what it had done and to limit it. But the decision had its roots in earlier cases holding that the First Amendment protected the right of listeners as well as speakers, readers as well as publishers. And there, too, Justice Brennan had played an important part.

In *Lamont v. Postmaster General* in 1965 the Court held unconstitutional a law requiring the post office to hold up any "communist political propaganda"—copies of *Pravda,* for instance—unless and until the person to whom it was addressed sent in a card asking to have it delivered. (It was the first time ever that the Court had found a federal statute in violation of the First Amendment.) Justice Douglas wrote the opinion of the Court. But there was a more thoughtful concurring opinion by Justice Brennan. The First Amendment, he wrote, "contains no specific guarantee of access to publications." But such a right is necessary to make freedom of expression meaningful. "The dissemination of ideas can accomplish nothing if otherwise willing addressees are not free to receive and consider them. It would be a barren marketplace of ideas that had only sellers and no buyers." And of course potential receivers might be hesitant to say they wanted "communist political propaganda."

Press Exceptionalism

The American press, the freest in the world, sometimes acts as if its freedom were separate from others' in our constitutional system. When its own interest is at stake, as in the *Pentagon Papers* case, it rallies its forces like King Henry at Harfleur. When the Supreme Court imposes lifetime censorship on an important source of information, dismissing the First Amendment offhandedly, the press hardly notices. (In a 1980 case, for example, Frank Snepp, a former CIA official, was savagely penalized for publishing a book about Vietnam. Justice Brennan was among the dissenters.)

Justice Brennan tried to teach the press that it must respect others' freedom as it values its own. He did not believe, for example, that the protections of *New York Times v. Sullivan* were for the press alone; he thought individuals who were sued for libel were entitled to the same First Amendment guarantees. (A good example is his 1985 dissenting opinion in *Dun & Bradstreet v. Greenmoss Builders,* where he argued that a credit reporting agency that released erroneous credit information was protected under the First Amendment.)

The speech and press clauses of the First Amendment were for Justice Brennan an integral system of freedom embracing all. Newspapers, magazines, and broadcasters benefited from the same understanding of America that led him to end his opinion of the Court in the second flag-burning case, one of his last, by saying: "Punishing desecration of the flag dilutes the very freedom that makes this emblem so revered, and worth revering."

We Hardly Know It When We See It: Obscenity and the Problem of Unprotected Speech

Jeffrey Rosen

> As the Judge remarked the day
> that he acquitted my Aunt Hortense:
> "To be Smut, it must be ut-
> terly without redeeming social importance."
> —Tom Lehr, "Smut"

In his opinions about unprotected speech in general, and obscenity in particular, Justice Brennan gave civil libertarians so much more than they expected from him that it seems peevish to withhold gratitude from him. And yet it was Justice Brennan who spoke most often for the Court during the anxious period between his *Roth* decision in 1957 and his repudiation of *Roth* in 1973, a period during which the justices struggled to distinguish obscenity (which can be banned) from pornography (which must be protected). During those sixteen years, the Court handed down seventeen major obscenity cases; Justice Brennan wrote for the majority or plurality ten times, and he dissented twice. Had Justice Brennan confessed error a year or so earlier than he did—had he announced his new position that obscenity should be decriminalized in 1970 rather than 1973, for example—he almost certainly would have had a majority for overturning his own handiwork in *Roth*. For a justice who was such a master at counting to five, Justice Brennan's timing, in retrospect, seems surprisingly ingenuous.

But in a larger sense, it's hard not to admire the painstakingly incremental quality of Justice Brennan's intellectual evolution from his majority position in *Roth* (that obscenity "is not within the area of

The author is legal affairs editor of the *New Republic*.

---

constitutionally protected speech or press") to his dissenting position in *Miller* and *Paris Adult Theater* (that the Court should "reconsider the attempt altogether under *Roth* to define a category of all sexually oriented expression that may properly be subject to outright suppression by government"). In addition to being one of the most dramatic mea culpas in the history of the Court, Justice Brennan's evolution—worked out in majority opinions and concurrences, in private memoranda to his colleagues, and in speeches and law review articles—represents an unusually candid attempt to reconcile the categorical formalisms of obscenity doctrine with the lived experiences of actual judges struggling to make sense of actual cases. Justice Brennan's increasing focus on the nature of the state's interests in suppressing speech, rather than the nature of speech that the state sought to suppress, helped to guide him through the most important free speech battles of the 1970s and 1980s. In obscenity cases and in other cases, Justice Brennan's growing skepticism about the categorical distinction between protected and unprotected speech led usually, but not invariably, to speech-protective results.

JUSTICE BRENNAN DEFINES OBSCENITY

Roth was Justice Brennan's first free speech opinion, decided during his first term on the Court; and of course it was a product of its times. Still, it's striking to revisit the opinion and to note how casually Justice Brennan dismissed concerns that he would soon come to view as crucial. His holding that the First Amendment does not protect obscenity was based on several questionable judgments. First, Justice Brennan hastily surveyed the history of the First Amendment to support his conclusion that "the protection given speech and press was fashioned to assure unfettered interchange of ideas for the bringing about of political and social changes desired by the people." Implicit in First Amendment history, Justice Brennan concluded, "is the rejection of obscenity as utterly without redeeming social importance." Second, Justice Brennan distinguished between high-value, protected speech and low-value, unprotected speech. He adapted the conclusion of *Chaplinsky v. New Hampshire,* a case declaring that "fighting words" are unprotected: Obscene utterances, he observed, "are no essential part of any exposition of ideas, and are of such slight social value as a step to truth that any benefit that may be derived from them is clearly outweighed by the social interest in order and morality." Finally, Justice Brennan rejected the

Hicklin test, which measured obscenity by its effect on the most susceptible viewer, in favor of a more nuanced test: "whether, to the average person, applying contemporary community standards, the dominant theme of the material, taken as a whole, appeals to prurient interest." Justice Brennan's emphasis on the "dominant interest" of the disputed material, rather than isolated passages, represented an improvement over *Hicklin,* as did his focus on the sensibility of the "average person," rather than the most vulnerable person. But Justice Brennan was too quick to dismiss the dangers of subjectivity and imprecision that would continue to plague the Court.

Before long, Justice Brennan came to repudiate each of the judgments at the heart of *Roth.* His first public doubts concerned the notion that prurience could be objectively determined by applying "contemporary community standards." Who was the relevant community—the entire United States or the local audience at which the allegedly obscene material was targeted? Initially undecided on this point, Justice Brennan merely concurred in the result in *Manuel Enterprises* (1962), in which the Court embraced a national standard and added the opaque requirement that obscene material had to be "patently offensive." But two years later, in *Jacobellis v. Ohio,* Brennan made clear that the "contemporary community standards" test under *Roth* was national, not local. He also emphasized that the requirement that material be "utterly without social importance" was not only a reason for excluding obscene material from First Amendment protection, but also part of the constitutional definition of obscenity.

In the *Memoirs* case in 1966, involving a conviction for publishing *Fanny Hill,* Justice Brennan, again speaking for the Court, announced that "three elements must coalesce" before material can be judged legally obscene:

> It must be established that (a) the dominant theme of the material taken as a whole appeals to a prurient interest in sex; (b) the material is patently offensive because it affronts contemporary community standards relating to the description or representation of sexual matters; and (c) the material is utterly without redeeming social value.

The metaphysics of these distinctions were a little elusive: As Professor Harry Kalven of the University of Chicago noted, it is hard to imagine material that has "valuable, patently offensive pruriency." But because the trial judge had acknowledged the minimal literary value of *Fanny Hill,* Justice Brennan emphasized that it could not be banned:

> A book cannot be proscribed unless it is found to be utterly without re-deeming social value. This is so even though the book is found to possess the requisite prurient appeal and to be patently offensive. Each of the three federal constitutional criteria is to be applied independently; the social value of the book can neither be weighed against nor canceled by its pruri-ent appeal or patent offensiveness.

In *Memoirs,* Justice Brennan was clearly groping for a solution to the subjectivity of *Roth.* But he was not yet ready to abandon entirely the enterprise of distinguishing obscenity from pornography. In two other decisions announced the same day as *Memoirs*—*Mishkin v. New York* and *Ginzburg v. United States*—Justice Brennan again wrote the principal opinions, affirming two obscenity convictions for the first time since *Roth.* In *Mishkin,* the defendant argued that sadomasochis-tic materials were not obscene because they did not appeal to the pruri-ent interest of the "average person." Justice Brennan rejected the argument, holding that when materials are aimed at a "clearly defined deviant sexual group, rather than the public at large," their prurient ap-peal was to be judged by the sensibilities of the audience at which they were aimed. Of course, one man's deviance is another man's lyric; and Justice Brennan's casual suggestion that the obscenity standard could be both national and variable introduced further subjectivity into the law. Furthermore, as a *Yale Law Journal* article argued at the time, by ex-panding the concept of prurience, and emphasizing the effects on the most susceptible audience, Justice Brennan seemed to be returning to the regime of *Hicklin,* which he had earlier repudiated.

Justice Brennan's most disappointing decision, however, was the *Ginzburg* case, which involved an obscenity protection for *Eros,* a so-phisticated erotic magazine. Artistically photographed, and promoted as "the magazine of sexual candor," *Eros* might not have been proscrib-able under the three-part *Memoirs* test. But Justice Brennan unexpect-edly relied on the new concept of "pandering." In "close cases," he stressed, material need not be judged on its own terms, but could be considered in the context of its promotional materials. Merely adver-tising material as obscene would make it increasingly vulnerable, Jus-tice Brennan held. As the dissenters emphasized, the Court had upheld a conviction on a different theory from the one invoked at trial, which was an arguable denial of due process.

JUSTICE BRENNAN ABANDONS OBSCENITY RULES

In his published opinions in the mid-1960s, Justice Brennan seemed to be adhering faithfully to the framework of *Roth*. But in other arenas, he was beginning to confess his doubts. In his Meiklejohn Lecture at Brown University in April 1965, for example, he confessed that "the line between protected and unprotected portrayal [of sex] is dim and uncertain, and judges do experience great difficulty in marking it. The standard against which challenged material must be measured is not perfect; perhaps the problem does not lend itself to precise standards." And before the beginning of the 1962 term, as W. Wat Hopkins describes in *Mr. Justice Brennan and Freedom of Expression* (1991), Justice Brennan circulated a 140-page private memorandum challenging his colleagues to address the host of questions raised by the evolving doctrine, including whether the Constitution permits any suppression of obscene material and whether the *Roth* test should be modified. In his memorandum, Justice Brennan reiterated his position in *Roth*, that it is necessary to define a category of legal obscenity to avoid watering down other First Amendment protections. But in a candid acknowledgment of his growing dissatisfaction with *Roth*, Justice Brennan concluded that if obscenity is "not susceptible of clear, legal definition, I am prepared to say that government suppression of the obscene violates the First Amendment in all but the rare cases in which a private-injury, public-nuisance, or clear-and-present-danger rationale is applicable."

The most significant development in Justice Brennan's memorandum was his growing emphasis on the states' interests in suppressing pornography, rather than the formal distinction between protected and unprotected speech. Rejecting as unsubstantiated the notion that pornography causes sexual crimes, Justice Brennan found only two convincing arguments for suppressing sexually explicit speech: the evils of commercial exploitation, and the emotional injury inflicted on juveniles. Based on these two state interests, Justice Brennan concluded: "There is substantial legitimate social interest in a general criminal law forbidding the dissemination of pornography."

If Justice Brennan had publicly expressed his growing misgivings about *Roth* before the 1970 term, he almost certainly could have persuaded a majority of his colleagues to overturn *Roth*. Alas, it was not until the 1971 term that the Court confronted its next important obscenity decision, *Miller v. California;* and by then, the Court had been transformed by the retirement of Justices Black and Harlan. Chief Justice Warren Burger circulated a memorandum purporting to support Justice Brennan's *Memoirs* test, but suggesting two "refinements" that made the test far less speech protective. The "contemporary community standards," Burger suggested, should be local rather than national; and he questioned the "utterly without redeeming social value" test, which he felt allowed pornographers to pander with impunity by adorning their wares with a pretense of seriousness. As Professor Hopkins relates, Brennan reacted with alarm to the Chief Justice's memorandum, and he circulated another memorandum of his own:

> With all respect, the Chief Justice's proposed solution to the obscenity quagmire will, in my view, worsen an already intolerable mess. I've been thinking for some time that only a drastic change in applicable constitutional principles promises a way out. I've decided that I shall use this case as a vehicle for saying that I'm prepared to make that change. I'll write in effect that it has proved impossible to separate expression concerning sex, called obscenity, from other expression concerning sex, whether the material takes the form of words, photographs or film; . . . that we should treat obscenity not as expression concerning sex excepted from First Amendment speech but expression, although constituting First Amendment speech, that is regulable to the extent of legislating against its offensive exposure to unwilling adults and dissemination to juveniles. I'll try in due course to circulate my views.

In his landmark dissent in *Paris Adult Theater I v. Slaton* (1973), issued the same day as *Miller,* Justice Brennan finally circulated his new view. "I am convinced," he began dramatically, "that the approach initiated 16 years ago in *Roth v. United States,* and culminating in the Court's decision today, cannot bring stability to this area of the law without jeopardizing fundamental First Amendment values, and I have concluded that the time has come to make a significant departure from that approach." What follows is remarkable for its candor:

> After 16 years of experimentation and debate I am reluctantly forced to the conclusion that none of the available formulas, including the one announced today, can reduce the vagueness to a tolerable level while at the same time striking an acceptable balance between the protections of the

First and Fourteenth Amendments, on the one hand, and on the other the asserted state interest in regulating the dissemination of certain sexually oriented materials. Any effort to draw a constitutionally acceptable boundary on state power must resort to such indefinite concepts as "prurient interest," "patent offensiveness," "serious literary value," and the like. The meaning of these concepts necessarily varies with the experience, outlook, and even idiosyncrasies of the person defining them. Although we have assumed that obscenity does exist and that we "know it when [we] see it" . . . we are manifestly unable to describe it in advance except by reference to concepts so elusive that they fail to distinguish clearly between protected and unprotected speech.

After reviewing and rejecting the various alternatives embraced by other members of the Court—the *Miller* emphasis on "serious literary, artistic, political, or scientific value"; the possibility of general deference to lower courts; and the absolutist position of Justices Black and Douglas, who held that the First Amendment bars the suppression of any sexually oriented expression—Brennan concluded that more "sensitive tools" were necessary to distinguish between legitimate and illegitimate speech. "Because we assumed—incorrectly, as experience has proved—that obscenity could be separated from other sexually oriented expression without significant costs, . . . we had no occasion in *Roth* to probe the asserted state interest in curtailing sexually oriented speech." Turning to the state's general interests in suppressing obscenity to regulate morality, Brennan concluded that they remained "essentially unfocused and ill defined," were "predicated on unprovable . . . assumptions about human behavior, morality, sex, and religion," and could not, therefore, "validate a statute that substantially undermines the guarantees of the First Amendment." Finally, Justice Brennan announced his meticulously wrought conclusion: "at least in the absence of distribution to juveniles or obtrusive exposure to unconsenting adults," the state cannot attempt "wholly to suppress sexually oriented materials on the basis of their allegedly 'obscene' contents."

Weighing the State's Interest in Suppression

Justice Brennan's careful weighing of the state interests in *Paris Theater,* and his insistence that the interests be specifically defined and "empirically provable" when fundamental constitutional interests are involved, would be the hallmark of his attempt to distinguish protected from unprotected speech during his remaining two decades on the Court. He never formally repudiated *Chaplinsky's* formal distinction between high-value, protected speech and low-value, unprotected speech: In the two flag-burning cases, for example, he took care to emphasize that flag burning did not fall into one of the traditional *Chaplinsky* exceptions.

But in the decades following *Miller,* Justice Brennan was more concerned with weighing the power of the state's interest in suppressing speech than in assigning cases to rigid doctrinal categories. As Dean Geoffrey Stone has noted, between 1956 and 1990, Justice Brennan rejected a free speech claim that the Court accepted in only two cases, and in both, the regulation of free expression was designed to "improve" the marketplace of ideas: *Federal Election Commission v. National Conservative Political Action Committee* (1985) and *First National Bank of Boston v. Bellotti* (1978). Rather than writing separately, Justice Brennan joined Justice White's dissents in both cases, each of which argued that limits on electoral spending by corporations and political action committees might serve First Amendment values, promoting the free marketplace of ideas by preventing corporate domination of political debate.

All in all, Justice Brennan rejected the First Amendment claim in only thirty-one cases during his entire career. Approximately half of them involved regulations designed not only to "improve the marketplace of ideas," but also to promote competing interests of equality, such as *Austin v. Michigan Chamber of Commerce* (1990), upholding a state limitation on corporate political spending during elections, or *Roberts v. United States Jaycees* (1984), upholding a state statute requiring Jaycees to admit women. Justice Brennan accepted the free speech claims in 88 percent of the 252 free speech cases in which he participated, while the Court as a whole accepted only 59 percent of the claims.

Justice Brennan never worked out a comprehensive theory of how to weigh the state's interests in suppressing sexually explicit speech; nor was he interested in a comprehensive enumeration of how compelling interests should be identified in the first place. The methodology that served him in *Paris Theater*—rejecting broadly defined interests that could not be empirically tested, such as promoting morality—was not the methodology he used in the campaign finance cases, where he accepted the state's claim that regulation would, in fact, improve the marketplace of ideas without demanding empirical support.

Perhaps the landmark *New York Times* case epitomizes Justice Brennan's mature views about the central meaning of the First Amendment, and his emphasis on "the principle that debate on public issues should be uninhibited, robust, and wide-open" helps to explain his willingness to tolerate occasional regulation to improve the quality of public debate. In his Meiklejohn Lecture, Brennan himself noted the similarities between his view, expressed in *Garrison v. Louisiana* (1964), that "speech concerning public affairs is more than self-expression; it is the essence of self-government" and Meiklejohn's own view that "the freedom that the First Amendment protects is not, then, an absence of regulation. It is the presence of self-government."

But even those who are more skeptical of the Meiklejohnian project, and would give self-expression *and* self-government equal weight in the pantheon of First Amendment values, can only consider Justice Brennan's First Amendment legacy with gratitude and awe. His candid evolution from the categorical formalism of *Roth* to the more flexible, interest-oriented approach of *Paris Theater, Bellotti,* and *Garrison* epitomizes a skeptical intelligence at work. Although Justice Brennan never, in his later years, worked out a comprehensive theory for distinguishing protected speech from unprotected speech, his case-by-case scrutiny of the state's purported interests in First Amendment cases is a testament to the value of what Professor Cass Sunstein has called "incompletely theorized arguments."

In the years since he retired from the Court, the revival of free speech formalism in cases concerning unprotected speech has not always led the Court to positions that are more protective of speech than Justice Brennan's more flexible approach. With Justice Black, whose absolutist view of the First Amendment he rejected, Justice Brennan surely ranks among the most important defenders of free speech in the history of the Court.

Freedom of Association

Robert L. Carter

In 1938, when I was a student at Howard Law School, I attended the oral argument at the Supreme Court in the case of *Missouri ex rel. Gaines v. Canada.* This case, which challenged the exclusion of a black student from the University of Missouri's law school, was one of the first in the National Association for the Advancement of Colored People's strategic use of the court system to battle segregation at the state university level. When Charles Hamilton Houston, chief counsel of the NAACP, rose to begin his oral argument, Justice McReynolds turned his chair around and presented his back to Houston. Later, not surprisingly, he dissented from the Court's holding that Mr. Gaines was entitled to admission to the law school. Thus, despite the beneficial holding, my first view of the Supreme Court was of justice turning its back on black people and manifesting indifference to their needs and aspirations.

Throughout much of this century, the federal courts, and the Supreme Court in particular, have been the only forum realistically available to many disenfranchised, disfavored minorities. But as Justice McReynolds's behavior indicates, the Supreme Court was not always entirely receptive to the call for equal justice and equal opportunities. It took the compassion, intelligence, and understanding of great minds such as Justice William J. Brennan to ensure that the Constitution's guarantees of freedom of speech and freedom of association included the guarantee that voices raised in lawful protest would be heard and answered.

THE FIRST AMENDMENT'S GUARANTEE OF FREEDOM OF ASSOCIATION

The First Amendment secures to Americans the freedom of religion, speech, and the press, and the right "peaceably to assemble, and to peti-

The author is a senior judge on the United States District Court for the Southern District of New York. As a lawyer with the NAACP, and general counsel from 1957 to 1968, he litigated numerous groundbreaking civil rights cases.

tion the Government for a redress of grievances." Although the Constitution does not explicitly mention freedom of association, that right has generally been understood to be an essential element of the First Amendment; as the Supreme Court affirmed in *Griswold v. Connecticut* (1965), "its existence is necessary in making the express guarantees [of the First Amendment] fully meaningful." Associational rights were of obviously central importance to the Framers of the Constitution, who had recently fought a war over, among other things, meaningful political participation and the right to assemble and raise their voices in lawful protest to their own government. The Supreme Court has repeatedly reaffirmed these values, stating in *United States v. Cruikshank* in 1876, for example, that "the very idea of a government, republican in form, implies a right on the part of its citizens to meet peaceably for consultation in respect to public affairs and to petition for a redress of grievances."

As this country has struggled to eliminate discrimination and to recognize the value of a multiethnic, multiracial, diverse society, constitutional doctrine has endeavored to keep pace. Freedom of association has come to be a protection, a refuge that enables members of unpopular, weak, or disfavored minority groups to band together to pool their resources. Individuals working in isolation, forced to fight and refight the same battles, can accomplish far more lasting change when they join together in groups and organizations. In banding together, individuals gain strength not only from numbers but from an affirmation of group identity and value. Thus, the freedom to associate and exercise the right to petition the government has been a central, enabling aspect of the struggles for justice and equality of ethnic and racial minorities, such as African Americans and Latino Americans; religious groups, such as Jews and Catholics; women; and other groups subjected to discrimination and repression, such as gays and lesbians.

Justice Brennan understood the importance of this meaning of freedom of association. His presence on the Supreme Court helped to ensure that the right of disfavored groups to raise their voices in lawful protest would be meaningful and secure.

No opinion better reflects Justice Brennan's understanding of associational freedom than his opinion for the Supreme Court in *NAACP v. Button* (1963), which related the abstract language of constitutional doctrine to the realities of the situation faced by black Americans in the 1960s.

NAACP v. Button

The case arose out of the line of desegregation cases, beginning in 1954, when the Supreme Court held in *Brown v. Board of Education* that the "separate but equal" doctrine was unconstitutional with regard to public grade-school education. Southern legislators and officials immediately began a campaign to frustrate the implementation of *Brown.* They initiated a concerted effort to destroy the NAACP, which had brought *Brown* and other cases challenging segregation: They sought to drive it out of existence by attacking its tax-exempt status and by smothering the organization's efforts to speak to, meet with, and organize blacks for future lawsuits. It was individual black citizens, however, who bore the brunt of these attacks. The aim was to render the organization powerless through harassment and economic and physical reprisals on its members, and to make membership in the organization too heavy a price for the average black to bear because it might mean loss of a job or exposure to violence and attacks on family members.

From 1956 and onwards, the NAACP engaged in battle after battle in the federal courts to counter the attacks to oust it from the South. In a series of cases, the Supreme Court agreed with the NAACP that various states' demands for our membership lists violated the freedoms of speech and association. Justice Harlan, in *NAACP v. Alabama ex rel. Patterson* (1958), Justice Stewart, in *Bates v. City of Little Rock* (1960), and Justice Goldberg, in *Gibson v. Florida Legislative Investigation Committee* (1963), asserted that the symbiotic relationship between the rights to free speech and free assembly had long been recognized and that the due process clause of the Fourteenth Amendment protected these rights against state action absent a controlling justification. The justices elucidated the principles of the First Amendment in these cases in which the government's evidence clearly failed to satisfy the close scrutiny applicable to constitutionally protected rights. However, it was Justice Brennan, in *NAACP v. Button,* who breathed life into the First Amendment freedom to associate by explicitly relating these principles to the very real danger that faced the NAACP, and black people generally, in the United States.[1]

Button arose from Virginia's attempts to drive the NAACP from the state. In the years following *Brown,* Virginia amended several state statutes to make the activities of the NAACP fall within the definition of barratry and champerty, or improper solicitation of legal business. (Arkansas, Florida, Georgia, Mississippi, South Carolina, and Tennessee also passed laws following the *Brown* decision which brought within the reach of their barratry statutes cases in which the organization urged blacks to file lawsuits testing various laws or undertook to supply lawyers and represent the litigants without charge.) The NAACP believed that the enforcement of those statutes outlawed its litigation efforts to assert the civil rights of black Americans. Therefore, suits were filed in federal and state courts on the grounds that the Virginia laws violated First Amendment freedoms, protected against state action by the Fourteenth Amendment. We argued that the Virginia statute infringed the right of the NAACP and its members and lawyers to associate for the purpose of assisting persons who sought legal redress for infringements of their constitutionally guaranteed rights. We believed that the First Amendment guaranteed the freedoms to express and advocate that racial discrimination was constitutionally and morally infirm. The Supreme Court agreed.

In an opinion written by Justice Brennan, the Court held that First Amendment protection of communication extended beyond the protection of abstract discussion to include within its shelter active opposition to governmental intrusion. Litigation, as used strategically by the NAACP and black Americans, was no longer just a technique for resolving private differences. It was vigorous advocacy: in Justice Brennan's words, "a means for achieving the lawful objectives of equality of treatment by all government, federal, state, and local, for the members of the Negro community in this country."

Justice Brennan recognized that the NAACP and black Americans turned to the courts because litigation was most likely "the sole practicable avenue open to a minority to petition for redress of grievances," when avenues of legislative action had been foreclosed. When Virginia law criminalized the person who advised another that his legal rights had been infringed and referred him to a particular attorney or group of at-

---

1. It is useful in the context of this discussion to note that besides the upheavals of the civil rights movement, the 1960s also marked the emergence of this nation from the dark cloud of McCarthyism. The right of freedom of association took severe blows from demagoguery and the use of popular fear of and antipathy to communism. These turbulent times gave some indication of what might happen if guilt by association became an acceptable, even a constitutional, principle. Justice Brennan's response to the attacks on the NAACP by many southern states should be viewed in light of the widespread denial of the freedom of association in the 1950s.

torneys for assistance, and criminalized the attorney who knowingly gave assistance in this situation as well, the law "smother[ed] all discussion looking to the eventual institution of litigation on behalf of the rights of members of an unpopular minority." After describing the great risk to lawyers, members, and sympathizers of the NAACP as cause for hesitation by black Americans to publicly support the NAACP's causes, Justice Brennan struck down the vague and overbroad statute. He stated:

> We cannot close our eyes to the fact that the militant Negro civil rights movement has engendered the intense resentment and opposition of the politically dominant white community of Virginia; litigation assisted by the NAACP has been bitterly fought. In such circumstances, a statute broadly curtailing group activity leading to litigation may easily become a weapon of oppression, however evenhanded its terms appear. Its mere existence could well freeze out of existence all such activity on behalf of the civil rights of Negro citizens.

Justice Brennan's recognition of litigation as a form of political expression for the NAACP reconciled the loftiness inherent in the ideals of freedom of speech and association and the right to petition the government with the practical realities of our putatively egalitarian society. Drawing from Justice Harlan's opinion in *NAACP v. Alabama ex rel. Patterson*, Justice Brennan did more than reaffirm the principle that the First and Fourteenth Amendments protect the right "to engage in association for the advancement of beliefs and ideas." For those striving to vindicate the civil rights of black Americans, *NAACP v. Button* recognized that the NAACP's "litigation . . . makes possible the distinctive contribution of a minority group to the ideas and beliefs of our society." The case gave constitutional protection not only to group litigation efforts, but to direct protest activity as well, such as sit-ins at lunch counters and street marches. Such actions were necessary to ensure that the words of the Constitution extended to all, regardless of race, creed, or color.

FURTHER DEVELOPMENTS IN FREEDOM OF ASSOCIATION DOCTRINE

The freedom of association, asserted in such ringing tones in *Button* and similar cases, is not always such a straightforward concept, however. Associational rights of one individual can run counter to those of another, when the freedom to associate becomes entangled with the freedom to exclude. (This tension comes into play in other First Amendment areas as well: most recently, for example, in the battles over university speech codes.) Associational rights entail the freedom to form groups and organizations along selected lines—the freedom to associate with people of one's own choosing. But what happens when these rights are exercised in such a way as to impinge on the rights of others to associate or to participate equally? In later cases on the subject, Justice Brennan addressed the central tension between freedom of association as a means of participation and a guarantee that voices will be heard and freedom of association as a means of exclusion, asserted to enforce and perpetuate historical iniquities.

In the 1984 case of *Roberts v. United States Jaycees,* the Supreme Court addressed a challenge to the Jaycees organization's policy of excluding women from full membership. Two chapters of the young men's civic group had begun to admit women members, and the national leadership had imposed sanctions against those chapters. The chapters filed discrimination claims with the Minnesota Department of Human Rights, under a Minnesota law which provided that

> it is an unfair discriminatory practice . . . [t]o deny any person the full and equal enjoyment of the goods, services, facilities, privileges, advantages, and accommodations of a place of public accommodation because of race, color, creed, religion, disability, national origin or sex.

After the Department of Human Rights ordered the Jaycees to cease their discriminatory practices in refusing to admit women, the organization filed suit in federal court against state officials, claiming that opening their doors to women would impinge on the rights of male members to free speech and free association.

In his opinion for the Supreme Court, Justice Brennan explained that freedom of association is not an absolute right; it is subject to restriction by a compelling state interest if it is unrelated to the suppression of ideas and if there exists no significantly less restrictive means to accomplish the regulatory end. This sort of test is not unfamiliar in constitutional doctrine; similar standards have been erected to guide judicial scrutiny of the constitutionality of laws and regulations that affect various classes and communities of people. For example, any laws impacting directly on groups of people defined by their race or national origin must meet a similar test.

Justice Brennan's decision becomes most interesting to our examination of his role in the development of freedom of association doctrine, however, in his willingness to apply constitutional principles as informed by his understanding of the social and historical underpinnings of the situation. His decision is written with an awareness of the systematic, historical exclusion of women not only from positions of power, but from the opportunities that would allow them to develop the skills and contacts necessary to achieve preeminence. He recognized that the "stigmatizing injury" resulting from denials of equal access to publicly allocated goods and services is as potent and debilitating to those discriminated against on the basis of sex as those who face discrimination because of their race.

Justice Brennan's deep understanding is illustrated in his interpretation of the Minnesota statute in question. The statute forbade discrimination in the provision of "goods, services, facilities, privileges, advantages, and accommodations." The Jaycees were not engaged in selling goods or offering services for hire in a conventional way; instead, they provided less tangible advantages to members, such as business contacts and leadership training. In holding that the statute applied to the Jaycees and that it furthered a compelling state interest in this case, Justice Brennan defined the statute to extend to consideration of economic advancement generally. His broad view of commercial activity included intangible benefits. He acknowledged

> the changing nature of the American economy and . . . the importance, both to the individual and to society, of removing the barriers to economic advancement and political and social integration that have historically plagued certain disadvantaged groups, including women.

As with his recognition of the legal strategy of the NAACP as political speech, this understanding of employment opportunities as "goods" or "privileges" displays his ability to look to underlying realities of commercial activity, to the historical and social forces that shape the law and are in turn transformed by it.[2]

Thus, the importance of Justice Brennan's decision in *Roberts v. United States Jaycees*, as in *NAACP v. Button*, lies in its recognition of the historical and political context surrounding, underlying, and giving meaning to the legal decisions. It was Justice Brennan who truly understood the practicalities behind the principles, the realities behind the rights; he knew that the statement that a right exists, made without any awareness of how implementation of that right might be carried out, can be a nullity.

Thus informed by an understanding of the realities behind the rights, Justice Brennan indicated that freedom of association should be safeguarded only insofar as it in turn engenders the expression of ideas. In Justice Brennan's view, as expressed in *Roberts v. United States Jaycees,* freedom of association doctrine concerns the protection not of a thing but of a process, a potential. Freedom of association is a crucial right, one which can safeguard the unpopular speech of a group desperate to ameliorate its situation. But it must not be used as a means of excluding minority voices and perpetuating discrimination. This is a relatively narrow definition of freedom of association, with an emphasis on modality and implementation. But it is an expansive view of rights, one which turns its back on no one.

Conclusion

Freedom of speech is an extremely complicated and slippery concept. Justice Brennan's commitment to a legal analysis informed by the instrumentality of rights and the ways in which they work themselves out in people's lives; his extraordinary ability to clothe bare legalities in the garb of history, reality, and justice; and his refusal to allow simplistic, rigidly patterned legal analysis all help to ensure that freedom of association doctrine will be responsive to the needs and aspirations of Americans of all types. Justice Brennan is justly celebrated as a protector of the First Amendment. His opinions on freedom of association and his role in shaping that doctrine demonstrate the ways in which free speech to Justice Brennan is not merely an academic or jurisprudential matter but a living concept that plays a role in the lives of each one of us.

2. This insight derives in part from *The Supreme Court, 1983 Term: Freedom of Association,* 98 Harv. L. Rev. 195 (1984).

Conditions and Conscience:
Free Exercise of Religion

Robert F. Drinan, S.J.

When Republican President Eisenhower in 1956 nominated a Democratic judge named William Brennan from New Jersey to be a justice of
the United States Supreme Court no one could have predicted that in
his thirty-four years on the Court Justice Brennan would be one of the
principal architects of the flowering of protection for the free exercise
of religion. Indeed, at that time there were many suspicions and questions about whether a Catholic justice would bring to the Court some
of his own religious convictions. Judge Brennan answered "categorically
that . . . in every office I have held in my life or that I shall ever do in
the future, what shall control me is the oath that I took to support the
Constitution of the United States."

When Justice Brennan took the oath of office in 1956, the Supreme
Court had ruled on an amazingly small number of cases involving the
free exercise clause of the First Amendment, which provides that "Congress shall make no law . . . prohibiting the free exercise" of religion.

The free exercise clause obviously prohibits laws that directly target
a religion or religious practice. The difficult cases have been those in
which a law designed to apply to all has the effect of prohibiting or burdening a religious practice or observance. Before 1956, the handful of
cases drew murky boundaries on the obligation of the government to
exempt particular religious groups from the operation of laws that apply
to all.

On the one hand, the Court in *Reynolds v. United States* in 1877 had
not been sympathetic to the claim of the Mormons that laws against
bigamy infringed their religious liberty. On the other hand, in *Follett v.*

The author, a professor at Georgetown University Law Center, was a member of Congress from
1971 to 1981. Before serving in Congress, he was dean of Boston College Law School for thirteen years.

Town of McCormick in 1944 the Court held unconstitutional a flat license tax on booksellers as applied to a Jehovah's Witness who sells religious literature. And in *Cantwell v. Connecticut* in 1940 the Court held that the free exercise clause (which by its terms applies only to Congress) was applicable to the states as well, in a decision that invalidated a statute restricting the right of Jehovah's Witnesses to proselytize.

Justice Brennan therefore had little precedential guidance in 1961 when he encountered his first religion cases, a pair of cases about Sunday closing laws. Brennan joined the majority opinion in *McGowan v. Maryland*, rejecting the claim that the Sunday closing laws amounted to the unconstitutional establishment of religion. But he protested strongly in *Braunfeld v. Brown*, the companion case, against the enforcement of a Sunday closing law to the extent that it burdened a merchant's free exercise of his religion. Specifically, the law forbade Orthodox Jews to open their businesses on Sunday even though they were required by their faith to abstain from labor from sundown Friday to sundown Saturday.

In his dissent in *Braunfeld* Justice Brennan demonstrated for the first time how deeply he felt about government infringements on the right of a person to follow his or her conscience. Justice Brennan complained that the Pennsylvania law forced the "individual to a choice between his business and his religion." Justice Brennan may have overstated the case since the Pennsylvania law did not require the Orthodox Jew to affirm beliefs repugnant to him or to work on the Sabbath; the law was neutral and the impact on Orthodox Jews was unintended. But Justice Brennan compared the Sunday closing law to the tax on religious literature, which the Court struck in *Follett*.

Braunfeld did not last long. At Justice Brennan's first chance to write a majority opinion on the free exercise clause, in *Sherbert v. Verner* in 1963, he practically overruled *Braunfeld*, seizing the opportunity to begin a pilgrimage, almost a crusade, to expand the protection of the free exercise clause.

The facts in *Sherbert* were appealing. Adell Sherbert, a Seventh Day Adventist, was forbidden by her faith from working on Saturday. She was fired as a result of her refusal to work on the day she worshiped God, and was denied unemployment benefits on the ground that she declined job offers that would have required her to work on Saturdays.

The majority in *Sherbert* could have rested its case on the narrow ground that the statute in South Carolina guaranteed a day of rest to all on Sunday and protected them from work on Sunday; hence, the Court could have found compliance with the principle that if a state guarantees a benefit to one group it must guarantee it to similarly situated persons. But Justice Brennan and the majority of the Court wanted to make the *Sherbert* decision the new Magna Carta for the rights of persons claiming that a law, even if it is neutral on its face, can violate the free exercise clause if it infringes on the dictates of conscience of some believers. Thus, *Sherbert* became the first case in which the Supreme Court struck down a statute based *only* on the free exercise clause.

Justice Brennan reached back to his dissent in *Braunfeld* and held that "if the purpose or effect of a law is to impede the observance of one or all religions that law is constitutionally invalid even though the burden may be characterized as being only indirect." In this case, Justice Brennan concluded, the state law "forces her to choose between following the precepts of her religion and forfeiting benefits, on the one hand, and abandoning one of the precepts of her religion in order to accept work, on the other hand."

The *Sherbert* decision did not explicitly overrule *Braunfeld* although logically it probably should have. At least that was the view of the dissent. Justice Harlan, joined by Justice White, concluded that *Sherbert* "necessarily overrules" *Braunfeld*. Indeed, he reasoned, the financial burden of the South Carolina law is far less onerous than the law in *Braunfeld* which required a store owner to close his business on Sunday. Justice Stewart, concurring in the majority view in *Sherbert*, also stated that *Braunfeld* should be reversed.

The profound determination of Justice Brennan to protect the diversity of religious views was articulated eloquently in *Sherbert*—more eloquently than in any of his numerous opinions on religious freedom.

For over twenty years, the Court continued to build upon the foundation that Justice Brennan laid in *Sherbert*. In 1965 Brennan joined the majority of the Court in *United States v. Seeger*, where the Court defined "religion" in an expansive manner which allowed Seeger to claim conscientious objection to the draft. And then in 1972, the nearly unanimous decision in *Wisconsin v. Yoder* broadened the thrust of the free exercise clause in a ruling that held that a state may not enforce compulsory attendance laws (at least after the age of sixteen) against students whose Amish parents are conscientiously opposed to their children being required to attend a school that they considered a secular institution.

In 1978, in *McDaniel v. Paty*, the Supreme Court had an easy case where it ruled that the free exercise clause invalidated a Tennessee statute which forbade "ministers of the gospel" from serving as delegates to the state's constitutional convention. Justice Brennan, in concurring, emphasized that the free exercise clause meant that the state could not constitutionally suppress religious ideas, thoughts, and actions in an attempt to avoid political divisiveness.

Until 1990 the Supreme Court remained fairly firm in its commitment to the principles set forth by Justice Brennan in *Sherbert*. That decision was hailed by all religious groups as a reassurance by the Court that it would protect the dissenters, conscientious objectors, and members of small and vulnerable religious minorities.

There were, of course, limits to the requirements of accommodation. Even Justice Brennan drew the line in a 1982 case in which an Amish employer desired an exemption from paying Social Security taxes. The Justice concurred in *United States v. Lee*, which held that the free exercise clause does not extend that far.

Nevertheless, twice in the 1980s, the Court reaffirmed *Sherbert*. In 1981, in *Thomas v. Indiana Employment Security Division*, the Court held that a Jehovah's Witness who for reasons of conscience withdrew from his job at a munitions factory was entitled to unemployment benefits. In *Hobbie v. Unemployment Appeals Commission* in 1987 the Court ruled that a person who became a Seventh Day Adventist after beginning her employment and was then fired for refusing to work on Saturdays, her Sabbath, was entitled to unemployment compensation.

But the favor which the *Sherbert* decision and the free exercise clause enjoyed shifted in 1986 when the Supreme Court in *Goldman v. Weinberger* refused to allow Captain Goldman, a psychologist in the military, to wear the yarmulke characteristic of Orthodox Jews. Justice Brennan's stirring dissent is a moving and eloquent defense of a generous interpretation of the free exercise clause.

> Our constitutional commitment to religious freedom and to acceptance of religious pluralism is one of our greatest achievements. . . . [A]lmost 200 years after the first amendment was drafted, tolerance and respect for all religions still set us apart from most other countries and draws to our shores refugees from religious persecution from around the world.

Justice Brennan openly asked the Congress to review and reverse the wooden regulation of the military on what headgear may be worn.

The Congress responded and in essence reversed the *Goldman* decision.

The retrenchment continued with *Lyng v. Northwest Indian Cemetery Protection Association* in 1988. The majority sustained a decision of the United States Forest Service to build a road through a tract of land in California that had long been sacred to an Indian tribe.

Justice Brennan in dissent harkened back to his dissent in *Braunfeld.* He noted that the religious plaintiffs in the case had shown that the government's proposal would effectively prevent them from practicing their religion. Consequently the free exercise clause had been violated. One reads Justice Brennan's dissent wondering if he sensed that his opinion in *Sherbert* was living on borrowed time.

The heaviest blow to *Sherbert* came in 1990 with a 5–4 ruling in *Employment Division v. Smith.* The two claimants there were dismissed from employment in a private drug rehabilitation organization because they had ingested peyote for sacramental purposes at a ceremony of the Native American church to which they belonged. The Oregon Supreme Court, relying on *Sherbert,* held that the claimants were entitled to unemployment benefits because their conduct was the result of their religious convictions. The use of peyote for sacramental purposes was an essential part of the faith of the two dismissed persons. It should be noted that the use of peyote for religious purposes is specifically allowed in the laws of several western states and in at least one federal law.

The twenty-seven-year tenure of the *Sherbert* decision did not deter the majority in *Smith* from qualifying *Sherbert,* although not expressly overruling it. The opinion of Justice Scalia reversed the Oregon Supreme Court, writing that "we have never held that an individual's religious beliefs excuse him from compliance with an otherwise valid law prohibiting conduct that the state is free to regulate." Scalia sought to isolate the *Sherbert* decision, stating that *Sherbert, Thomas,* and *Hobbie* do not apply to any governmental action except the denial of unemployment compensation. Scalia concluded that *Sherbert* and its progeny do not apply to the criminal statute in Oregon forbidding the use of peyote.

Justice Brennan must have found the *Smith* decision distressing. It came in his last year on the bench. He protested by joining in the dissenting opinions of Justice O'Connor and Justice Blackmun. We do not know why Justice Brennan did not write his own dissent in a case which clearly cast a giant shadow over the results and the reasoning in *Sherbert.* Justice O'Connor, although concurring in the result, opened her dissent by declaring that "today's holding dramatically departs from well settled First Amendment jurisprudence . . . and is incompatible with our nation's fundamental commitment to individual religious liberty."

Justice Blackmun was equally vigorous in denouncing the Scalia opinion. He declared that the majority "effectuates a wholesale overturning of settled law concerning the religious clauses of our Constitution." Blackmun also expressed the view that "one hopes that the Court is aware of the consequences, and that its result is not a product of overreaction to the serious problems the country's drug crisis has generated."

Shortly after *Smith* was handed down, an unprecedented group of religious organizations and civil libertarian groups took up Justice Brennan's challenge in *Goldman* to have Congress restore the freedoms the Court had cut out. The groups sponsored and helped to enact the Religious Freedom Restoration Act (RFRA). This measure directly qualifies and even reverses the *Smith* decision. RFRA makes it clear that the moment a plaintiff alleges that a government law infringes on his religious freedom the burden of proof shifts to the government to justify the law. In order to prevail, the government must demonstrate that the challenged restriction on religious freedom is required by a compelling concern of the government and that it is narrowly tailored to achieve that objective.

Thus, three years after the *Smith* decision, which altered Justice Brennan's view on religious freedom as set forth in *Sherbert,* the Congress restored the thrust of the *Sherbert* ruling. There has never been anything quite like the Religious Freedom Restoration Act in all of American history. Its provisions are now being aggressively advanced in a wide variety of ways in federal and state courts. It is not clear as yet whether RFRA will have a radical effect on the way the free exercise clause will be construed. But it is clear that RFRA has restored religious freedom to the same stature it had in the twenty-seven years from *Sherbert* to *Smith.*

History may reveal that the legacy which Justice Brennan bequeathed on the free exercise of religion has now been codified in federal law. This may well turn out to be one of the most important and lasting achievements among the Justice's countless contributions.

Separation Most Strict: Discovering an Unpublished Establishment-Clause Opinion

NATHAN LEWIN

When I rose to argue in the Supreme Court on behalf of the estate of Donald Thornton on November 7, 1984, I did not think there was any real likelihood that I would lose the vote of Justice Brennan. My client had been a Sunday-observing Presbyterian, who had been fired by Caldor's Department Store because he had refused to work on Sundays. And Justice Brennan had, by 1984, shown his understanding of the plight of Sabbath-observant employees in two important cases.

BRENNAN'S EARLY VIEW OF SABBATH OBSERVANCE

Braunfeld v. Brown (1961) concerned the impact of Pennsylvania's Sunday laws on Orthodox Jewish merchants who were required by their faith to close their shops on Saturdays. They claimed that the free exercise clause of the First Amendment entitled them to an exemption from Sunday-closing laws. Chief Justice Earl Warren spoke for the majority in rejecting the constitutional claim on the ground that the Sunday law did not prohibit observance of Orthodox Judaism; it only made, in Warren's words, "the practice of their religious belief more expensive." While acknowledging that a statutory exemption for Sabbath observers might be "the wiser solution to the problem," the Chief Justice rejected the argument that an exemption is constitutionally required because if Sabbath observers were permitted to keep their stores open on Sunday, they might well have "an economic advantage over their competitors who must remain closed on that day."

The author is a partner in the law firm Miller, Cassidy, Larroca & Lewin in Washington, D.C. He has litigated many landmark cases on the religion clauses of the First Amendment.

Justice Brennan had no patience with this hairsplitting. He recognized that, in the real world of commerce, Sabbath observers do not enjoy competitive advantages; they routinely confront obstacles. Brennan described the issue in *Braunfeld* as "whether a State may put an individual to a choice between his business and his religion." The effect of the Sunday-closing law on the Orthodox Jewish shopkeeper, he said, is a "clog upon the exercise of religion," and he dismissed Warren's assertion that the Sabbath observer would gain an advantage as "more fanciful than real."

Dissenting in *Braunfeld* was no small step. Justice Brennan was still a junior justice in 1961, and he was building the bridge to Earl Warren that would make Brennan the true behind-the-scenes manager of what came to be known as the Warren Court. Yet he felt so strongly for the Sabbath observer that he published a dissent that was sharply critical of the Chief Justice—the colleague whom he had most frequently joined in the Court's cases during the two preceding terms.

Little more than two years later came the strongest blow that the Supreme Court has struck for the freedom to observe one's Sabbath—the landmark Brennan opinion in *Sherbert v. Verner* (1963). Justice Brennan articulated the constitutional rule that the free exercise of religion may be overcome only by a "compelling state interest." The Court's ruling was that a state unemployment-compensation system may not constitutionally disqualify an employee who refuses to accept a job requiring her to work on her Sabbath. An individual may not be forced "to choose between following the precepts of her religion and forfeiting benefits, on the one hand, and abandoning one of the precepts of her religion in order to accept work, on the other." Brennan rejected the argument that upholding the constitutional right would lead others who are not truly religious to make similar claims in order to be able to take Saturdays off and still receive unemployment benefits. His response was that "there is no proof whatever to warrant such fears of malingering or deceit."

A justice less sensitive to the tribulations of religious observance would have rejected Adell Sherbert's claim on the ground that no one forced her to be a Seventh Day Adventist. Her personal religious choice, it could be said, carried with it certain consequences that she might have to endure. Her religious observance might make her life "more expensive" by rendering her ineligible for unemployment benefits if she rejected a job requiring Saturday work. Justice Stewart's concurrence and

Justice Harlan's dissent also noted that the "singling out of religious conduct for special treatment may violate the constitutional limits on state action" because it might be tantamount to favoring religion in violation of the establishment clause. Justice Brennan bought none of that. South Carolina's law was unconstitutionally applied, he said, because it "constrain[ed] a worker to abandon his religious convictions respecting the day of rest."

Donald Thornton's Case

And so we come to the Connecticut law that was before the Court in 1984 in Donald Thornton's case—more than two decades after *Sherbert v. Verner.* The Connecticut legislature had repealed its Sunday law in 1976. In order to protect religious employees of stores that would now be open on Sundays from being forced to work on their day of rest, the following clause was tucked into the repealer legislation:

> No person who states that a particular day of the week is observed as his Sabbath may be required by his employer to work on such day. An employee's refusal to work on his Sabbath shall not constitute grounds for his dismissal.

Notwithstanding this provision, Caldor's Department Store fired Thornton, the manager of its men's and boys' clothing department, when he refused to work on Sundays. The Connecticut Supreme Court rejected his claim that the Sabbath observer provision shielded his job. It found the statute unconstitutional because the word "Sabbath" in the law indicated that the statutory right "comes with religious strings attached" and this made it "clearly violative of the establishment clause."

When the Surpeme Court granted the certiorari petition I filed for Thornton's estate, I assumed—mistakenly as matters turned out—that the justices understood the Sabbath observer's plight and were ready to repudiate the reasoning and result of the Connecticut Supreme Court. The state court had not, by the way, ever construed the Connecticut law to determine whether the excuse from work it gave to Sabbath observers was "absolute." Could a Sabbath-observing employee invoke the protection of the law to be excused on Sunday even if his presence on that day was absolutely essential to the conduct of the employer's business?

Federal law has qualifications built into the language of the applicable statute. The Civil Rights Act of 1964 had prohibited discrimination on account of "religion" in private employment, but it had failed to define "religion." The Supreme Court twice divided 4–4, once in 1971 and again in 1976, on the question whether Sabbath observance was "religion" within the meaning of the law, and whether an employee fired (or an applicant not hired) because of his or her Sabbath observance may maintain a federal civil rights action. Between those two cases, Congress amended the act by adding a definition of religion that I personally drafted and transmitted to West Virginia Senator Jennings Randolph— a Sabbath-observing Baptist—in 1972. Congress defined "religion" to include "all aspects of religious observance and practice unless an employer demonstrates that he is unable to reasonably accommodate to an employee's or prospective employee's religious observance or practice without undue hardship on the conduct of the employer's business."

Caldor's Department Store was happy to compare the federal statute with Connecticut's and to argue in the Supreme Court—as it had *not* done in the Connecticut courts—that the law permitted no exceptions and was, therefore, an invalid "absolute" preference for religion. It was helped, in this respect, by another event. After the Connecticut Supreme Court had declared the Sabbath protection provision unconstitutional, some well-meaning legislators, prodded by a group of Sabbath observers, had drafted and enacted a new Connecticut law that mirrored the text of the federal statute. There were, therefore, *two* Connecticut statutes on the books protecting Sabbath observers by the time the case arrived at the door of the Supreme Court.

The state surprisingly did not defend the constitutionality of the 1976 law while the case was in the Connecticut courts. When the certiorari petition was filed, however, Connecticut's newly elected attorney general—now United States Senator Joseph I. Lieberman—moved to intervene. The solicitor general of the United States also supported our position with *amicus* briefs endorsing our petition and our argument on the merits. His office's representative was a young lawyer who has subsequently made a national reputation as an academic expert and ace litigator on the religion clauses—Professor Michael W. McConnell of the University of Chicago Law School.

The "Question Presented" in my petition was: "Whether a Connecticut statute that protects religious observers against being compelled to work on the day of the week they observe as their Sabbath violates the Establishment Clause of the First Amendment." Caldor's brief in opposition responded that the case concerned an "odd statute and odd factual situation . . . designed for consideration by moot courts and not by the Supreme Court of the United States."

The Court's decision to grant certiorari seemed to bode well for our side. Had a majority of the Court been sympathetic to the argument that protection could not be given to Sabbath observers without violating the establishment clause, it could easily have refused to take the case. And in light of Justice Brennan's staunch support for Sabbath-observing employees, I had little doubt how he would rule on the constitutionality of this protection for religious minorities.

My confidence took a jolt about one minute after I began my argument. Justice Brennan—hardly loquacious during oral arguments—asked me whether the 1976 and the more recent Connecticut laws could "stand side by side" and whether it was not true that "the legislature intended to make a change in the law and simply forgot to repeal this one." I responded that the 1976 law deliberately remained on the books. And Attorney General Lieberman, during his argument, was also questioned by Justice Brennan when Lieberman said that the second law was merely a "stopgap" designed to provide protection if the earlier law was invalidated. Lieberman argued that the "two statutes can stand side by side," and he emphasized that the law had not been read by the Connecticut courts as absolute. The "reasonable accommodation" and "undue hardship" qualifiers of federal law might still be read in as implied provisions of the Connecticut law.

Much of the argument was devoted to discussion of the seemingly "absolute" terms of the statute and the alleged unfairness of allowing a Sabbath observer to be excused from work on a Saturday or Sunday while a parent of a child playing a Little League game could be required to work all weekend. Maddening as this was, it still did not seem to be destructive of our position. If an "absolute" exemption from Sabbath employment is required by statute, it is merely a legislative decision to guarantee that religious employees will not be victims of discrimination in the workforce. If an employer may be required to spend money in order to prevent or cure *racial* discrimination or discrimination based on a handicapping condition, why may he not be required to spend money to prevent *religious* discrimination? And if a fellow employee may be inconvenienced or his promotion may be delayed because of nondiscrimination efforts undertaken on behalf of a sick co-worker or to assist a black or Hispanic applicant, must accommodation to religious conscience be given less respect?

An Unhappy and Disappointing Result

The Court took months to decide the case, and the ruling against Thornton's estate did not come down until a few days before the term closed—June 26, 1985. The Court's opinion, written by Chief Justice Burger, was seven pages long, and its reasoning covered less than three pages in the *United States Reports*. Burger read the Connecticut law as requiring the Sabbath observer to be excused "no matter what burden or inconvenience this imposes on the employer or fellow workers." As he understood it, the law "arms Sabbath observers with an absolute and unqualified right not to work on whatever day they designate as their Sabbath."

The Burger opinion continued with a description of the law that was wholly foreign to the reason for its enactment. "The State thus commands that Sabbath religious concerns automatically control over all secular interests at the workplace; the statute takes no account of the convenience or interests of the employer or those of other employees who do not observe a Sabbath." A footnote described the Sabbath observer's right to be excused on his Sabbath as "the valuable right to designate a particular weekly day off—typically a weekend day, widely prized as a day off." Burger did not appreciate that a religious believer does not personally "designate" any day that fits his fancy. Nor is the *only* consequence of his religious observance that he may be indolent on that one day. Serious Sabbath observance is ordinarily accompanied by worship and religious limitations that secular co-employees would find confining. Burger's footnote ended with a tone that belittled the problems faced by Sabbath observers and turned the effort to protect them into the grant of a special privilege: "Those employees who would like a weekend day off, because that is the only day their spouses are also not working, must take a back seat to the Sabbath observer."

Only Justice Rehnquist dissented, and he did so without an opinion. Justices O'Connor and Marshall joined Burger with a short opinion that also spoke enviously of "the right to select the day of the week in which to refrain from labor." It described this "right" as a "valued and desirable benefit" conferred by the law "only on those employees who adhere to a particular religious belief." The O'Connor-Marshall opinion distinguished the 1972 amendment to the federal Civil Rights Act because it called for reasonable, rather than absolute, accommodation.

Where was Justice Brennan? I could not believe, when the opinions came out, that he had veered so drastically from the course he marked in *Braunfeld* and in *Sherbert* and had joined the Burger opinion. But by the nature of Supreme Court decision-making, there was no way to learn how so promising a case had come to such a dismal end.

How *Thornton v. Caldor* evolved and why the opinions were so unsatisfactory remained a mystery for years. Some of us who participated in the case speculated that the drafting of the majority opinion had been delayed by other projects that Chief Justice Burger deemed were more pressing, and that the case was caught up in the end-of-the-term crush. The issues, we feared, had not been given serious and thoughtful attention by the justices.

Truth Revealed

How wrong we were. When Justice Thurgood Marshall's papers became public after his death, the secret history of *Thornton v. Caldor* became accessible. The Marshall files revealed a first draft of an opinion for the Court circulated by the Chief Justice on March 13, 1985—little more than four months after the oral argument. The draft was sixteen pages long, and it took great pains to distinguish between legislative accommodation for religious observances—which it recognized as a desirable means to avoid "tensions between governmental power and religious institutions"—and "governmental coercion of conduct on behalf of particular religious adherents"—which is how it described the Connecticut law. In that first draft, the Burger opinion contained a paragraph explicitly distinguishing the Connecticut provision from the 1972 amendment to the federal civil rights statute and from the laws of ten states that followed the federal model.

A separate section of the Burger draft explained that difficult "line drawing" was necessary to reconcile conflicting constitutional obligations under the establishment and free exercise clauses. It reaffirmed the doctrine Brennan had announced in *Sherbert* and the decision in *Thomas v. Review Board* (1981), a more recent application of the *Sherbert* principle. It extolled the conscientious-objector exemption from the military draft and Burger's 1970 decision *(Walz v. Tax Commission)* upholding the constitutionality of property-tax exemptions for churches. It then compared these accommodations with the Connecticut law, which, it said, "coercively burdens a host of others to conform their conduct in order to facilitate the religious activity of Sabbath observers." Burger never specified where, other than in the domain of pure theory, the "host of others" are to be found. He simply declared that "the State is reaching out into the private sector to compel absolute deference to a certain religious practice—this goes beyond accommodation."

What the Burger draft did *not* do is what apparently troubled Justice Brennan. It did not apply to the Connecticut law the three-pronged establishment clause test of another landmark Burger opinion—*Lemon v. Kurtzman* (1971). By 1985, Chief Justice Burger had become disenchanted with his own 1971 formulation and was prepared to describe it as only "a convenient shorthand" or "a helpful signpost." The first draft of his opinion even called it "a mechanistic inquiry" and spoke of "the limited utility of fixed tests in that category of cases where the Court must decide whether a particular governmental accommodation of religion violates the prohibition against the establishment of religion." Just one year before, in *Lynch v. Donnelly* (1984), Burger had repudiated "any single test or criterion" in establishment clause cases. And a perceptive passage in his *Thornton* first draft (minus citations)—that, as matters turned out, never appeared in the *United States Reports*—was the following:

> By definition efforts toward accommodation inevitably implicate consideration of religious factors; such consideration, however, does not necessarily contravene the Establishment Clause, as *Lynch* demonstrates. To pigeonhole analysis in all cases into fixed inquiries may well obscure rather than illuminate the sensitive issues surrounding accommodation of religion. No single "test" or formula fits every case raising Establishment Clause questions. Courts must look beyond the rhetoric of any single approach to determine whether the values protected by the Religion Clauses have been offended.

Burger's first draft apparently satisfied none of his colleagues. The Marshall papers show no justice joining it during the following two months. On May 13, 1985, a second try at an opinion for the Court was circulated by the Chief Justice. This draft toned down the criticism of *Lemon* and removed the first three sentences of the excerpt quoted above. It also inserted a curious passage arguing that a law singling out Sabbath observance discriminated against "persons belonging to Eastern religions such as Buddhism and Hinduism." The second Burger draft generated no enthusiasm, and it was met, almost immediately, with the circulation of a draft concurring opinion that Justice Brennan had obviously been preparing for some time.

The Brennan concurrence made its first rounds on May 17, 1985. The opening passage explains why Justice Brennan is writing separately:

> I join in affirming the judgment of the Connecticut Supreme Court that Con. Gen. Stat. § 53-303e(b) violates the Establishment Clause of the First Amendment. I believe that this result is required by our consistent understanding of the Establishment Clause, as applied in this Court's precedents over at least the past 40 years. However, I do not agree with the Court's evident distaste for the Establishment Clause guidelines derived from our prior cases and set forth in *Lemon v. Kurtzman*. . . . Because I believe that resolution of the sensitive issues in this case is best advanced by concentrating on the *Lemon* analysis, I therefore write separately to offer a less innovative explanation for today's result.

Justice Brennan's thirteen-page draft begins with a description of the two "perspectives" from which Connecticut's law could be viewed—as a protection against religious discrimination and as a promotion of Sabbath observance. These two differing understandings, he says, turn the case into one that "raises sensitive and difficult issues concerning the scope of permissible state action under the Establishment Clause." But Brennan's initial summary of the law assumes one point that was vigorously debated in the briefs and during the oral argument. He says that the law "requires employers absolutely to accommodate the needs of employees who desire not to work on their Sabbath, regardless of the resulting impact on the employer or other employees."

The *Lemon* standard, he insists, should control the outcome of *Thornton v. Caldor*. I had argued in my brief that the *Lemon* standard does not apply to a law that is designed to accommodate religious observance in private employment because "religious freedom is a constitutionally encouraged means of implementing the values of the Free Exercise Clause." Brennan's concurrence rejects that understanding of the free exercise clause as "deeply at odds with our interpretation of both Religion Clauses." That argument could be invoked, he says, to defend every legislative effort to help religion, including state subsidies for the salaries of parochial-school teachers and state sponsorship of school prayers. They could all be characterized as "accommodation."

The Brennan draft goes on for almost five pages to discuss the "secular purpose" prong of the *Lemon* test and to reject the argument that a "facial reference to religion" is enough to invalidate a law. "Where the government seeks to expand the domain of civil liberty by protecting the rights of all citizens to participate on an equal basis, without regard to religion, in important public and private aspects of our national life, its purpose is wholly legitimate." In this portion of his concurrence, Justice Brennan explicitly approves the 1972 federal "reasonable accommodation" Civil Rights Act amendment:

> A state may reasonably believe . . . that a reasonable accommodation by private employers to the employees' religious needs is necessary fully to permit them to participate in the state's economic life. Thus, although the statute may require private parties to give particular attention to their treatment of members of religious groups, this special attention would be required only in service of the goal of equal opportunity and full participation, not as an effort to institute a religious preference.

The Connecticut law, he says, is different because "a statute so sweeping on its face could only be motivated by the forbidden purpose of granting religious observers a position of primacy in the workplace." This depends, says Justice Brennan, on the validity of the claim that "the statute will necessarily enlist the powers of government positively to promote religion." As a result, he says, it is more "profitable" to turn to the second *Lemon* prong—the principal or primary effect of the law.

THE CALLOUS JUSTICE BRENNAN

One may quarrel with some of the rhetoric in the first eight and one-half pages of the Brennan concurrence, but much of it sounds like the Justice Brennan that Sabbath observers and other religious minorities came to admire in *Braunfeld* and *Sherbert*. When the Justice turns to the effect of the Connecticut Sabbath observer protection, however, the benevolent Dr. Jekyll is suddenly transmogrified into a terrifying Mr. Hyde.

Hyde-Brennan begins by distorting why the Sabbath observer does not work on his Sabbath, making it sound as if he frivolously chooses to take a "day off" and as if he or she has no religious limitation or required observance on the Sabbath other than the privilege of laziness. Hyde-Brennan declares, "The right not to work on a day of one's choice is surely a scarce and valued benefit in our society." Jekyll-Brennan had been more perceptive in *Braunfeld* and *Sherbert*. He knew then that Sabbath observance was not "one's choice" of a day off but a divinely ordained command that the believer could not "choose" to defy. The Court majority may have thought that a storekeeper's "choice" of the day on which to close his shop was a "scarce and valued benefit," but Justice Brennan in 1961 knew that Orthodox Jewish merchants were not simply exercising a "choice." And Justice Brennan in 1963 knew that Adell Sherbert had no "choice" on whether to accept a job requiring her to work on Saturdays.

Hyde-Brennan, however, contrasts this seemingly arbitrary "choice" by the Sabbath observer with the "strong but non-religious reasons for wanting a day off" that non-Sabbatarian employees might give. None of the hypothetical reasons he ascribes to the non-Sabbatarians is frivolous. None goes to the racetrack, none does couch-potato service at the Sunday football TV specials, and none lies on the beach. Brennan's wholesome and deserving secular employees are deprived of their weekend days off by the selfish Sabbatarian even though they want "to be with their family, to participate in community activities, to undertake a part-time educational program." According to the Brennan draft, these employees must "sacrifice days off that would otherwise be available to them in order to 'accommodate' their religious colleagues."

The quotation marks that surround the word "accommodate"—a word that Justice Brennan had invoked respectfully in earlier free exercise opinions and would use again in subsequent opinions construing the free exercise clause—sting as sharply as the cruel text of this draft opinion. The Brennan concurrence turns the oft-victimized Sabbath observer into a predatory beast. He or she exercises a "right to impose whatever cost is necessary on others in order to have one's religious preferences satisfied." (Note, too, the word "preferences." Like the word "choice," it reduces the conscientious believer's practice to mere self-gratification.)

In several decades of handling discrimination claims of Sabbath observers I have yet to encounter a single Sabbatarian employee who wants to "impose costs" on fellow employees to satisfy his or her own "preferences." Sabbath-observing employees are invariably self-conscious and apologetic over the limitations that their beliefs impose on their availability. Their request always is to find some way of squaring their religious convictions with the desires—be they worthy or frivolous, sound or senseless—of their fellow workers. Justice Brennan obviously knew this in 1961, when he brushed aside the assertion that Sabbath-observing shop owners would enjoy a competitive advantage if they were closed on Saturdays and open on Sundays, and he knew in 1963 that South Carolinians were unlikely to flock to the Seventh Day Adventist Church just in order to be able to turn down Saturday work. Why was he ready to presume in 1985 that Connecticut's Sabbatarians are so secure in their employment that the law's protection had "the effect of advancing a particular religious practice at the expense of those, whether they profess a religion or not, who do not engage in that practice"? And how could Brennan, even in his Hyde persona, say that the exception for Sabbath observers "places the imprimatur of governmental endorsement and encouragement on a particular religious practice"?

Brennan's May 17 draft collected concurrences in quick sequence. On May 20, Justice Blackmun concurred, and on May 22, Justices Marshall and Stevens asked that they be joined. Justice Powell did not join Brennan's language, but circulated on May 23 a short concurrence agreeing that "the proper framework for analysis of this case" was the three-pronged test of *Lemon v. Kurtzman.* He said he would hold "simply and briefly that the Connecticut statute—at least as applied in this case—violates the 'effects' prong of the *Lemon* test."

On receiving Powell's concurrence—which left him with no chance to speak for a Court majority—the Chief Justice replied that "the duty of each of us is to execute an assignment as a majority vote," and he said he would redraft his opinion. He concluded with the following paragraph:

> I suspect it is the time of the year that makes it very difficult for me to see how Bill Brennan's opinion and mine are at great odds except that he believes *Lemon* is "the test for all seasons."

Burger's next draft—distributed on May 23—paid lip service to *Lemon.* It quoted the three prongs from the *Lemon* opinion, and followed with the observation that "although *Lemon* provides no rigid, fixed formula applicable to all Establishment Clause cases, the criteria properly focus on whether the values protected by the Religion Clauses have been undermined." Burger also added that "the *Lemon* criteria themselves are designed generally to determine whether government has respected" the requirement that it neither impair the free exercise of religion nor coerce adherence to any religion. The third draft retained some of the language describing the difficulty of drawing the line between acknowledgment and accommodation of religion, on the one hand, and coercion to aid religion, on the other.

This draft won over Justice White, who said on May 28 that he "would not be averse to modifying the *Lemon* test," but was willing to join Burger's opinion. At this point, O'Connor—who was then the junior justice—first circulated a separate opinion.

O'CONNOR TO THE RESCUE

The Court's papers reveal that Justice O'Connor was the only member of the Court who had been ready to agree with our reading of Connecticut's law. On April 30—while Burger's first draft was the only opinion on the table—she proposed that the case be vacated and remanded in light of the then-pending public-school moment-of-silence decision, *Wallace v. Jaffree. Wallace v. Jaffree* was, in fact, decided on June 4, 1985, with an opinion which found that the Alabama moment-of-silence law was enacted with the unconstitutional purpose of encouraging prayer. A remand, O'Connor said in April, would enable the Connecticut Supreme Court to determine the purpose of the law, to decide whether the challenged statutory provision was an endorsement of Sabbath observance, and to rule on whether the law was, in fact, absolute.

Burger replied the next day and defended his first draft. He said that such a remand would send "obscure and puzzling signals" to the Connecticut Supreme Court. He also noted that the Court, at its conference on the case, had decided that the law was absolute. Burger then circulated his second draft on May 13, and this provoked the May 17 concurrence issued by Brennan.

In late May, in response to Burger's May 23 draft, O'Connor joined what were then Parts I and III of the Burger opinion. Her separate concurrence stated that she would prefer to have the case remanded so that Connecticut courts could apply the *Lemon* test and determine whether the law is absolute. If forced to reach the merits, she expressed her belief that the message of the Connecticut law is "endorsement of a particular religious belief." Thornton's case did not justify discussion of "accommodation," said Justice O'Connor, because the Connecticut law did not "lift a government-imposed burden," and it is only government-imposed burdens that are subject to an "accommodation" analysis.

It appears from the Marshall papers that Justice Rehnquist remained aloof from the whirlwind of activity in *Thornton v. Caldor* until after the O'Connor concurrence circulated. On June 3, Rehnquist sent a short note to the Chief Justice:

> Please add at the end of your opinion, "JUSTICE REHNQUIST dissents."

When he had circulated his second draft on May 13, the Chief Justice noted in a covering memorandum that *Thornton v. Caldor* was "a close-to-the-line case, as are most of the Establishment Clause cases." By early June, after Brennan's concurrence had collected four votes and Powell and O'Connor had expressed their views that *Lemon* doomed Connecticut's statute, the "closeness" of the case was less obvious (even though Rehnquist was cryptically dissenting). Burger circulated a memo on June 7 promising "another effort to resolve the 'logjam' in this case." And on June 12, a fourth Burger draft emerged. All talk of accommodation was removed. The approval given in earlier drafts to the antidiscrimination provision of federal law requiring "reasonable accommodation" by employers was excised. *Sherbert* and *Thomas* were not cited or discussed. Burger continued to ignore the difficulty of being a Sabbath observer in a secular world. The Connecticut law, said the Chief Justice, "arms Sabbath observers with an absolute and unqualified right not to work on whatever day they designate as their Sabbath," regardless of the "burden or inconvenience this imposes on the employer or fellow workers."

Evisceration of the opinion did the trick. Powell immediately joined the fourth draft and withdrew his "little concurring opinion." O'Connor as promptly agreed with the Burger draft and substantially revised her concurrence to remove any suggestion that the case should be remanded. And Brennan extorted one more concession. Burger had said in his fourth draft that the Court "has frequently relied on our holding in *Lemon* for guidance," but Brennan insisted that he say, instead, "We apply the criteria set out in *Lemon.*"

And so Burger's fifth draft, changed per Justice Brennan's request, was circulated on June 18. Blackmun joined the opinion on that day, and Justice Brennan sent Burger a brief note:

Please join me in your fifth draft in this case. I appreciate the changes you have made and I will withdraw my separate concurring opinion.

CONTINUED DEFENDER OF RELIGIOUS FREEDOM

Notwithstanding the language in his unpublished opinion, Justice Brennan continued after the 1984 term vigorously to defend minority religious rights. In a case I argued during the 1985 term, *Goldman v. Weinberger* (1986), he spoke eloquently of "our constitutional commitment to religious freedom and to acceptance of religious pluralism," which he described as "one of our greatest achievements." He added that "tolerance and respect for all religions still set us apart from most other countries and draws to our shores refugees from religious persecution from around the world."

The issue this time was the right of an Orthodox Jew to wear a yarmulke while in military service. This was, to be sure, not as obviously "a substantial public benefit" as was the right to be absent from work on Saturdays or Sundays. But the record indicated that other religious denominations were requesting, or could be expected to request, the right to wear or carry their religious garb. And nonreligious military personnel might also want to wear unconventional headgear for personal secular reasons. Nonetheless, requiring an exemption for the religious observer did not, in Justice Brennan's view, implicate the establishment clause.

In other free exercise clause cases involving religious practices that are more difficult to accommodate than is Sabbath observance, Brennan continued to vote for the religious minority. In *Lyng v. Northwest Indian Cemetery Protection Association* (1988), he would have sustained a religious claim that prevented the federal government's construction of a road through a national forest. "Mutual accommodation" (without quotation marks around the second word) is required, he said, if the government's conduct threatens a "central" or "indispensable" religious practice. Sabbath observance is, of course, "central" to many religious faiths, including Orthodox Judaism and Seventh Day Adventism. Permitting private employers to require their employees to work on their Sabbaths undermines the practice of these religions, just as Brennan concluded that construction of the road could do in *Lyng*.

The issue in *Employment Division v. Smith* (1988) was whether employees fired for ingesting peyote in a religious ceremony could claim unemployment compensation benefits. Justice Brennan vigorously argued that to deny these benefits is unconstitutionally to burden religious practice. He called the Court's remand a "foray into the realm of the hypothetical"—an apt description of the establishment clause discussion in his unpublished *Thornton* opinion.

WHY?

The mystery that remains is *why* Justice Brennan took a stance in *Thornton v. Caldor* that was so hostile to Sabbath observers. To be sure, it was rational to draw the line in his unpublished opinion between cases where accommodation is constitutionally required because "the government itself has . . . imposed requirements that burden or penalize individuals in the exercise of their religion" and cases in which the religious burden results from wholly private action. But he acknowledged later in the opinion that "ridding the workplace of . . . barriers to equal participation and achievement is a state purpose fully in keeping with our deepest national aspirations." Yet his vote and much of the language in his unpublished opinion were contrary to these "aspirations."

The answer to the riddle lies, I believe, in the other religion clause cases that the Court was considering in the 1984 term. It was a busy year for the first sixteen words of the Bill of Rights. *Thornton v. Caldor* was the least significant of the church-state disputes that came before the Court that year.

I have already mentioned *Wallace v. Jaffree* (1985), which concerned Alabama's minute-of-silence law. Six justices found the law unconstitutional on establishment clause grounds, and the case was among the most publicized on the Court's docket.

This was also the year when the Court went over the precipice in invalidating public assistance to students in parochial schools. The issue in *Grand Rapids School District v. Ball* (1985) and *Aguilar v. Felton* (1985) was whether assigning full-time public-school teachers to visit and teach in private religious schools violates the establishment clause. *Ball* involved "enrichment" and "remedial" secular classes; *Aguilar* concerned federally financed programs under Title I of the Elementary and Secondary Education Act of 1965—directed to disadvantaged and learning-disabled children ("educationally deprived" in the politically correct terminology).

A Supreme Court majority ruled, contrary to Franklin D. Roosevelt's exhortation, that the Constitution requires us to fear fear itself. Brennan's opinion for five justices in the *Ball* case held that the loan of public-school teachers to religious schools is impermissible because "in the pervasively sectarian environment of a religious school, a teacher may knowingly or unwittingly tailor the content of the course to fit the school's announced goals." This creates a "substantial risk" of religious indoctrination with public funds, particularly since "no attempt is made to monitor . . . for religious content." No evidence supported this apprehension, just fear itself.

In *Aguilar,* where the state showed that it had attempted to "monitor for religious content," Brennan invoked Catch-22. The "pervasive monitoring," he said, "infringes precisely those Establishment Clause values at the root of the prohibition of excessive entanglement." And so New York's parochial-school students were deprived of essential educational assistance because of two wholly unsubstantiated fears—(1) that nonreligious public-school teachers would inculcate religion if they visited religious schools and (2) that state monitoring to prevent this would inhibit the religious schools' independence.

Aguilar v. Felton is, to my mind, the second worst opinion Justice Brennan wrote in thirty-four distinguished years on the Court. (It is exceeded only by *Ginzburg v. United States* [1966], in which a criminal defendant went to jail on a novel legal theory declared by Justice Brennan that no one, including the government's lawyer and the defendant's counsel, had any reason to anticipate.) A majority of the current Supreme Court indicated during the oral argument and in their opinions in *Kiryas Joel Board of Education v. Grumet* (1994) that it is prepared to overrule *Aguilar.* It is an opinion that stretches the establishment clause to its farthest reach, and does so at great human expense.

The unpublished concurrence in *Thornton v. Caldor* has the same doctrinaire inflexibility that marks *Ball* and *Aguilar.* Justice Brennan's usual understanding of human nature and the needs of minorities and of the disadvantaged is absent in all three opinions. Rather than considering the issues in light of the real-life needs of those affected by the legislation, the Brennan opinions subordinate the real world to sheer separationist theory.

My theory that the justices were thinking of the minute-of-silence and of *Ball* and *Aguilar* when they decided Thornton's case finds some support in the Marshall files. The memorandum from Justice Powell following Burger's circulation of a second draft noted, "I agree with Bill that the *Lemon* test that will be reaffirmed in *Grand Rapids* and *Aguilar*, applies to and disposes of this case." And Powell's memorandum ends with the following sentence:

> Your opinion is at odds with the reasoning in *Wallace, Grand Rapids* and *Aguilar* and my concurring opinions in these cases.

Driven by the result the Court was reaching in *Aguilar*, Justice Brennan failed to respect religious observance in *Thornton v. Caldor*. Terrible as Burger's majority decision became as a result of Brennan's disagreement, it is fortunate for Justice Brennan's place in history that it will always remain only a draft opinion.

Reproductive Rights and Liberties: The Long Road to *Roe*

David J. Garrow

Justice Brennan's contributions to the establishment of constitutional protections for Americans' reproductive and sexual liberties—Fourteenth Amendment due process rights that often have been addressed under the rubrics of "privacy" or "autonomy"—have been important both in cases in which Brennan authored much-cited opinions, cases such as *Eisenstadt v. Baird* (1972) and *Carey v. Population Services International* (1977), and in cases where Brennan made substantively crucial behind-the-scenes contributions to well-known opinions written by colleagues, cases such as *Griswold v. Connecticut* (1965) and *Roe v. Wade* (1973).

However, Justice Brennan's significant contributions to the "privacy" doctrine cases that reach from *Griswold* through *Eisenstadt* and *Roe* to *Carey* all rest upon a foundation created by the outcome of an earlier case, *Poe v. Ullman,* a 1961 decision in which an intensely torn Justice Brennan finally concluded that he could not vote to endorse the plaintiffs' constitutional challenge to a Connecticut criminal statute prohibiting the use or prescription of birth control devices—a statute which the Court *would* void four years later in *Griswold. Poe v. Ullman* thus was not only Justice Brennan's somewhat stressful introduction to the family of reproductive rights issues that would be most famously addressed in *Griswold, Eisenstadt,* and *Roe,* but *Poe* was also a most ironic antecedent for the subsequent contributions that William J. Brennan, Jr., would make toward constitutional protection of Americans' fundamental reproductive rights.

The author is Distinguished Historian in Residence at the American University. He is the author of *Liberty and Sexuality: The Right to Privacy and the Making of Roe v. Wade* and won the Pulitzer Prize in biography in 1987 for *Bearing the Cross: Martin Luther King, Jr. and the Southern Christian Leadership Conference.*

THE FORTY-YEAR CRUSADE FOR REPRODUCTIVE FREEDOM

The Supreme Court's consideration of *Poe v. Ullman* came only four years after Justice Brennan had first taken his seat on the Court. The Planned Parenthood League of Connecticut (PPLC) had been struggling for decades against the state's unique and extremely intrusive criminal law that prohibited any use of birth control devices by anyone, and that also prohibited all doctors and other medical professionals from counseling or advising patients in the use of such devices. The criminal statute was an 1870s legacy of anti-obscenity crusader P. T. Barnum—a man far better known as a nineteenth-century circus magnate than as a Connecticut state legislator.

The Barnum prohibition had stood without challenge until the 1920s, when Katharine Houghton Hepburn, one of the founders of Connecticut Planned Parenthood and the mother of the famous actress, launched the first effort to repeal the law. Hepburn and her fellow birth control proponents, working in close alliance with national birth control champion Margaret Sanger, hoped to open a network of free or low-cost clinics that could provide vaginal diaphragms to poor or working-class women who could not afford a private physician. The Barnum statute represented an explicit obstacle to their hopes.

Hepburn and her allies—a combination of early, upper-class feminists and a smattering of liberal physicians—found limited receptivity and no success in the Connecticut legislature. The growing number of Catholic legislators—representing urban districts filled with first- and second-generation Italian, Eastern European, and French-Canadian immigrants—gave vociferous voice to the Roman Catholic Church's unbending doctrinal opposition to any state authorization of "unnatural" birth control methods.

Stymied again and again with their legal reform efforts in the Connecticut legislature, Hepburn and her co-workers in the mid-1930s quietly resolved to open an initial clinic in Hartford and to expand to other Connecticut cities if prosecutors made no move to enforce the Barnum law against them. For four years, from 1935 until 1939, their initiative succeeded. A quiet expansion into Waterbury, Connecticut's most heavily Catholic city, however, generated public complaints by local Roman Catholic clergymen, resulting in the arrest and prosecution of the nurse and two young doctors who staffed the clinic.

In the wake of the Waterbury arrests, Connecticut Planned Parenthood immediately closed all its clinics and sought unsuccessfully to challenge the Barnum statute in the Connecticut Supreme Court. Two years later, following another failed push for legislative reform, Hepburn's allies mounted a constitutional challenge, *Tileston v. Ullman,* that was turned aside both by Connecticut state courts and finally by the U.S. Supreme Court as well.

Following that 1943 defeat, Connecticut's birth control proponents endured twelve more years of looking without success for some channel that would allow them to reopen their clinics. Then, in the mid-1950s, under the leadership of a new executive director, Estelle Trebert Griswold, the Connecticut women and their medical allies resolved to mount another courtroom challenge to the constitutionality of the Barnum statute. They framed a set of cases around Dr. Lee Buxton, the head of Yale University's obstetrics and gynecology department, and several of Buxton's female patients who had to avoid pregnancies for either extremely serious reasons of health or, in one particular case, a likely danger to her very life.

Dr. Buxton and the women (who chose pseudonyms like Poe and Doe to protect their privacy) sued Abraham Ullman, the same New Haven prosecutor who had held office since the 1943 litigation. The cases met with no success in Connecticut state courts. Early in 1960 Connecticut Planned Parenthood's lead attorney, well-known Yale Law School professor Fowler Harper, appealed *Poe v. Ullman* and the companion cases to the U.S. Supreme Court. In his petition, Harper challenged the Barnum law's criminalization of the *use* of birth control devices by married couples. He argued that the law represented "an unreasonable and arbitrary intrusion into the private affairs of the citizens of Connecticut. . . . When the long arm of the law reaches into the bedroom and regulates the most sacred relations between a man and his wife, it is going too far." The Poes, the Does, and their physician, Dr. Buxton, "insist that marital intercourse may not be rationed, censored, or regulated by priest, legislator, or bureaucrat. Certainly, they contend, the 'liberty' guaranteed by the due process clause includes this, among the most sacred experiences of life." In May of 1960, five members of the high court, one more than was necessary, including Justice Brennan, voted to hear Harper's appeal.

Justice Brennan Grapples with *Poe*

Not until March of 1961 was *Poe* argued before the Supreme Court. In advance of the hearing, one of Justice Brennan's young law clerks, Richard S. Arnold—later in life to be chief judge of the Eighth Circuit Court of Appeals—warned his boss that the *Poe* cases suffered from insufficient factual development in the courts below. It was not clear that the state would actually prosecute—or had even threatened to prosecute—married couples for merely *using* contraceptives. Arnold advised Brennan that "on a properly constructed record a holding of unconstitutionality would be required," but that the sparse record in *Poe* was a poor invitation for overturning such a long-standing state statute.

At argument, Justice Brennan queried Harper about whether other states had anti–birth control laws similar to Connecticut's—Massachusetts came the closest—and he questioned the state's lawyer as to whether the statute allowed for the sale or use of condoms, and was told no. Indeed, unbeknownst to either the justices or the *Poe* lawyers, that very week in the Connecticut town of Wallingford a salesman was arrested, convicted, and fined $75—along with the loss of his merchandise—for distributing condoms to service stations.

In the final moments of Harper's closing argument, Brennan pointedly asked, "Isn't the operation of clinics what's at stake here really?" When Harper answered yes, Brennan replied, "I take it that the Poes and Does can get what they need almost anyplace in Connecticut," providing that they could both find and afford a sympathetic doctor and a quietly cooperative pharmacy.

Those comments directly foreshadowed the position Brennan took when the nine justices met privately the next day to discuss and vote on how they would decide *Poe*. He told his colleagues that the cases failed to meet the constitutional requirement of representing a "case or controversy," which meant, in essence, that the plaintiffs had presented a merely theoretical dispute. Four of his colleagues—Chief Justice Warren and Justices Frankfurter, Clark, and Whittaker—felt likewise, making for a five-vote majority to turn the *Poe* challenge aside.

Three months later, in early June, Felix Frankfurter circulated an initial draft of his opinion for the *Poe* majority. But Justice Brennan now was having second thoughts about his vote. The final conference of the term was right at hand, and at that gathering he informed his fellow justices that rather than join Frankfurter, he would submit a brief separate concurring opinion of his own before the end of the day. Formally issued three days later, Brennan's opinion took no position on the constitutional merits of the Barnum law—privately he told Arnold and fellow clerk Dan Rezneck that were he to address the merits he would vote to void the statute—but agreed with the Frankfurter quartet that the appeal should be dismissed. *Poe* failed to present "a real and substantial controversy" and was based upon "a skimpy record." The "true controversy" in Connecticut was not over the Poes' and Does' access to birth control devices, but—as in 1939—"over the opening of birth-control clinics on a large scale." Unless Connecticut made "a definite and concrete threat to enforce these laws against individual married couples," the Supreme Court could "decide the constitutional questions urged upon us when, if ever, that real controversy" over clinics "flares up again."

BRENNAN DEVELOPS A RIGHT TO PRIVACY

Connecticut Planned Parenthood immediately announced that it would take up that challenge, and less than five months after the defeat in *Poe* PPLC publicly opened a birth control clinic for married women in downtown New Haven. Local prosecutors made no immediate move against them, but a Roman Catholic layman, James G. Morris, began complaining both to the press and to elected officials that the authorities were failing to carry out their duties by declining to enforce a still-valid law. With some reluctance, two police detectives were detailed to question Estelle Griswold about the clinic's activities. Eager to launch a case that this time the Supreme Court could not duck, Mrs. Griswold enthusiastically answered their questions and agreed to find several patients who would willingly testify that Mrs. Griswold's and Dr. Buxton's assistance to them did indeed violate the anti–birth control provisions of the Barnum law. Just nine days after the clinic's opening, a local judge issued arrest warrants for Griswold and Buxton, and later that day both defendants were released on bond after turning themselves in to New Haven police.

Given Connecticut state courts' long track record of upholding the Barnum statute, no one was surprised when both Griswold and Buxton were found guilty following a one-day trial early in 1962 or when their convictions were upheld by an appellate panel and then by the Connecticut Supreme Court. Those reviews took more than two full years, and only in September of 1964 was Fowler Harper able to appeal *Griswold v. Connecticut* to the U.S. Supreme Court. In early December the justices unanimously agreed that the case should be heard, and in late March Yale law professor Thomas Emerson—who inherited *Griswold* upon his friend Harper's death that January—argued Griswold and Buxton's appeal challenging the constitutionality of the Barnum statute before the Court. When the justices caucused privately three days later, Brennan agreed with six of his eight colleagues that Griswold and Buxton's convictions had to be reversed.

Chief Justice Warren assigned William O. Douglas to write the majority's opinion in *Griswold,* but when Douglas sent an initial draft of his handiwork to Justice Brennan's chambers, the reaction was far from enthusiastic. Brennan's clerk Paul Posner prepared a long and substantive letter of advice for Brennan to send his colleague, recommending that Douglas replace his draft's primary reliance upon a First Amendment "freedom of association" protection for the sanctity of married couples' procreative choices with a principal focus on a right to privacy argument. The Brennan letter explained:

> Instead of expanding the First Amendment right of association to include marriage, why not say that what has been done for the First Amendment can also be done for some of the other fundamental guarantees of the Bill of Rights? In other words, where fundamentals are concerned, the Bill of Rights guarantees are but expressions or examples of those rights, and do not preclude applications or extensions of those rights to situations unanticipated by the Framers. Whether, in doing for other guarantees what has been done for speech and assembly in the First Amendment, we proceed by an expansive interpretation of those guarantees or by application of the Ninth Amendment admonition that the enumeration of rights is not exhaustive, the result is the same. The guarantees of the Bill of Rights do not necessarily resist expansion to fill in the edges where the same fundamental interests are at stake.

"All that is necessary for the decision of this case," Brennan told Douglas, "is the recognition that, whatever the contours of a constitutional right to privacy, it would preclude application of the statute before us to married couples."

Three days later Douglas circulated a revised draft that fully adopted and incorporated Brennan's advice. When *Griswold v. Connecticut* was publicly handed down some six weeks later, Douglas's majority opinion quickly became well known for its signal recognition of how the Constitution fully protected a fundamental right to privacy for married couples' choices concerning birth control. Not publicly announced or acknowledged, however, was the fact that William J. Brennan rather than William O. Douglas was indisputably the primary progenitor of *Griswold's* famous right to privacy analysis. *Griswold's* constitutional analysis not only overrode the evasiveness of *Poe v. Ullman* and successfully concluded the forty-year battle that Connecticut Planned Parenthood had waged against the Barnum law; *Griswold's* privacy analysis also opened the constitutional door to an argument that prior to 1965 not a single judge or constitutional scholar had yet suggested: that the right to privacy protected by the Bill of Rights could cover a woman's decision to abort an unwanted pregnancy just as well as it could cover a married couple's choice to use contraceptives.

Brennan Paves the Road to *Roe v. Wade*

Between 1967 and 1970 a number of young attorneys, led first and foremost by the audacious, twenty-five-year-old Roy Lucas, developed and refined the constitutional argument that a *Griswold*-style right to privacy did indeed protect a pregnant woman's desire to choose abortion. One early case potentially raising that issue, *United States v. Vuitch,* was derailed by procedural questions, but in early 1971 Justice Brennan joined with four colleagues to vote in favor of hearing two right-to-abortion cases from Georgia and Texas, *Doe v. Bolton* and *Roe v. Wade.*

But less than four weeks before *Doe* and *Roe* were argued before the Court in December of 1971, the justices also had to confront a Massachusetts case that likewise was based upon *Griswold.* Freelance birth control advocate Bill Baird, a frequent speaker on the college lecture circuit, had been arrested by Boston police after finishing a speech at Boston University by distributing several packets of vaginal foam to young women from the audience. Massachusetts prosecutors alleged that Baird had thereby violated a state statute prohibiting the distribution of contraceptive items other than to married people by a physician. After a two-hour trial, Baird was found guilty, and the Massachusetts Supreme Judicial Court affirmed the constitutionality of his conviction by a 4–3 vote. Baird was then sentenced to three months' imprisonment. Following an initial Supreme Court refusal to hear his appeal, Baird served thirty-five days in a Boston jail before a federal appeals court ordered his release. Eighteen months later, after the appeals court had voided the state law and Massachusetts filed an appeal, *Eisenstadt v. Baird* was heard by the U.S. Supreme Court.

At the oral argument, Justice Brennan responded to Massachusetts's effort to defend its statute with a raft of questions, and finally told the state's lawyer, "I'm sorry, I just don't follow you, that's all." At conference, Brennan told his colleagues that Baird's conduct was clearly protected by "the penumbra of *Griswold,*" and one week later it was decided that Brennan would write for the majority of justices who were in agreement that Baird's conviction had to be voided.

While Brennan was preparing that *Eisenstadt* opinion, the justices also cast their initial private votes concerning *Roe* and *Doe*. Brennan believed that both Texas's anti-abortion law and Georgia's slightly more liberal abortion statute were constitutionally unacceptable. Chief Justice Warren Burger assigned preparation of the principal opinions to junior justice Harry A. Blackmun, but William O. Douglas set out to write a *Doe* opinion of his own and, as in *Griswold,* quickly shared his first draft with Bill Brennan. Agreeing with Douglas that both the Georgia and Texas statutes infringed upon the constitutional right to privacy, Brennan explained that privacy

> is a species of "liberty" . . . but I would identify three groups of fundamental freedoms that "liberty" encompasses: *first,* freedom from bodily restraint or inspection, freedom to do with one's body as one likes, and freedom to care for one's health and person; *second,* freedom of choice in the basic decisions of life, such as marriage, divorce, procreation, contraception, and the education and upbringing of children; and, *third,* autonomous control over the development and expression of one's intellect and personality.

Brennan reminded Douglas that his own discussion of *Griswold* in the initial draft of the *Eisenstadt* opinion—which he had circulated to his colleagues on the very day that *Roe* and *Doe* had been argued—"is helpful in addressing the abortion question." He concluded that "the right of privacy in the matter of abortions . . . means that the decision is that of the woman and her alone," aside from the state's authority to require that abortions be performed by physicians.

Brennan's eleven-page letter to Douglas laid out a full analysis of how the Court might persuasively decide both *Doe* and *Roe*. Twelve weeks later, when Brennan's opinion for four of the seven justices who had heard *Eisenstadt v. Baird* was publicly released, everyone could see for themselves just what Brennan had told Douglas about *Eisenstadt's* helpfulness in extending *Griswold's* privacy analysis to the issue of abortion. By failing to demonstrate any "rational basis" for distinguishing between married and unmarried individuals in the felony statute under which Baird had been convicted, the Massachusetts law unconstitutionally violated "the rights of single persons under the Equal Protection Clause" of the Fourteenth Amendment.

Brennan emphasized that "whatever the right of the individual to access to contraceptives may be, the rights must be the same for the unmarried and the married alike." He explained:

> If under *Griswold* the distribution of contraceptives to married persons cannot be prohibited, a ban on distribution to unmarried persons would be equally impermissible. It is true that in *Griswold* the right of privacy in question inhered in the marital relationship. Yet the marital couple is not an independent entity with a mind and heart of its own, but an association of two individuals each with a separate intellectual and emotional makeup. If the right of privacy means anything, it is the right of the *individual,* married or single, to be free from unwarranted governmental intrusion into matters so fundamentally affecting a person as the decision whether to bear or beget a child.

No one, neither justice nor clerk nor interested attorney or journalist, could fail to note how clear the implication of that "bear or beget" sentence might well be for the constitutional question of a pregnant woman's right to choose abortion.

JUSTICE BRENNAN INFLUENCES *Roe*

Two months later Harry Blackmun circulated a first draft of his *Roe* opinion. Blackmun's draft completely avoided the crucial issue, focusing instead on the question of statutory vagueness. Justice Brennan was quick to advise Blackmun that a majority of justices certainly felt that the crux of the matter had to be confronted and disposed of in both the Texas and Georgia cases. Blackmun's *Doe* draft, distributed three days later, was considerably stronger, but after some internal disagreement the Court resolved to hold both *Doe* and *Roe* over for reargument in the fall.

Following those rearguments, in November 1972, Justice Blackmun distributed significantly revised drafts of both *Roe* and *Doe*, asking Bill Brennan, as the Court's only Roman Catholic justice, to pay particular attention to the opinions' comments about the history of Catholic religious opposition to abortion. Brennan responded by discussing the opinions privately with Blackmun. His principal suggestion to his junior colleague was that Blackmun consider extending the point in pregnancy before which intrusive state regulation of abortion would be impermissible from the end of the first trimester to some later period. Blackmun indicated his willingness to shift that "cut-off" point to the stage of fetal viability. Two days later Brennan sent Blackmun a letter suggesting that the Court should adopt a three-stage rather than two-stage view of pregnancy. "I have no objection," Brennan wrote,

> to moving the "cut-off" point (the point where regulation first becomes permissible) from the end of the first trimester (12 weeks) as it now appears to a point more closely approximating the point of viability (20 to 28 weeks), but I think our designation of such a "cut-off" point should be articulated in such a way as to coincide with the reasons for . . . creating such a "cut-off" point. . . . [R]ather than using a somewhat arbitrary point such as the end of the first trimester or a somewhat imprecise and technically inconsistent point such as "viability," could we not simply say that at that point in time where abortions become medically more complex, state regulation—reasonably related to protect the asserted state interests of safeguarding the health of the woman and of maintaining medical standards—becomes permissible? . . . Then we might go on to say that at some later stage of pregnancy (i.e. after the fetus becomes "viable") the state may well have an interest in protecting the potential life of the child and therefore a different and possibly broader scheme of state regulation would become permissible.

Blackmun welcomed Brennan's suggestions, and, as the final texts of the *Roe* and *Doe* opinions very much reflected when the decisions were handed down several weeks later, Blackmun indeed completely adopted the analytical substance of Brennan's recommendations. Just as with William O. Douglas's much-cited majority opinion in *Griswold*, much of the crucial substance of Harry Blackmun's landmark opinions in *Doe v. Bolton* and *Roe v. Wade* likewise came without public acknowledgment or credit from the mind and pen of William J. Brennan.

BRENNAN EXPANDS REPRODUCTIVE RIGHTS

Four years after *Roe* and *Doe, Carey v. Population Services International* (1977) presented the Court with a challenge to a New York law which prohibited the distribution of contraceptives by anyone other than a pharmacist and also banned any distribution to anyone under age sixteen. Speaking for a six-justice majority that voided the statute, Justice Brennan reiterated that "the teaching of *Griswold* is that the Constitution protects individual decisions in matters of childbearing from unjustified intrusion by the State." Access to contraceptives "is essential to exercise of the constitutionally protected right of decision in matters of childbearing that is the underlying foundation of the holdings in *Griswold, Eisenstadt v. Baird,* and *Roe v. Wade.*" Regarding the second question at issue, Brennan further held that "the right to privacy in connection with decisions affecting procreation extends to minors as well as to adults."

In cases where a majority of the Burger Court refused to acknowledge the constitutional necessity of public funding for poor women's abortions, Justice Brennan consistently wrote in dissent. Likewise, when the Burger Court refused to consider or review early challenges to state criminal statutes penalizing consensual sodomy, Brennan again repeatedly dissented. Brennan also wrote forcefully in cases where local governments penalized public employees for engaging in consensual, nonmarital intimate relationships, and in 1986 Brennan was among the minority of four justices who strongly protested the majority's constitutional affirmance of Georgia's criminal sodomy statute in *Bowers v. Hardwick.* Three years later, Brennan likewise was in dissent when a five-member majority of the Rehnquist Court threatened to void the underpinnings of *Roe v. Wade* in *Webster v. Reproductive Health Services* (1989).

But, as history's record memorably indicates, in the crucial family of cases reaching from *Griswold* and *Eisenstadt* to *Roe* and *Carey,* Justice William J. Brennan, Jr.—sometimes writing in his own name, and sometimes by dint of his extensive but publicly unacknowledged contributions to the well-known majority opinions of others—played a landmark role in the development of constitutional protection for the reproductive and procreative rights of American citizens. Absent the Supreme Court's 5–4 rejection of *Poe v. Ullman,* the doctrinal watershed of *Griswold v. Connecticut* would not have come to pass, and, absent *Griswold,* the recognition of a woman's constitutional right to choose abortion in *Roe v. Wade* would have been an unlikely and perhaps impossible judicial development as well. Thus, beyond Justice Brennan's own statements in *Eisenstadt* and *Carey,* and beyond his crucial private contributions to *Griswold* and *Roe,* looms the paradoxical possibility that William J. Brennan, Jr.'s decisive vote in *Poe v. Ullman* may ironically have been just as significant a boon to the creation of constitutional protection for Americans' reproductive choices as were his analytical insights in *Griswold, Eisenstadt,* and *Roe.*

The Family and Responses of the Heart

Anna Quindlen

It is difficult to read the Supreme Court decision in *Moore v. City of East Cleveland* (1977) without thinking in passing of the girlhood of Marjorie Leonard. She was five when her father died and eleven when her mother followed, and she was raised by her two older sisters, who shared a household with her in upstate New York and worked as schoolteachers.

In 1928 Marjorie Leonard married a young man named William J. Brennan, Jr., and almost fifty years later he would feel compelled to write a concurring opinion in *Moore,* a case that mirrored his wife's childhood. The city of East Cleveland had prosecuted a woman living with her grandsons because of zoning regulations that narrowly defined the meaning of family—defined it, in fact, in a fashion that would have prohibited Marjorie and her sisters from living together.

"I write only to underscore the cultural myopia of the arbitrary boundary drawn by the East Cleveland ordinance in light of the tradition of the American home that has been a feature of our society since our beginning as a nation," Justice Brennan wrote, "a tradition . . . 'of uncles, aunts, cousins and especially grandparents sharing a household along with parents and children. . . .' The line drawn by this ordinance displays a depressing insensitivity toward the economic and emotional needs of a very large part of our society."

Cultural myopia, insensitivity—neither afflicted Justice Brennan when he considered issues of family law during his decades as a justice of the Supreme Court. Perhaps it is a mistake to identify a great man's biography too closely with his body of work. Perhaps Justice Brennan was not especially influenced by his own family life, by his roles as son,

The author won the Pulitzer Prize for commentary for her opinion column in the *New York Times.* A reporter and editor for seventeen years, she is now a novelist. The author gratefully acknowledges the research assistance of Liz Galst and Rebecca Glaser.

husband, father. But to look to his life in this area of his work must be forgivable, for he seems always to be speaking not as an Olympian observer of the Constitution but as one who has participated in the small rituals of everyday family life, understands its variety and its difficulties, and honors always its centrality in human existence and the obligation of living law both to protect it from encroachment and to safeguard it from those of smaller minds. His decisions in the area of family matters reflect what was the omnipresent tension in his work, between the rights of citizens to be free of intrusive government and the obligation of that same government to safeguard its citizens' well-being. The compassion and empathy that were the hallmark of so many of his decisions in so many areas are much in evidence when he writes of marriage, parenthood, and the privacy and protections that may extend to both. He understood how we live now.

Justice Brennan seems always to be guided by a description of his judicial character rendered by Arthur Vanderbilt, the chief justice of the New Jersey Supreme Court, who was instrumental in persuading the lawyer, against his inclinations, to turn jurist and become a superior court judge. "For Mr. Justice Brennan," Justice Vanderbilt wrote,

> the law is a living reality concerned with human beings, rather than a series of judicial declarations embalmed in judicial opinions. . . . [W]hile he is keenly conscious of the fact that we live in a constantly changing world, he is equally aware of the fact that human nature changes very little. He is, therefore, instinctively inclined to preserve the essentials of all that is good in the past and to adapt them to the needs of the times.
>
> But one must know Mr. Justice Brennan personally to understand the great joy which he takes in human contacts and especially in his family life.

Justice Vanderbilt made that assessment of the Brennan judicial character in 1957, shortly after William J. Brennan had become, at age fifty, the Supreme Court's youngest member. And throughout his thirty-four years on the Court Justice Brennan concerned himself with the "living reality" of the law in ways large and small, in decisions that considered the component parts of family life—marital privacy, divorce restrictions, social welfare oversight, paternity—and the notion of what family means. Many of those opinions reflect those issues for which he is most remembered as a jurist: gender equity, sexual and reproductive privacy, the rights of the disenfranchised, above all the rights of the individual. In the process he wrote opinions that were often intensely commonsensical, and sometimes deeply moving.

He wrote the majority opinion in *Orr v. Orr* (1979), in which the Court declared unconstitutional a state law that required husbands, but not wives, to pay alimony. "There is no reason," Justice Brennan observed dryly, "to use sex as a proxy for need." In deciding that procedures for removing children from foster homes afforded sufficient due process protection, he nonetheless added with compassion, "We deal here with issues of unusual delicacy, in an area where professional judgments regarding desirable procedures are constantly and rapidly changing. In such a context, restraint is appropriate on the part of courts."

And when he authored a 1987 dissent arguing that paternity should be proven by more than a mere preponderance of the evidence, he added a passionate coda on the nature of fatherhood. "I cannot agree with the Court that a determination of paternity is no more significant than the resolution of 'a monetary dispute between private parties,' " he began, adding, "Most of us see parenthood as a lifelong status whose responsibilities flow from a wellspring far more profound than legal decree. Some men may find no emotional resonance in fatherhood. Many, however, will come to see themselves far differently, and will necessarily expand the boundaries of their moral sensibility to encompass the child that has been found to be their own." The second of eight children of an ebullient, sometimes overbearing union leader and political official, the father of three children himself, Justice Brennan wrote as a man who knew fatherhood as well as he knew the Constitution.

But while Justice Brennan himself grew up in a conventional family and was later, with his wife Marjorie, the head of a similarly conventional one, his simultaneous appreciation of the bonds of love and the liberty protections implicit in the United States Constitution led him to have a deep appreciation for family arrangements distinct from his own, and to refuse to enshrine traditional family ties or mores when to do so would cause constitutional or individual harm. With one sentence in a case regarding Louisiana inheritance laws, he decimated societal prejudice against illegitimate children: "The formality of marriage primarily signifies a relationship between husband and wife, not between parent and child." And while in the landmark case *Griswold v. Connecticut* (1965) Justice Brennan agreed with the majority that a statute prohibiting the distribution of contraceptives was unconstitutional becuase it invaded the intimate relationship between husband and wife, by the time he wrote the opinion in *Eisenstadt v. Baird* (1972), he could see no reason to treat unmarried couples differently. In an oft-quoted section, he wrote, "the marital couple is not an independent entity with a mind and heart of its own, but an association of two individuals, each with a separate intellectual and emotional makeup. If the right of privacy means anything, it is the right of the *individual,* married or single, to be free from unwarranted governmental intrusion into matters so fundamentally affecting a person as the decision whether to bear or beget a child." By 1977 he had extended that right even further in *Carey v. Population Services International,* ruling that a provision in a New York state law prohibiting the distribution of contraceptives to those under sixteen was too restrictive. "The right to privacy in connection with decisions affecting procreation extends to minors as well as adults," said Justice Brennan, writing for the majority.

But government intrusion into family life was sometimes not unwarranted, but compelled, as it was in the case of *Joshua De Shaney v. Winnebago County Department of Social Services* (1989). The Court majority held that a child whose father had beaten him so brutally that he became permanently retarded had no claim for damages against the state that was supposed to protect him. Justice Brennan disagreed. Spelling out the long history of those who had known Joshua was being abused and had reported it to authorities, noting that the social worker assigned to the case had once said, "I just knew the phone would ring some day and Joshua would be dead," Justice Brennan concluded that his colleagues failed to recognize "that inaction can be every bit as abusive of power as action, that oppression can result when a state undertakes a vital duty and then ignores it."

Perhaps one family law matter makes manifest not only Justice Brennan's jurisprudence in the area of family law, but also his overarching concept of the elasticity of the Constitution and his core argument with those who rely on the intent of its Framers. It is the withering dissent he wrote in *Michael H. v. Gerald D.* (1989). The matter was a tale of convoluted relationships: a child, Victoria, who was conceived when her mother was impregnated by one man while she was married to another. The Court's majority upheld the presumption that the husband was the father and said that the biological father did not have sufficient liberty interest in the relationship with Victoria to overcome the privacy interest of the family. Justice Scalia relied heavily on tradition in rendering an opinion for a plurality of the Court, and made clear his own view of unorthodox domestic arrangements when he began, "The facts of this case are, we must hope, extraordinary."

Justice Brennan's anger is vivid in his reply. "Pinched," he calls the majority's idea of family, "narrow." Of the reliance on tradition in the majority opinion, he writes, "Apparently oblivious to the fact that this concept can be as malleable and as elusive as 'liberty' itself, the plurality pretends that tradition places a discernible border around the Constitution." Justice Brennan continues, "Even if we could agree, moreover, on the content and significance of particular traditions, we still would be forced to identify the point at which a tradition becomes firm enough to be relevant to our definition of liberty and the moment at which it becomes too obsolete to be relevant any longer."

Michael H. v. Gerald D. was decided in June of 1989, just a year before Justice Brennan stepped down from the Court. It is tempting to hear in his dissent the summation of a career, the articulation of a worldview, at the very least a clarion cry for an America only rarely glimpsed, an America built on the bedrock of true tolerance:

> We are not an assimilative, homogeneous society but a facilitative, pluralistic one, in which we must be willing to abide someone else's unfamiliar or even repellent practices because the same tolerant impulse protects our own idiosyncracies. Even if we can agree, therefore, that family and parenthood are part of the good life, it is absurd to assume that we can agree on the content of those terms and destructive to pretend that we do. In a community such as ours, liberty must include the freedom not to conform. The plurality today squashes this freedom by requiring specific approval from history before protecting anything in the name of liberty.
>
> The document that the plurality construes today is unfamiliar to me. It is not the living charter that I have taken to be our Constitution; it is instead a stagnant, archaic, hidebound document steeped in the prejudices and superstitions of a time long past. This Constitution does not recognize that times change, does not see that sometimes a practice or rule outlives its foundations. I cannot accept an interpretive method that does such violence to the charter that I am bound by oath to uphold.

It's common to hear family court judges complain that they are the jugglers of the bench, dealing with an ever-changing panoply of mores and crises, bound to plumb the murky recesses of the human heart and concoct an uncomfortable marriage between the law and real life. Yet in his rulings on family law matters, writing both for the majority and in dissent, Justice Brennan instead seems to revel in this juggling act, even to embrace it as one of the most palpable manifestations of daily life to come before the Court and one of the greatest opportunities to reveal the living nature of the Constitution.

If his rulings on these matters were not rooted in his own family, they were surely rooted in his essential nature. As he said in a 1987 lecture, effective jurisprudence relies upon "the range of emotional and intuitive responses to a given set of facts or arguments, responses which often speed into our consciousness far ahead of the lumbering syllogisms of reason," responses that are "of the heart rather than the head."

Sticks and Carrots:
The Doctrine of Unconstitutional Conditions

Laurence H. Tribe

In 1892, while he was serving on the Massachusetts Supreme Judicial Court, Oliver Wendell Holmes, Jr., upheld the firing of a policeman for engaging in prohibited political activities on the job, writing, in *McAuliffe v. New Bedford,* that the officer "may have a constitutional right to talk politics, but he has no constitutional right to be a policeman. There are few employments for hire in which the servant does not agree to suspend his constitutional rights of free speech, as well as of idleness, by the implied terms of the contract. The servant cannot complain, as he takes the employment on the terms which are offered him."

Largely through the efforts of Justice Brennan, that case would come out differently today, for more than anyone in our history, Justice Brennan contributed to establishing the doctrine of unconstitutional conditions. In essence, that doctrine holds that government may not grant a benefit (such as a job on a police force) on the condition that the beneficiary surrender an unrelated constitutional right (such as the right to speak freely)—even if the government may withhold that benefit altogether.

The earliest articulation of the concept of unconstitutional conditions as a constraint on governmental authority came during the 1920s. At first the evolution of the doctrine was unconscious, and therefore slow and tentative. Its application was, until quite recently, confined almost totally to the protection of corporations from state regulation. For ex-

The author is Tyler Professor of Constitutional Law at Harvard Law School. He has written many scholarly articles and books, including the leading modern treatise on constitutional law. He has argued twenty-two cases before the Supreme Court since 1980. The author would like to express his appreciation to Melanie Oxhorn, J.D., Harvard Law School, 1994, for her assistance in the preparation of this essay.

ample, a state might try to prohibit an out-of-state corporation from expanding its business activities into the state unless the corporation gave up some federal privilege (such as the right to sue in federal court), and the doctrine of unconstitutional conditions would forbid bargains of that sort. The significant cases could be collected in a small pamphlet.

What Justice Brennan did was to expand the doctrine and shift its focus from corporate interests to the rights and liberties of individuals who seek or receive government benefits. Such a shift was necessary, Justice Brennan perceived, in view of the rise of the modern administrative state, which allowed government to affect conduct not only through criminal sanctions, but also, and indeed primarily, through spending, licensing, and employment decisions. Specifically, in the late nineteenth and early twentieth centuries government decisively abandoned any pretense to a genuinely minimalist "night-watchman" role—a role limited to enforcing supposedly well-defined spheres of physical liberty and tangible property surrounding private individuals and companies. Government bodies became more avowedly active participants in all aspects of American social and economic life. Simultaneously, those bodies acquired growing power to regulate conduct even more extensively through the selective disbursement of benefits than through the imposition of imprisonment or monetary fines or penalties.

Ordinarily, using the "carrot" of public benefits rather than the "stick" of criminal sanctions is an accepted tool of modern government. However, serious constitutional questions are raised when the method is applied in a manner calculated to affect the exercise of protected constitutional rights in a way that would be impermissible through a direct criminal prohibition. Thus, the typical question in unconstitutional conditions cases is whether government should be free to offer gratuitous benefits or privileges subject to the binding condition that, if those benefits or privileges are indeed accepted on the government's terms, the recipient must give up a constitutional right that the recipient could not otherwise be forced to sacrifice. "The central question," Justice Douglas observed in a 1971 dissent, "is whether the government by force of its largesse has the power to 'buy up' rights guaranteed by the Constitution." Or, put another way, when it comes to the scope of government's regulatory authority, is the carrot mightier than the stick?

This question has assumed great significance because, as the reach of government largesse at every level has increased, so too has the potential for abuse. Even as the precise sources and extent of such largesse have waxed and waned during periods of devolution from federal to state authority, and even during eras of budgetary stringency, the range of publicly funded benefits, or of publicly awarded contracts or licenses, over which *some* level or agent of government wields discretionary power has steadily expanded—and, with that expansion, the danger of indirect abridgement of constitutional rights has continued to swell.

Justice Brennan was one of the first to perceive that the welfare state, even when "welfare" as such may be out of favor, wields as much power by withholding benefits as by coercive force, and that, in a society where survival depends on *inclusion* in an economy dominated by government largesse of one sort or another, the consequences of *exclusion* may be more devastating than criminal punishment. The difficulty is that citizens ordinarily cannot claim an affirmative constitutional right to government aid. Since the government is under no obligation to provide benefits, should the government not be able to attach whatever conditions it wishes—even if it might thereby achieve indirectly that which it cannot do directly?

The unconstitutional conditions doctrine answers this inquiry. If the government were given *unlimited* power to attach conditions to the distribution of its largesse, this power—even if formally dependent on the individual recipient's voluntary assent to the conditions attached—could quickly overwhelm the core constitutional values of a free and democratic society by distorting the *system* of rights on which those values depend. Individual freedoms could be swallowed whole by conditioned benefits, rendering substantial parts of the Bill of Rights meaningless. Consequently, Justice Brennan concluded that, in the advent of the modern bureaucratic state, government's claimed authority to condition funding or other benefits on a recipient's seemingly voluntary agreement not to exercise a fundamental right cannot rest simply on the truism that "it's the government's money" coupled with the observation that the recipient was theoretically free simply to turn the government's offer down altogether. The "consent" at issue may be illusory where the benefit is desperately needed and, even when that is not so, there may be some offers the government cannot be left free to make at all if our basic system of rights is not to be radically circumvented.

There are two major cases on which we must focus in order to understand Justice Brennan's contribution, for they are the cornerstones of the unconstitutional conditions doctrine. One is *Speiser v. Randall* (1958), coming quite early in Justice Brennan's tenure on the Court; the other is *Sherbert v. Verner* (1963), coming later in his career and reflecting the maturation of his views in this area.

THE LANDSCAPE BRENNAN FACED

But first, it is worth taking a brief look at the legal landscape in this area as Justice Brennan assumed his seat on the Court—if only to see how far we have come. Quaint though Holmes's views about Officer McAuliffe may sound today, they lingered far into the twentieth century. As late as 1952—sixty years after *McAuliffe*—the Supreme Court, in *Adler v. Board of Education,* sustained the New York loyalty laws with the callous comment that state employees who did not like disclaimer oaths were always "at liberty to retain their beliefs and associations and go elsewhere." The underlying premises were that public employment and, of course, other types of government benefits as well were "privileges" rather than "rights"; since government was not legally required to provide these benefits at all, it could attach to the offer any conditions or restrictions it wished. Or, put another way, the "greater" power to deny the benefit outright presupposed the existence of a "lesser" power to restrict access or eligibility on any basis whatever. The result of this reasoning was to leave government largesse subject to virtually no constitutional limitations.

Two years later—a mere thirty months before Justice Brennan took his seat—the Court, in *Barsky v. Board of Regents* (1954), upheld by a 6–3 decision the power of New York State to suspend the license of a physician for refusing to produce documents demanded by the House Committee on Un-American Activities. The rationale was more revealing than the decision: "The practice of medicine in New York is lawfully prohibited by the State except upon the conditions it imposes. Such practice is a privilege granted by the State under its substantially plenary power to fix the terms of admission." The several internal security cases in the mid-1950s did little to improve the status of government beneficiaries. Essentially, the laws remained little changed from the rule that Justice Holmes had enunciated. While the Warren Court had already spoken with great force on the matter of school desegregation and other dimensions of civil rights, remarkably little had been done to protect civil *liberties* before the 1956 term.

BRENNAN CHANGES THE LANDSCAPE SUBTLY

Early in Justice Brennan's second term, a group of cases brought before the Court a California law requiring claimants for certain property-tax exemptions to submit loyalty affidavits. The California constitution made the tax benefits unavailable to persons and organizations who advocated the violent overthrow of the government of the United States or of the state; the legislature had required the loyalty oath as the mechanism for determining eligibility. The California Supreme Court had consistently upheld the tax exemption by reasoning that the state's interest "in protecting its revenue raising from subversive exploitation" sufficed to validate the procedure—and by drawing an analogy to the public employee oaths consistently upheld by the U.S. Supreme Court in the 1950s.

The issue eventually reached the U.S. Supreme Court in *Speiser v. Randall* (1958), involving eligibility of a non-signing World War II veteran for a tax exemption. One major contribution of the decision in *Speiser* was the rediscovery and new application of the doctrine of unconstitutional conditions. Without using the terminology or citing any of the old cases involving nonresident corporations, Justice Brennan, writing for the majority, unmistakably invoked the concept when he held that government may not arbitrarily restrict access even to a benefit which it is under no duty to create.

For the first time in the context of individual rights and liberties, the Court made clear that calling something a "privilege" did not immunize its allocation from judicial review. Justice Brennan rejected the state's argument that the disqualification at issue was lawful merely because it withheld a "privilege" rather than something which the recipient could claim as an independent "right": "To deny an exemption to claimants who engage in certain forms of speech is in effect to penalize them for their speech [and] necessarily will have the effect of coercing the claimants to refrain from the proscribed speech," because the "deterrent effect is the same as if the State were to fine them for this speech." For the first time, too, it was clear that a "greater" power to deny outright did not always include a "lesser" power to offer upon chilling or demeaning conditions, at least where constitutional freedoms might be jeopardized.

BRENNAN ANNOUNCES THE DOCTRINE EXPLICITLY

Justice Brennan regarded *Speiser* as a cornerstone of constitutional law, even though his colleagues had not yet appreciated its full implications, and he perceived its potential relevance to a far broader range of governmental beneficiaries than taxpayers seeking exemptions. His use of the unconstitutional conditions doctrine was to be more widely understood in later cases—especially after *Sherbert v. Verner* (1963). In that case, South Carolina's unemployment compensation payments, like those of most states, were offered only to persons deemed "available for work." Adell Sherbert had been steadily employed for some years in a cotton mill. Suddenly, the demand for the product increased and the mill converted to a six-day week, expecting its employees to be available for work on Saturday. Mrs. Sherbert, a Seventh Day Adventist, refused to work on Saturdays in contravention of her religious principles and was therefore discharged. She sought other work in the area but found none that would leave her Saturdays free—no doubt at least in part because the state of South Carolina had largely prohibited Sunday employment. Without questioning Mrs. Sherbert's good faith, the state's employment security commission ruled Mrs. Sherbert ineligible for benefits, finding her not "available for work" since she would not accommodate her schedule to the demands of employers in the area. Thus she was faced with a harsh, and partly state-induced, choice between her faith and her livelihood. Seeking relief from the ensuing dilemma, she filed suit for a declaration of eligibility for benefits. The state courts summarily denied her claim.

Justice Brennan, writing for a majority of seven, now had an opportunity to make explicit many of *Speiser*'s latent premises. After placing the case in the context of religious freedom, Justice Brennan stated his central premise: Although no criminal penalties were involved, the state agency's action "forces [Mrs. Sherbert] to choose between following the precepts of her religion and forfeiting benefits, on the one hand, and abandoning one of the precepts of her religion in order to accept work, on the other hand." Such a dilemma "puts the same kind of burden upon the free exercise of religion as would a fine imposed against [her] for her Saturday worship." (Justice Brennan also noted that the state of South Carolina "expressly saves the Sunday worshiper from having to make the kind of choice which we here hold infringes the Sabbatarian's religious liberty.") Lest there be any doubt about the constitutional significance of that finding, Justice Brennan then went on, as he had done in *Speiser*, to reject explicitly the state's proffered right/privilege distinction: "It is too late in the day to doubt that the liberties of religion and expression may be infringed by the denial of or placing of conditions upon a benefit or privilege." He provided a lengthy summary of and quotation from *Speiser*, serving to establish the link between the two cases and the debt of the *Sherbert* holding to the *Speiser* precedent.

In later cases, Justice Brennan continued to apply the rationale of *Speiser* and *Sherbert* to limit governmental power over public assistance—and indeed over all forms of benefits, regardless of whether they were denominated "rights" or "privileges"—in such opinions for the Court as *Keyishian v. Board of Regents* (1967), involving public employment; *Goldberg v. Kelly* (1970), involving welfare benefits; *Bell v. Burson* (1971), covering driver's licenses and auto registration; *Communist Party of Indiana v. Whitcomb* (1974), dealing with elective office; *Elrod v. Burns* (1976), a plurality opinion involving patronage dismissals in public employment; *FCC v. League of Women Voters* (1984), applying to grants to public television stations; and *Rutan v. Republican Party of Illinois* (1990), involving patronage in hiring, rehiring, transferring, and promoting.

The evolution of the doctrine of unconstitutional conditions has proceeded rapidly in the years since 1963. Both in the Supreme Court and in lower federal and state courts, the indebtedness to *Sherbert* has been substantial and direct. As Justice Brennan had recognized in showing solicitude for Mrs. Sherbert's plight, to place in proper perspective the constitutional rights of government beneficiaries one must look not only at the challenged constraints or requirements in isolation, but also at the dilemma created by collision between that external force and the beneficiary's own beliefs or circumstances, especially as those circumstances are shaped by surrounding provisions of state or federal law. It would no longer do (paraphrasing Justice Holmes) to say that Mrs. Sherbert had a constitutional right to be a Seventh Day Adventist but no right to receive unemployment benefits; realistically, the former without out the latter was a hollow right. To make the constitutional liberty meaningful, its exercise must not cause the forfeiture of public benefits. Likewise, in *Speiser*, Justice Brennan had inquired into the actual, practical effects of California's regulatory scheme, thus shifting the focus of judicial inquiry toward the impact of the legislation, as concretely embedded in its procedural setting, on concededly legitimate speech.

This principle has extended far beyond the First Amendment context of *Speiser* and *Sherbert*. For example, it has been applied in cases that implicate the Fifth Amendment takings clause, which preserves the right of a property owner to receive just compensation when the property is taken for public use. A prominent example is *Nollan v. California Coastal Commission* (1987), holding that the government may not require a person to give up the constitutional right to just compensation for a beachfront easement in return for a permit to enlarge a nearby building. (Interestingly, Justice Brennan dissented in *Nollan,* perhaps in part because the development permit itself arguably *constituted* just compensation.) Perhaps even more surprisingly, the doctrine has been applied when government has encroached upon the autonomy of a state by offering the state a conditioned benefit. An intriguing illustration is *South Dakota v. Dole* (1987), in which the Court upheld the conditioning of federal highway funding on a state's adoption of a minimum drinking age. Justices Brennan and O'Connor dissented, arguing that Congress had no power to condition a federal grant in a manner that abridges the states' Twenty-first Amendment right to regulate the minimum age for purchasing liquor.

Today, there can be little doubt that government benefits and privileges available in the modern regulatory and welfare state are pervasive. Various levels of government control the distribution of valuable licenses, subsidize everything from agriculture to art museums, transfer billions of dollars to both needy and not-so-needy recipients, and offer employment to millions of people. As a consequence, government also has very broad powers to dispense social benefits with strings attached— conditions that profoundly affect constitutionally protected rights. Attaching such conditions makes it easier for the government to be less cognizant of these protected rights than it would be if it had to confront more directly the way its programs affect the system of rights as such.

But, as Justice Brennan urged, courts should not permit a legislature to impose a rights-pressuring condition on a benefit or other dispensation simply because the legislature has the power to deny the benefit entirely. Such a blindly deferential approach may eviscerate the constitutional safeguards that protect individual and at times corporate rights and liberties against unwarranted government encroachment. Government may not do indirectly what it may not do directly; government may not "penalize" the exercise of constitutional rights; and government may not coerce persons into relinquishing constitutional rights through regulation, spending, and licensing, any more than it may do so through criminal sanctions.

The Penalty/Subsidy Distinction

It is true that a problem pervading much of contemporary constitutional law has been and is likely to remain that of drawing a workable distinction between government's undoubtedly broad power to decide which activities to subsidize or otherwise encourage and government's considerably narrower power to decide which activities to penalize or otherwise discourage, whether directly or by attaching conditions to various privileges or gratuities. Thus, the Court has recognized the principle that government may make relatively unconstrained value judgments about what its money supports, and that the state can decide to subsidize one sort of constitutionally protected activity while choosing not to subsidize another sort of constitutionally protected activity—even when this means government paying someone if he or she exercises a right of choice in one direction but not if he or she makes the opposite, equally protected choice. In other words, funding, regulating, and licensing decisions are indeed sometimes different from criminal punishment, and the fact that government may not penalize exercise of a right by withholding an otherwise discretionary benefit does not invariably imply that government must subsidize exercise of the right. For example, as the Court observed in *Harris v. McRae* (1980), parents have a constitutional right to send their children to private schools, but a government's decision to subsidize public schooling does not entail a constitutional duty to subsidize the private alternatives.

Although it is not always a simple matter to distinguish between the imposition of a penalty and the withholding of a subsidy, and to determine when the government has overstepped or abused its discretionary power to decide what to subsidize, Justice Brennan wisely recognized the need for a doctrine that would mediate the boundary between constitutional rights and government prerogatives in the areas of spending, employment, and licensing. He saw that the rise of the activist administrative state thus need not compel the elimination of constraints on governmental activities that burden constitutional rights, because the Constitution constrains not simply the imposition of fines and penalties but *all* governmental conduct—including local, state, or federal disbursements of funds or other gratuities. Because unfettered government power to condition the receipt of benefits may have powerful distorting effects on crucial constitutional values, Justice Holmes's position is unacceptable, and a new set of limits must be developed.

LAURENCE H. TRIBE

During his years on the Supreme Court, Justice Brennan continually reminded his colleagues of these limits on the excesses and abuses of governmental power. Through a long series of decisions, involving a broad range of government beneficiaries, Justice Brennan articulated a set of basic principles that composes the modern doctrine of unconstitutional conditions and protects individuals and businesses alike from unjustified government encroachment. The doctrine has assumed a vital protective role in a world in which the government has wide powers over social and economic life, powers exercised as often through conditioned benefits as through outright prohibitions. Under Justice Brennan's guidance, the United States came a very long way indeed from Justice Holmes's rigid view that Officer McAuliffe "may have a constitutional right to talk politics, but . . . no constitutional right to be a policeman." Today, within certain broad limits, Officer McAuliffe's right to talk may indeed imply, if not a right to any specific public position or job, at least a right to a *system* of benefit distribution in which the right to talk— and other rights as well—remains meaningful.

Criminal
Justice

The Tireless Warrior
for Racial Justice

CHARLES J. OGLETREE, JR.

My father, Charles J. Ogletree, Sr., was born in Birmingham, Alabama, in 1908, and in many respects never escaped the discrimination that raged like an epidemic during his childhood. Birmingham, like many other southern cities, was in the grip of racial segregation; Jim Crow laws during my father's youthful years mapped the territory of his growing up. He went to a segregated school, and after the fourth grade dropped out, as many African-American males did at that time, to find employment. His views about the legal system in general, and the criminal justice system in particular, were not very positive. Both he and my uncle, Robert Ogletree, would often tell stories of the special laws that existed in Alabama. In fact, they believed that there was such a thing as "eyeball rape," under which a black man could be prosecuted for simply looking at a white woman.

While this view of the legal system was somewhat exaggerated, it is worth noting how a 1953 Alabama case addressed the issue. In *McQuirter v. State* an African-American man was found guilty of attempt to commit an assault with intent to rape. A white woman was walking with her two children and a neighbor's child at about 8 P.M. As they were going toward their home, the woman noticed an African-American man in a parked truck. As she passed the truck, the African-American man mumbled something that was unintelligible, opened the truck door, and placed his foot on the running board.

She testified that the man followed her down the street and at one point came within two or three feet. However, he passed on, and she watched him stand in the area near the home for a period of time and

The author is a professor of law at Harvard Law School and the director of Harvard Law School's Criminal Justice Institute. He is the co-author of *Beyond the Rodney King Story: Minority Communities and Police Conduct* (Boston: Northeastern University Press, 1994) and has published a significant number of articles on race and the criminal justice system.

then he left. The chief of police testified that when he confronted the African American, he indicated he had walked behind the woman and that he was going to carry her into the cotton patch and, if she screamed, he was going to kill her. The defendant testified that he had been in the area, and that he was simply walking around and denied that he followed the woman or made any gestures toward her or her children. He also denied the statements of the police chief.

In deciding that there was sufficient evidence to convict the African American of attempt to commit an assault with intent to commit rape, the court made the following observation: "In determining the question of intention the jury may consider social conditions and customs founded upon racial differences, such as the prosecutrix was a white woman and defendant was a Negro man." On the basis of these customs, the court said the evidence was sufficient to sustain McQuirter's conviction. Should any African American have doubted the *legal* strength of these "customs," they were reminded over and over to keep their "customary" place. Death was often the legal penalty. It was also the extralegal penalty. In 1955, the beaten, swollen, and decomposed body of fourteen-year-old Emmett Till was discovered in a river. A northern African-American teenager, he clearly did not know the law of the South: he was tortured and murdered for allegedly whistling at a white woman.

It is precisely this form of justice that caused my father to have such a strong aversion to justice in Alabama, in particular, and in the country in general. William J. Brennan, Jr., who hails from New Jersey, grew up about the same time as my father. Although he has heard thousands of stories like this one, his life experiences are quite different. Justice Brennan was educated in some of the nation's finest institutions, including Harvard Law School, and was a distinguished state court judge before being appointed to serve on the United States Supreme Court.

The connections between Justice Brennan and my father are significant to me. While my father saw the Constitution as offering little solace for African-American people of his generation, Justice Brennan has spent his entire legal life trying to give that document life and meaning for African Americans. Justice Brennan's most profound work, in my view, has been his statements and actions in a criminal justice system that has forced the Supreme Court, other courts, and many institutions to recognize the importance of equal justice under the law. It is his fierce defense of the strong sense of constitutional law, and of equal justice, and his powerful dissenting opinions that lead me to praise his criminal justice efforts.

The Justice's view on the treatment of suspects was clear: "Why do we have those protections for the accused in the Constitution? . . . Obviously because we as a society have appreciated that a society's decency is best reflected in how it treats those who offend against its laws. That is not merely a matter of compassion. It's a way of securing for every one of us guarantees which will protect us when we're prosecuted."

Brennan located and extended to criminal justice many enduring constitutional principles, among which are "universal equality, freedom, and prosperity." The Justice explained the derivation of his principles by noting, "The philosophy of government that emerged from the depression of the 1930s . . . conceived of government as having an affirmative role, a positive duty to provide those things which give real substance to our cherished values of liberty, equality, and human dignity—jobs, social security, medical care, housing, and so forth. That duty was rather similar to the duty expressed in the Universal Declaration of Human Rights. . . . Utopian though it may be, unratified by the United States as is still the case, and unfulfilled for most of the peoples of the world, the declaration nonetheless helps point the way in which law and society should be moving."

Perhaps the most significant emphasis in his criminal justice jurisprudence is in Justice Brennan's tireless, incisive, and categorical opposition to capital punishment during his Court tenure.

He abhorred the death penalty: "I have . . . long held the view that the death penalty is in all circumstances an uncivilized and inhuman punishment inconsistent with the Eighth Amendment." He particularly abhorred its brutal consequences for anyone not white and well-off. Justice Brennan's views about capital punishment's tortuous connection with race were most eloquently presented in his dissenting opinion in *McCleskey v. Kemp* (1987). Warren McCleskey, an African American, was charged with the murder of a white police officer in Georgia. The government sought and obtained the death penalty. Following McCleskey's trial, his lawyers challenged the conviction on the ground that it violated the Eighth and Fourteenth Amendments. They submitted a substantial statistical study conducted by Professor David Baldus, which indicated that there was disparity in the imposition of the death penalty in Georgia on the basis of the race of the victim and of the defendant.

Baldus examined over 2,000 murder cases in Georgia during the

1970s. He also determined the race of the defendant and of the victims in those cases, and took into consideration a variety of variables to decide whether they had influenced the verdict. Baldus's findings indicated that the death penalty was assessed in disproportionate ways based on the race of the victim and of the defendant. His study indicated that defendants charged with killing white persons received the death penalty in 11 percent of the cases, while those charged with killing blacks received the death penalty in 1 percent of the cases. Moreover, his study indicated that the death penalty was imposed in 22 percent of the cases involving black defendants and white victims, and 8 percent of the cases involving white defendants and white victims. And in only 1 percent of the cases involving black defendants and black victims. Baldus found that prosecutors sought the death penalty in 70 percent of the cases involving black defendants and white victims, and in 32 percent of the cases involving white defendants and white victims. However, the prosecutors only sought the death penalty in 15 percent of the cases involving black defendants and black victims, and in 19 percent of the cases involving white defendants and black victims.

On the basis of these data, Baldus concluded that Warren McCleskey, like other black defendants, would have a greater likelihood of being subjected to the death penalty because he was black and his victim was white. While the Supreme Court, in a 5–4 opinion, accepted the validity of Baldus's studies, it concluded nonetheless that Warren McCleskey's death penalty conviction did not violate the Eighth or Fourteenth Amendment.

In a searing dissent, Justice Brennan stated precisely the conversation that McCleskey's lawyer would have to have with him to try to explain the Court's rationale in this case:

> At some point in this case, Warren McCleskey doubtless asked his lawyer whether a jury was likely to sentence him to die. A candid reply to this question would have been disturbing. First, counsel would have to tell McCleskey that few of the details of the crime or of McCleskey's past criminal conduct were more important than the fact that his victim was white. . . . Furthermore, counsel would feel bound to tell McCleskey that defendants charged with killing white victims in Georgia are 4.3 times as likely to be sentenced to death as defendants charged with killing blacks. . . . In addition, frankness would compel the disclosure that it was more likely than not that the race of McCleskey's victim would determine

whether he received the death sentence: 6 of every 11 defendants convicted of killing a white person would not have received the death penalty if their victims had been black, while among defendants with aggravating and mitigating factors comparable to McCleskey's, 20 of every 34 would not have been sentenced to die if their victims had been black. Finally, the assessment would not be complete without the information that cases involving black defendants and white victims are more likely to result in the death sentence than cases involving any other racial combination of defendant and victim. The story could be told in a variety of ways, but McCleskey could not fail to grasp its essential narrative line: There was a significant chance that race would play a prominent role in determining if he lived or died.

This stark reality of racism's role in the criminal justice system is a constant specter. Statistics like these—and there are more—screech of the inequality in our criminal justice system.

Justice Brennan set out to alter that course. And he meant to sound a clarion call: "Warren McCleskey's evidence confronts us with the subtle and persistent influence [of blacks' subordination by whites]. His message is a disturbing one to a society that has formally repudiated racism, and a frustrating one to a Nation accustomed to regarding its destiny as the product of its own will. *Nonetheless, we ignore him at our peril, for we remain imprisoned by the past as long as we deny its influence in the present* [italics added]."

Justice Brennan went on in his dissent to point out earlier evidence of racial disparity in the criminal justice system. It is amazing that the same points that he noted in his dissent were issues that my father often mentioned in his view about the lack of fairness in the criminal justice system in this country. In the 1977 case of *Coker v. Georgia,* Justice Brennan pointed out that, although the Supreme Court did not mention race, the Court recognized a racial disparity in the imposition of the death penalty for rape. The circumstances surrounding the death penalty for rape were particularly alarming in Georgia. Justice Brennan pointed out that by 1977 Georgia had executed sixty-two men for rape. Of those men, fifty-eight were black and only four were white. It is precisely this inequality in the imposition of punishment on the basis of race that has so powerfully illustrated the problem of disparity.

When my father talked about the lynchings and the unequal treatment of blacks, many thought it was simply rhetoric. However, it is astonishing to find that, in fact, his views were quite adequately documented in studies of the Georgia penal code. For example, at the time of the Civil War, there was a dual system of justice for blacks and whites. The Georgia penal code declared that any black convicted of murder would automatically receive the death sentence, while others could receive life in prison. Moreover, the penalty for a black raping a white female was death, while anyone else convicted of that crime would be punished by a period of two to twenty years. Moreover, the rape of a black woman was punishable by a fine and imprisonment rather than the death penalty.

When my father discussed the criminal justice system's ruthless treatment of black men, he probably did not know that since 1936, 405 of the 455 men who were put to death for rape were African American. That figure approaches 90 percent. Justice Brennan himself noted, "Over the last 17 years, 80 black defendants were executed for the murders of white victims (35% of all executions), and only *one* white defendant was executed for the murder of a black victim (0.44% of all executions)." My father, my uncle, all of us who heard them talking— none of us needed the statistics to prove the awful knowledge that, in a very real way, our lives depended on.

These disparities in the treatment of black men and women (although much less rarely criminals, black women were often victims of crime) created both my father's anxiety and Justice Brennan's challenge. In a variety of other instances, Justice Brennan did not hesitate to talk about his concern about racial bias in the criminal justice system, and to urge the Court to go even further in its recognition of the problem and to find appropriate remedies.

For example, in *Turner v. Murray* (1986), an African American was convicted of killing a white jeweler, and appealed on the basis that the court had not allowed the prospective jurors to be questioned about the victim's and the defendant's race to determine whether there was an issue of racial bias. In his usual powerful way, Justice Brennan firmly disagreed with the Court's refusal to reverse and order a new trial, stating:

> I cannot fully join either the Court's judgment or opinion. For in my view, the decision in this case, although clearly half right, is more clearly half wrong. After recognizing that the constitutional guarantee of an impartial jury entitles a defendant in a capital case involving interracial violence

to have prospective jurors questioned on the issue of racial bias, a holding which requires that this case be reversed and remanded for new sentencing, the Court disavows the logic of its reasoning in denying petitioner Turner a new trial on the issue of his guilt. It accomplished this by postulating a jury role at the sentencing phase of the capital trial, fundamentally different from the jury function at the guilt phase, and by concluding that the former gives rise to a significantly greater risk of a verdict tainted by racism. Because I believe that the Court's analysis improperly intertwined the significance of the risk of bias with the consequences of bias, and because in my view the distinction between the jury's role as a guilt trial and its role as a sentencing hearing is a distinction without substance insofar as juror bias is concerned, I join only that portion of the Court's judgment granting petitioner a new sentencing proceeding, but dissent from the portion of the judgment refusing to vacate the conviction.

Another example of Justice Brennan's tireless advocacy for fair criminal trials involved what might seem mundane: discovery, the process by which each side is allowed (or, in criminal cases, not allowed) to see the other side's case. Arguing that defendants should have better access to the state's case during discovery, Brennan asked, "Are the scales [in criminal trials] really evenly balanced? Who are our criminal defendants? . . . Judges know that the largest percentage of these people are indigent. . . . Do not these less privileged of our society present the particular problem that without resources to prepare a defense, they often don't have an adequate defense? Can we boast of a decent administration of the criminal law if we don't provide them some redress against this hard reality?"

As I evaluate the legal career of Justice William Brennan, I am in awe of his many accomplishments. He is the recipient of every significant award or honor that is associated with justice, fairness, and commitment. Nevertheless, Justice Brennan's greatest accomplishments, in my view, stem from the great work he has done for the faceless and voiceless masses. Men like my father respected the Supreme Court as an institution, but, for many years, lamented the decisions that undermined their manhood.

When Justice Brennan and, later, Justice Thurgood Marshall came along, they initiated a dialogue that acknowledged the pain and suffering of my father's generation. Justice Brennan's eloquent defense of these poor black men offered them a life with dignity, and it reflects his extraordinary capacity as an advocate for the powerless. I will be forever grateful to Justice Brennan for the power of his words and actions. I offer the gratitude, as well, of the thousands he has touched, even though they have not been able to acknowledge it to him personally.

Justice Brennan is the consummate warrior for racial justice, and no other can possibly fill his large shoes.

Search and Seizure: Fragile Liberty

Nat Hentoff

> These technicalities are basic to
> the kind of society we are.
> —William J. Brennan, Jr.

In his chambers, during conversations about the continually besieged Fourth Amendment, Justice Brennan would sometimes recite it, stressing each word—and then emphasizing "probable cause."

"It's a high standard the Framers wanted," he said. "Do you know that the evil of the general warrant is often regarded as the single immediate cause of the American Revolution?"

I saw what he meant when I came across a furious complaint delivered at a 1772 Boston town meeting: "Thus, our houses and even our bed chambers are exposed to be ransacked, our boxes, chests and trunks broke open, ravaged and plundered. . . . Those Officers may under the cloak of a general warrant destroy men's securities, carry off their property."

Two little-known cases especially illuminate Justice Brennan's passionate—and sometimes angry—devotion to the Framers' care in making the Fourth Amendment the most specifically detailed section of the Bill of Rights. Both were dissents and both were rebukes to the Court for denying review of these cases.

In *McCommon v. Mississippi* (1985), the petitioner's car had been searched pursuant to a warrant, and a considerable quantity of marijuana had been found in the trunk. The owner of the car moved, before trial, to have the evidence suppressed under the exclusionary rule. Yes, there had been a warrant, he said, but there had not been probable cause to issue that warrant.

The author is a columnist for the *Village Voice* and a syndicated columnist for the *Washington Post*. He is also a member of the steering committee of the Reporters' Committee for Freedom of the Press.

Brennan had, as usual, explored the record—in this case, the testimony from the pretrial hearing. The defense attorney had asked the judge if he had issued the warrant just because the police had asked for it—rather than because of "any particular thing they told you."

The judge readily told the truth. "That's right," he said. "If Sheriff Jones walked in and said, 'Judge, I need a search warrant to search John Doe for marijuana,' or drugs or whatever . . . , I'm going to go on his word because . . . I take him to be an honest law enforcement officer and he needs help to get in and search these places and it's my duty to help him to fulfill that."

Brennan told those of his colleagues who, by their silence in denying review, went along with that Mississippi judge: "Today the Court tacitly informs magistrates . . . they need no longer be neutral and detached in their review of supporting affidavits. . . . On whom may the citizens rely to protect their Fourth Amendment rights?"

As vital as Brennan's majority decisions are, his dissents have also deeply illuminated how much remains to be done to put the Bill of Rights back on course.

The justice differed with many of his colleagues, through the years, over the constitutional rights of young people. One morning I told him that I was about to spend a week at rural public schools in Pennsylvania—trying, to use his phrase, to get the Bill of Rights off the page and into their lives.

"Tell them stories," he said. "Tell them stories."

One of the stories I told them had to do with another of Brennan's dissents to the Court's denial of certiorari. The story did not have a happy ending, but it showed the students that at least one member of the distant, mysterious Supreme Court was on their side. I've told this story to other youngsters, and Brennan became a new kind of hero to them. He didn't play the guitar or move to a rock beat, but he sure was cool.

This is the story, with an angry coda, by Justice Brennan.

One morning in 1979, students in Highland, Indiana, at Highland Junior High and the adjacent high school were suddenly invaded by police and police-trained German shepherds. The police and the dogs were engaged in a mass random search for drugs and drug paraphernalia. No particular student was under suspicion. All were under general suspicion—like the American colonists raided by customhouse officers bearing a general search warrant.

For two and a half hours, the students were required to sit with their hands on their desks while each of them was examined by a German shepherd, sniffing between their legs.

One of the dog detectives started paying particular attention to thirteen-year-old Diane Doe. When no drugs were found in her pockets, she was taken to the nurse's office and strip-searched. It was later discovered that the girl had been playing with her own dog at home before coming to school, and that's why the police dog found her interesting. But no drugs were found on or in her.

Through her parents, Diane sued several school district officials and the police chief for conducting a search and seizure on her person in violation of the Fourth Amendment. There had been no warrant for this dragnet operation and thereby no probable cause for the invasion.

One of Diane's lawyers pointed out that "being a teen-aged schoolgirl is neither a crime nor a cause for suspicion." Nonetheless, a federal district judge dismissed her case, ruling that the warrantless mass detention and inspection were constitutional. The Seventh Circuit Court of Appeals agreed with the district court, except for the strip search: "It does not require a constitutional scholar to conclude that a nude search of a 13-year-old child is an invasion of constitutional rights."

But, according to the Seventh Circuit, the rest of the invasion—including the use of dogs as searchers in intimate places—was constitutional.

When the other justices refused to review the appellate decision, Brennan, as he later told me, was "really mad." Justices who dissent from denials of certiorari do not often explain the reasons for their objections, and even more rarely do they engage in a long written rebuke of their colleagues.

In *Diane Doe v. Renfrow*, Brennan did just that. He said that the use of the dogs was indeed an unconstitutional search, a warrantless search. He recalled that Diane had testified that "the experience of being sniffed and prodded by trained police dogs in the presence of the police and representatives of the press was degrading and embarrassing. [Also in class during the raid, the dog repeatedly jabbed its nose into her legs.] I am astonished that the Court did not find that the school's use of the dogs constituted an invasion of the petitioner's reasonable expectation of privacy."

As for the random search of all the students, Brennan said in his dissent:

At the time of the raid, school authorities possessed no particular information as to drugs or contraband, suppliers or users. Furthermore, they had made no effort to focus the search on particular individuals who might have been engaged in drug activity at school.

We do not know what class petitioner was attending when the police and dogs burst in, but the lesson the school authorities taught her that day will undoubtedly make a greater impression than the one her teacher had hoped to convey. . . . Schools cannot expect their students to learn the lessons of good citizenship when the school authorities themselves disregard the fundamental principles underpinning our constitutional freedoms.

In his last years on the Court, Brennan, though an optimist by temperament—and sometimes by force of will—began to fear that the protections of the Fourth Amendment were fading away. In *United States v. Leon* (1984), a majority of the Court had ruled that a law enforcement officer's execution of a defective warrant with, for instance, a wrong address—given to him by a magistrate—does not violate the Fourth Amendment if the officer didn't know the warrant was defective. Brennan, in dissent, warned that this creation of a "good faith" exception to the Fourth Amendment implicitly told judges that they didn't have to be all that careful in reviewing applications for a warrant because their mistakes would have hardly any consequences.

Then came *McCommon v. Mississippi,* which proved his point when the Court did not disturb a local judge who assumed the sheriff was always acting on "good faith" and therefore always had probable cause for a warrant because he was the sheriff.

Brennan was also increasingly concerned that the exclusionary rule—illegally seized evidence cannot be used at trial—was being eroded. He told *Legal Times* in 1986, "The Court has said now—over dissents— that the exclusionary rule is to be regarded merely as something that may be appropriate in some cases in order to deter [official] misconduct, but not otherwise. I think it's a very serious blow to the Fourth Amendment."

Not only the justices discounted the exclusionary rule. Many district attorneys excoriated it, as did newspaper columnists and even some judges. The prevailing fear has been of crime, and the corollary belief, among the citizenry, is that far too many criminals are set loose because of such "technicalities" as the exclusionary rule.

Acting as a devil's advocate and aware that Justice Brennan had often been accused of nurturing these "technicalities," especially in search-and-seizure cases, National Public Radio's Nina Totenberg asked him in 1987: "Why do you let some of those creeps go? They do such bad things, and on some technicality you let them go."

Justice Brennan, raising his voice—in an uncommon show of irritation—said, "Honestly, you in the media ought to be ashamed of yourselves to call the provisions of the Bill of Rights 'technicalities.' They're not. They're very basic to our very existence as the kind of society we are. We are what we are *because* we have those guarantees, and this Court exists to see that those guarantees are faithfully enforced. *They are not technicalities!* And no matter how awful may be the one who is the beneficiary time and time again, guarantees have to be sustained, even though the immediate result is to help some very unpleasant person. Those 'technicalities' are there to protect all of us."

Not long before he retired from the Court, Brennan told me that he was not depressed that a majority of the justices seemed to be a good deal less passionate about preserving those guarantees than he was. "This sort of thing has happened before," he said, "and eventually the Court has finally righted itself."

But it was not only the Supreme Court that thought justice would become more durably efficient if some of those guarantees were curtailed—the exclusionary rule, habeas corpus et al. There is also the Congress as an enemy of the Bill of Rights.

In February 1995, the House of Representatives, by a vote of 289 to 142, passed a bill that would eliminate the exclusionary rule—and permit warrantless searches if they are carried out in "circumstances justifying an objectively reasonable belief that they were in conformity with the Fourth Amendment." Brennan's prophecy that the *Leon* decision could lead to the evisceration of the Fourth Amendment had been borne out. The "good faith" exception had been greatly broadened to move from a magistrate's mistake to police deciding on their own whether to search and seize in the belief that they were honoring the Fourth Amendment even though they had ignored the core of the guarantee—the need for a warrant.

The House had paid no attention at all to the Framers, to the legacy of Justice Brennan, and to the prophecy of Justice Robert Jackson in *Johnson v. United States* (1948): "[To justify] officers in making a search without a warrant would reduce the Fourth Amendment to a nullity and leave the people's homes secure only in the discretion of police officers."

It is worth noting that the president of the United States, who had taught constitutional law at the University of Arkansas, offered no objection to this termination of the Fourth Amendment.

One member of Congress, Melvin Watt of North Carolina, introduced an amendment to the removal of the exclusionary rule. The amendment was the exact language of the Fourth Amendment, but it was not identified as such. The amendment was resoundingly defeated. Watching its fate on the House floor, I nonetheless felt that the spirit of Justice Brennan was still abroad in the land—fighting, through Melvin Watt, against the odds, as usual.

Moreover, Brennan's view of the always crucial need to safeguard the explicit provisions of the Fourth Amendment—which would disintegrate without the exclusionary rule—has considerable support among a fair number of law enforcement officers.

In 1987, a law student, Myron Orfield, published in the *Chicago Law Review* an empirical study of how the exclusionary rule was working in Chicago. For that report, which has since been widely quoted in Fourth Amendment studies, Orfield interviewed a sizable number of narcotics agents, as well as the head of the Narcotics Section of the Organized Crime Division of the Chicago Police Department. That command officer said: "I would not do anything to the exclusionary rule. It makes the police department more professional. It enforces appropriate standards of behavior. In this unit, seldom if ever does the law of search and seizure keep us from making the searches we would be able to make."

Several years later, I spent six months with homicide detectives on New York's Lower East Side. Over time, I asked each of them, separately, what they thought of the exclusionary rule. All said they were contemptuous of the rule when they first joined the force. ("It comes from judges who never spent a night, in danger, on the streets.")

With experience, however, they had changed their minds. They found they went into court with stronger cases when they had to show they had followed the Fourth Amendment rules in building their case.

In 1995, when the House bill to extinguish the exclusionary rule was being debated, homicide detectives in Cobb County, Georgia, told Ted Koppel on *Nightline* that they did not want the power to forget about the exclusionary rule, nor did they want the freedom to make warrantless searches.

One of them said: "It's been my experience that it's better to have a legal search warrant issued by a judge. That way, when you're entering, you know that you're legally entering and legally gathering evidence."

Said a colleague on the force: "The very best case is made through probable cause, with a warrant, and we intend to hold to that standard."

Those homicide detectives may or may not know who Justice Brennan is, but they are keeping alive the long line between him and the Framers of the Fourth Amendment.

The line may snap. As Justice Brennan told me while he was still on the bench, "Look, pal, we've always known—the Framers knew—that liberty is a fragile thing. A very fragile thing."

If the line does snap, Justice Robert Jackson will have been proved right:

> These [Fourth Amendment rights], I protest, are not mere second-class rights but belong in the catalogue of indispensable freedoms. Among deprivations of rights, none is so effective in cowing a population, crushing the spirit of the individual and putting terror in every heart. Uncontrolled search and seizure is one of the first and most effective weapons in the arsenal of every arbitrary government.

Justice Brennan carried that news to the nation all the years he was on the bench.

The Death Penalty in the Court: How It All Began

ALAN M. DERSHOWITZ

The first substantive conversation I ever had with Justice Brennan was about the death penalty. I had just arrived at the Supreme Court as a clerk to Justice Arthur J. Goldberg. My initial assignment was to write a memorandum on the possible unconstitutionality of the death penalty. I set to work but found no suggestion in the case law that any court had ever considered the death penalty to be of questionable constitutionality. Just five years earlier, Chief Justice Earl Warren had written in *Trop v. Dulles* (1958) that "whatever the arguments may be against capital punishment, both on moral grounds and in terms of accomplishing the purposes of punishment—and they are forceful—the death penalty has been employed throughout our history, and, in a day when it is still widely accepted, it cannot be said to violate the constitutional concept of cruelty."

I duly reported this to Justice Goldberg, suggesting that if even the liberal chief justice believed that the death penalty was constitutional, what chance did he have of getting a serious hearing for his view that the cruel and unusual punishment clause should now be construed to prohibit the imposition of capital punishment? Justice Goldberg asked me to talk to Justice Brennan and see what his views were. Unless Justice Brennan agreed to join, the entire project would have to be scuttled, since Justice Goldberg, the Court's rookie, did not want to "be out there alone," against the Chief Justice and the rest of the Court.

I had previously met Justice Brennan several times over the preceding few years, since his son, Bill, was my classmate and moot-court partner at Yale Law School. I had also had lunch several times with the Justice and his friend Judge David Bazelon, for whom I had clerked the previous year. But none of our discussions had been substantive, and I ner-

The author is Felix Frankfurter Professor at Harvard University Law School.

vously anticipated the task of discussing an important issue with one of my judicial heroes.

I brought a rough draft of the memorandum I was working on to the meeting, but Justice Brennan did not want to look at it then. He asked me to describe the results of my research to him, promising to read the memorandum later. I stated the nascent constitutional case against the death penalty as best I could. I told him that the Supreme Court case law, especially the Court's 1910 decision in *Weems v. United States,* could be read as recognizing the following tests for whether a punishment was "cruel and unusual": (1) Giving full weight to reasonable legislative findings, a punishment is cruel and unusual if a less severe one can as effectively achieve the permissible ends of punishment (that is, deterrence, isolation, rehabilitation, or whatever the contemporary society considers the permissible objectives of punishment). (2) Regardless of its effectiveness in achieving the permissible ends of punishment, a punishment is cruel and unusual if it offends the contemporary sense of decency (for example, torture). (3) Regardless of its effectiveness in achieving the permissible ends of punishment, a punishment is cruel and unusual if the evil it produces is disproportionally higher than the harm it seeks to prevent (for example, the death penalty for economic crimes).

In addition to these abstract formulations, I also told Justice Brennan that our research had disclosed a widespread pattern of unequal application of the death penalty on racial grounds. I cited national prison statistics showing that between 1937 and 1951, 233 blacks were executed for rape in the United States, while only 26 whites were executed for that crime.

Justice Brennan encouraged me to continue my research, without making any promise that he would join any action by Justice Goldberg. Several weeks later, Justice Goldberg told me that Justice Brennan had agreed to join a short dissent from the denial of certiorari in *Rudolph v. Alabama* (1963)—a case involving imposition of the death penalty on a black man who was convicted of raping a white woman. Justice William O. Douglas signed on as well. The dissenters invited the bar to address the following questions, which they deemed "relevant and worthy of argument and consideration":

(1) In light of the trend both in the country and throughout the world against punishing rape by death, does the imposition of the death penalty by those States which retain it for rape violate

> "evolving standards of decency that mark the progress of [our] maturing society," or "standards of decency more or less universally accepted"?
>
> (2) Is the taking of human life to protect a value other than human life consistent with the constitutional proscription against "punishments which by their excessive . . . severity are greatly disproportioned to the offenses charged"?
>
> (3) Can the permissible aims of punishment (e.g., deterrence, isolation, rehabilitation) be achieved as effectively by punishing rape less severely than by death (e.g., by life imprisonment); if so, does the imposition of the death penalty for rape constitute "unnecessary cruelty"?

As soon as the dissent was published, there was an immediate reaction. Conservative journalists had a field day lambasting the very notion that a court could strike down as unconstitutional a long-standing punishment that is explicitly referred to in the Constitution. One extreme criticism appeared in the *New Hampshire Union Leader* under the banner headline "U.S. Supreme Court Trio Encourages Rape":

> In a decision handed down last week three U.S. Supreme Court justices, Goldberg, Brennan, Douglas, raised the question of whether it was proper to condemn a man to death for the crime of rape if there has been no endangering of the life of the victim. This incredible opinion, of course, can serve only to encourage would-be rapists. These fiends, freed from the fear of the death penalty and knowing the saccharin sentimentality of many parole boards, will figure the penalty for their foul deed will not be too serious and, therefore, they will be inclined to take a chance.
>
> Thus, not content with forbidding our school children to pray in school, not content with banishing Bible reading from our schools, and not content with letting every type of filthy book be published, at least three members of the Supreme Court are now out to encourage rape.

Several state courts went out of their way to announce their rejection of the principle inherent in the dissenting opinion. This is what the Georgia Supreme Court said:

> With all due respect to the dissenting Justices we would question the judicial right of any American judge to construe the American Constitution contrary to its apparent meaning, the American history of the clause, and its construction by American courts, simply because the numerous nations and States have abandoned capital punishment for rape. First we believe

the history of no nation will show the high values of woman's virtue and purity that America has shown. We would regret to see the day when this freedom loving country would lower our respect for womanhood or lessen her legal protection for no better reason than that many or even all other countries have done so. She is entitled to every legal protection of her body, her decency, her purity and good name.

There was scholarly criticism as well. In the *Harvard Law Review,* Professor Herbert Packer of Stanford wrote:

In an interesting development, some members of the Supreme Court appear disposed to employ [recent constructions of the "cruel and unusual punishments" clause] to regulate the appropriate relation between crime and punishment. Three Justices recently noted their dissent from a denial of certiorari in terms that invite speculation about the role of constitutional adjudication in solving the age-old problem of whether and how the punishment may be made to fit the crime. . . . [However,] [s]ympathy with the legislative goal of limiting or abolishing the death penalty should not be allowed to obscure the difficulties of taking a judicial step toward that goal on the theory outlined by Justice Goldberg [in *Rudolph v. Alabama*]. . . . If one may venture a guess, what Justice Goldberg may really be troubled about is not the death penalty for rape but the death penalty. The problem may not be one of proportionality but of mode of punishment, the problem which concerned the framers of the eighth amendment and to which its provisions still seem most relevant. The Supreme Court is obviously not about to declare that the death penalty *simpliciter* is so cruel and unusual as to be constitutionally intolerable. Other social forces will have to work us closer than we are now to the point at which a judicial *coup de grâce* becomes more than mere fiat. Meanwhile, there may well be legitimate devices for judicial control of the administration of the death penalty. The burden of this Comment is simply that the device proposed by Justice Goldberg is not one of them.

These were the short-term reactions. Far more important, however, was the long-term reaction of the bar, especially the American Civil Liberties Union and the NAACP, which combined forces to establish a death penalty litigation project designed to take up the challenge of the dissenting opinion in *Rudolph*. The history of this project has been recounted brilliantly by Professor Michael Meltsner in his book *Cruel and Unusual,* and I could not possibly improve upon it here. But the results achieved were dramatic. Meltsner and the other members of the Legal Defense Fund, a group which included a number of talented and committed lawyers, litigated hundreds of cases on behalf of defendants sentenced to death and, in many of these cases, succeeded in holding the executioner at bay until the Supreme Court was ready to consider the constitutionality of the death penalty. The strategy was simple in outline: The Supreme Court should not be allowed the luxury of deciding the issue of capital punishment as an abstraction; instead, it must be confronted with the concrete responsibility of determining the immediate fates of many hundreds of condemned persons at the same time. In this way, the Court could not evade the issue, or lightly refuse to decide it, if the Court's refusal would result in the specter of mass executions of hundreds of convicts. However, the Court could decline to decide the ultimate issue—the constitutionality of capital punishment—if in doing so it could find some other way of keeping alive those on death row. And the litigants always provided the Court with this other way—a narrower issue, usually in the form of an irregularity in the procedure by which the death penalty was imposed or administered. Thus in the late 1960s, the Supreme Court decided a number of cases involving the administration of the death penalty; in each of these cases the Court declined to consider the ultimate issue, but it always ruled in favor of the doomed, thereby sparing their lives—at least for the moment. With the passage of each year, the number of those on death row increased and the stakes grew higher and higher.

Then in 1971 the Court took its first turn toward the noose: In *Mc-Gautha v. California*, it held that a condemned person's constitutional rights were not violated "by permitting the jury to impose the death penalty without any governing standards" or by permitting the imposition of the death penalty in "the same proceeding and verdict as determine the issue of guilt." At that point it looked like the string might have been played out; there were no more "narrow" procedural grounds. The Court would have to confront the ultimate issue. But it was not the same Court that had been sitting when the strategy was originally devised; there were four new Nixon appointees, and it was clear that at least some of them believed the death penalty to be constitutional. The umpires—if not the rules—had been changed after the strategy of the game had been worked out and irretrievably put into action. Now there was no pulling back.

The drama intensified. The Court let it be known that finally it was ready to decide the ultimate issue. Knowledgeable lawyers—counting noses on the Court—were predicting that the death penalty would be sustained. Some thought that it might be struck down for rape but sustained for murder. Some predicted that the Court would once again find—or contrive—a reason for avoiding the ultimate issue. A few, of optimistic bent, kept the faith and expressed the belief that the Court—even this Court—would simply not send hundreds to their death.

And then a major and unanticipated break. The California Supreme Court—perhaps the most influential state court in the nation—ruled that *its* constitution (which had substantially similar wording as the federal Constitution) forbade the death penalty. Then, on the last day of the United States Supreme Court's 1971 term, the decision was rendered: The death penalty, as administered in this country, was unconstitutional.

When the Court decided *Furman v. Georgia* in 1972, there were 600 condemned prisoners awaiting execution on America's death rows. The Court ruled, in a 5–4 decision, that the death penalty, as implemented in the United States, was unconstitutional because of the randomness of its application. Never in the history of the courts had a single decision resulted in the saving of so many lives. Never in the history of the American judiciary had so many laws—both state and federal—been struck down with one judicial pronouncement. And never before had so important a social change been accomplished by the courts in so short a period of time.

In *Furman,* each of the five justices voting for reversal of the death sentence wrote separately, including Justice Brennan, who for the first time articulated his view that the imposition of the death penalty, under all circumstances, was *per se* unconstitutional. According to one commentator, Justice Brennan reached this conclusion using a mixture of "precedent, legal reasoning, moral imperatives, and overall—hope—that the power of the Court could improve a society that appeared ambivalent about death as a punishment." Justice Brennan begins his attack on the death penalty in *Furman* by discussing the history surrounding the adoption of the Eighth Amendment, and concluding that it is impossible to determine "exactly what the Framers thought 'cruel and unusual punishments' were." Given this ambiguity, Justice Brennan deemed it the Court's responsibility to interpret and apply this portion of the Eighth Amendment:

> The very purpose of a Bill of Rights was to withdraw certain subjects from the vicissitudes of political controversy, to place them beyond the reach of majorities and officials and to establish them as legal principles to be applied by the courts.

Were the Court to abdicate this responsibility, by blindly accepting the unreviewability of the power of the legislative branch to prescribe punishments for crimes, Justice Brennan warned that the "Cruel and Unusual Punishments Clause would become, in short, 'little more than good advice.' "

Having decided that the courts must interpret the open-ended language of the clause, Justice Brennan reasoned that it "must draw its meaning from the evolving standards of decency that mark the progress of a maturing society." He then elaborated on this idea:

> At bottom, then, the Cruel and Unusual Punishments Clause prohibits the infliction of uncivilized and inhuman punishments. The State, even as it punishes, must treat its members with respect for their intrinsic worth as human beings. A punishment is "cruel and unusual," therefore, if it does not comport with human dignity.

In an effort to provide more specific content to the meaning of the phrase "does not comport with human dignity," Justice Brennan offered the following test:

> The test, then, will ordinarily be a cumulative one: If a punishment is unusually severe, if there is a strong probability that it is inflicted arbitrarily, if it is substantially rejected by contemporary society, and if there is no reason to believe that it serves any penal purpose more effectively than some less severe punishment, then the continued infliction of the punishment violates the command of the Clause that the State may not inflict inhuman and uncivilized punishments upon those convicted of crimes.

Justice Brennan proceeded to analyze the death penalty under this paradigm, after which he concluded:

> In sum, the punishment of death is inconsistent with all four principles: Death is an unusually severe and degrading punishment; there is a strong probability that it is inflicted arbitrarily; its rejection by contemporary society is virtually total; and there is no reason to believe that it serves any penal purpose more effectively than the less severe punishment of imprisonment. The function of these principles is to enable a court to determine whether a punishment comports with human dignity. Death, quite simply, does not.

Justice Brennan declared that the death penalty is surely the most severe and degrading punishment that society can inflict upon an individual, as evidenced by the following facts: the existence of a national debate over the death penalty where there is no such debate over other forms of punishment; the death penalty has been continually restricted by the states, and many have even abolished it; death is reserved for only the most heinous crimes; cases in which the death penalty is available are treated differently by lawyers, judges, and state legislatures; the death penalty is unique in its finality and enormity; and, finally, the death penalty, unlike all other punishments, ensures that the executed person has "lost the right to have rights."

On the issue of arbitrariness, Justice Brennan began his argument with the observation that the death penalty is actually imposed very infrequently in modern society, with the numbers decreasing in every year since 1930, even though the population of the United States and the number of capital crimes committed by its citizens have been growing steadily. Based upon the fact that in a country of over 200 million people, fewer than 50 people per year were being executed, Justice Brennan argued that we should draw a strong inference of arbitrariness in the application of the death penalty. In response to the argument that these statistics can be explained by the fact that only the most "extreme" cases receive the death penalty, Justice Brennan observed that there is no logical distinction based in fact which separates those individuals who are condemned to die from those who are sentenced to life imprisonment. Justice Brennan also observed that the Court's prior decision in *McGautha v. California*, which rejected a defendant's claim that due process had been violated since the jury that condemned him was permitted to make that decision wholly unguided by standards governing the choice, serves to undercut the argument that the criminal justice system can systematically and non-arbitrarily separate the most "extreme" cases from the others.

Justice Brennan then turned to the third principle, whether a punishment has been rejected by contemporary society, and concluded that the death penalty has been almost totally rejected, both in the United States and in other countries. As circumstantial evidence of this conclusion, Justice Brennan noted that our society has gradually moved toward less inhumane methods of execution, from firing squads and hanging to lethal gas and "more humane" electrocutions, as well as the fact that public executions, once thought to enhance deterrence, have been completely done away with. In addition, the class of crimes for which the death penalty is actually being imposed is constantly shrinking; at the time Justice Brennan wrote his dissenting opinion in *Furman,* nine states had abolished the death penalty altogether, many others had not employed the punishment in many years, and the highest court of one state, California, had already declared that punishment unconstitutional under that state's counterpart of the Eighth Amendment.

The final principle that Brennan used to disqualify the death penalty from the range of possible punishments authorized by the Eighth Amendment was the notion that a punishment may not be excessive in view of the purposes for which it is inflicted. The primary argument that Justice Brennan was required to answer is that execution deters murder and certain other heinous crimes better than life imprisonment. Justice Brennan first denied that the death penalty provides specific deterrence any better than life imprisonment; techniques of isolation, as well as focusing on the effective administration of the state's parole laws, can eliminate or minimize the danger of future crimes while the individual is confined. With respect to claims of increased general deterrence, Justice Brennan denied the possibility that there exist a significant number of persons in society who would commit a capital crime knowing that the punishment is long-term, perhaps even life, imprisonment, but who would not commit the crime knowing that the punishment is death. In addition, although Justice Brennan admitted that the statistical evidence available in 1972 was inconclusive with respect to the deterrent value of the death penalty as opposed to life imprisonment, he buttressed his argument by observing that to a person contemplating a murder or rape, the risk of being executed, taking into account the method under which the death penalty was currently administered, was remote and improbable whereas the risk of long-term imprisonment was near and great. Given these incentives, Justice Brennan concluded that there is simply no reason to believe, or any hard, statistical evidence to support, the claim that the death penalty provides greater deterrence, either general or specific, than does life imprisonment.

Aside from deterrence, Justice Brennan also rejected the suggestion that the death penalty serves the retributive goal of punishment any better than life imprisonment. First of all, Justice Brennan denied that a sentence of death, since it is inflicted so rarely in the United States relative to the number of capital crimes committed, serves either to prevent private enforcement of the laws, to inculcate a respect for the laws in our citizens, or to satisfy some sense of just desert for these criminals better than life imprisonment; in fact, he took the position that executing so few people actually undermines each of these values that comprise the retributive goal of punishment. Justice Brennan summed up his position in the following passage:

> When this country was founded, memories of the Stuart horrors were fresh and severe corporal punishments were common. Death was not then a unique punishment. The practice of punishing criminals by death, moreover, was widespread and by and large acceptable to society. Indeed, without developed prison systems, there was frequently no workable alternative. Since that time successive restrictions, imposed against the background of a continuing moral controversy, have drastically curtailed the use of this punishment. Today death is a uniquely severe punishment. When examined by the principles applicable under the Cruel and Unusual Punishments Clause, death stands condemned as fatally offensive to human dignity. The punishment of death is therefore "cruel and unusual," and the States may no longer inflict it as a punishment for crimes. Rather than kill an arbitrary handful of criminals each year, the States will confine them to prison. "The State thereby suffers nothing and loses no power. The purpose of punishment is fulfilled, crime is repressed by penalties of just, not tormenting, severity, its repetition is prevented, and hope is given for the reformation of the criminal."

The moratorium on the imposition of the death penalty which had been achieved in *Furman* turned out to be short-lived. In 1976, a majority in *Gregg v. Georgia* reinstated the death penalty for murder on the ground that adequate procedural safeguards had been adopted which made the imposition of the death penalty no longer violative of the Eighth Amendment. In a dissenting opinion co-authored by Justice Marshall, Justice Brennan attacked the majority's holding.

The fatal constitutional infirmity in the punishment of death, they observed, is that it treats "members of the human race as nonhumans, as objects to be toyed with and discarded. [It is] thus inconsistent with the fundamental premise of the Clause that even the vilest criminal remains a human being possessed of common human dignity." As such it is a penalty that "subjects the individual to a fate forbidden by the principle of civilized treatment guaranteed by the Clause." Justice of this kind is obviously no less shocking than the crime itself, and the new "official" murder, far from offering redress for the offense committed against society, adds instead a second defilement to the first.

In the cases following *Gregg v. Georgia*, Justice Brennan continued to adhere to his position that the death penalty is *per se* unconstitutional, offering additional arguments and statistical evidence to support this claim. For example, in his dissenting opinion in *McCleskey v. Kemp* (1987), Justice Brennan refuted the Court's claim that Georgia and other states have enacted appropriate safeguards to ensure fair determinations in the special context of capital punishment by citing a study which suggests that taking into account some 230 nonracial factors that might legitimately influence a sentencer, the jury more likely than not would have spared McCleskey's life had his victim been black, instead of white. In addition, Justice Brennan cited statistics indicating that in Georgia, race accounts for a six percentage point difference in the rate at which capital punishment is imposed, 11 percent for white-victim cases and 5 percent for black-victim cases, and thus, the rate of capital sentencing in a white-victim case is 120 percent greater than the rate in a black-victim case. These statistics provide support for Justice Brennan's arguments about the probability of arbitrary imposition of the death penalty that he first promulgated in *Furman;* however, rather than confirming his claim that the death penalty is *arbitrarily* imposed—that is, not imposed in only "extreme" cases—these statistics indicate that the death penalty is being systematically imposed against the killers of white victims more than the killers of blacks.

In the following passage from *McCleskey,* Justice Brennan used these statistics to draw an analogy about the imposition of the death penalty to the burden of proof:

> In determining the guilt of a defendant, a State must prove its case beyond a reasonable doubt. That is, we refuse to convict if the chance of error is simply less likely than not. Surely, we should not be willing to take a person's life if the chance that his death sentence was irrationally imposed is more likely than not. In light of the gravity of the interest at stake, petitioner's statistics on their face are a powerful demonstration of the type of risk that our Eighth Amendment jurisprudence has consistently condemned.

In addition to the statistical evidence, Justice Brennan also noted that prosecutors in Georgia have limitless discretion in the decision to seek the death penalty and that Georgia provides no list of aggravating and mitigating factors, or any standard for balancing them against one another, in making the sentencing determination. Both of these facts, Justice Brennan asserted, raise the specter of arbitrary enforcement of the death penalty and suggest reasons why the statistical evidence should be regarded as valid. In the concluding paragraph of his dissent in *Mc-Cleskey,* Justice Brennan made the following haunting statement:

> It is tempting to pretend that minorities on death row share a fate in no way connected to our own, that our treatment of them sounds no echoes beyond the chambers in which they die. Such an illusion is ultimately corrosive, for the reverberations of injustice are not so easily confined. "The destinies of two races in this country are indissolubly linked together," and the way in which we choose those who will die reveals the depth of moral commitment among the living.

Only time will tell whether Justice Brennan's views on the constitutionality of the death penalty will ultimately prevail, as have the views of other great dissenters of the past. They surely will continue to prick the conscience of a nation which today seems bent on increasing the number of executions. Whatever the outcome of this great debate, Justice Brennan should certainly be credited with having helped to save the lives of more Americans who had been condemned to die than any judge in our history.

The Hope of Justice: The Great Writ

Bryan Stevenson

When you're wrongly convicted of a crime, illegally sentenced to death or life in prison at twenty years of age, you quickly become desperate. You arrive in one of the growing hundreds of prisons and jails in America where the grim reality of extended confinement robs you of your identity, freedom, family, dreams, and aspirations, and you fear that ultimately it will take your life. Your insistent protestations about innocence, your complaints about an unfair trial, and your enraged cries of an unjust verdict are immediately silenced by the isolation of prison. Slowly you begin to realize that it's just a matter of time before you're going to lose the one thing you absolutely must have to get out and ever succeed again, your hope.

The struggle against hopelessness may be the greatest challenge of imprisonment. Finding the courage to persevere against an unlawful detention in a system of justice that is deliberately indifferent to its mistakes and arbitrariness may be considerably harder than facing the constant dangers, treachery, and anguish of extended confinement. The sense of rage and frustration emanating from the certain belief that you've been convicted in violation of the law is destructive and disorienting. Your assumptions about what's fair, right, and legitimate in the administration of criminal justice are radically altered.

To some it is ironic that correct application of the law is so important to prisoners. Yet the moral authority to punish someone for breaking the law is dependent on a commitment by organized society to follow the law. To the condemned and imprisoned, violating the Constitution to obtain a conviction reveals a cynicism about the law so that the violation can never adequately be described as a technicality. It feeds the bitterness and resignation that breed recidivism among those convicted of crimes. Worse, it deconstructs the morality of criminal law leaving

The author, director of the Equal Justice Initiative of Alabama, was awarded a MacArthur Fellowship in 1995 for his work in fighting the death penalty and protecting civil rights.

the powerful to exercise power against the powerless without a commitment to demand lawful conduct of everyone.

Thousands of men, women, and juveniles have found themselves in jails and prisons across America struggling against the oppressive reality of an unjust conviction. Their only hope for justice is a single obscure remedy: the writ of habeas corpus.

The Great Writ. The renowned English legal historian Blackstone described the writ of habeas corpus as the "most celebrated writ in the English law." Justice Brennan, in *Fay v. Noia* (1963), defined the writ of habeas corpus as a device to protect the principle that "in a civilized society, government must always be accountable to the judiciary for a man's imprisonment: if the imprisonment cannot be shown to conform with the fundamental requirements of the law, the individual is entitled to immediate release." Yet, despite the lofty office of habeas corpus in Anglo-American legal jurisprudence, it has devolved into a process that elevates form over substance.

EARLY CONFUSION ABOUT THE WRIT

Before Justice Brennan took the bench, jurists could not agree upon the proper scope of the Great Writ. The constitutional command was plain enough: Except in rare circumstances "the privilege of the Writ of Habeas Corpus shall not be suspended." And scholars agreed that historically habeas corpus emerged from English common law as a remedy for the prisoner who was being held indefinitely without ever appearing in court. Yet there was tremendous disagreement about precisely what privilege was guaranteed. Some jurists saw the writ as a narrow remedy for essentially pretrial detentions that failed to satisfy some minimal conception of due process. The legal force of the writ was no greater than the congressional statutes that codified its parameters. To these legal theorists, habeas corpus was less about collateral attacks on illegally obtained criminal convictions than about protection against unlawful surrender to government without *any* process or hearing.

Other legal historians saw writs of habeas corpus serving a much broader function. They pointed to seventeenth-century English law that recognized the applicability of petitions for writ of habeas corpus for wrongful imprisonment that did not satisfy due process even though some process had been afforded. The Great Writ was a tool, as Blackstone put it, for "all manner" of illegal confinement. The range of cases and instances where writs had been granted made it clear that restraints contrary to fundamental law, even when legitimated by some authority or process, were subject to redress by writ of habeas corpus.

In this country, the debate about the scope of habeas corpus was complicated by advance and retreat in the jurisprudence of the United States Supreme Court. It was further complicated by questions surrounding the extent to which state court convictions were subject to review by federal judges. Congress expressly extended the habeas statute in 1867 to cover state prisoners. However, observers disagreed even about the significance of that act. To some it served merely to confirm that the scope of habeas is entirely in Congress's hands. Others viewed Congress's act as an acknowledgment that the Constitution commands Congress to preserve English common-law practice of applying the Great Writ to protect personal liberty from all manner of government oppression.

BRENNAN REENERGIZES THE GREAT WRIT

It was in the midst of this considerable clamor over federalism, comity, history, and precedent around the scope of habeas corpus ad subjiciendum (as it is more formally known) that William Brennan's remarkably clear vision emerged in 1963 to radically influence the development of habeas corpus. To say that Justice Brennan's majority opinion in *Fay v. Noia* looms as the most influential opinion on the scope of federal habeas corpus nonetheless understates all that was accomplished in this single opinion.

The facts in *Fay v. Noia* were unusually simple. Noia, a state prisoner in New York, had been illegally coerced into confessing to a murder, through police techniques that one court described as "satanic." The confession was the only evidence against him when he was convicted and sentenced to life imprisonment. Noia was too poor to adequately appeal his conviction and sentence and he additionally feared that he might be subject to the death penalty if successful. His two codefendants, who were also forced to confess, did appeal their convictions and in subsequent proceedings were able to prove that the confessions of all three men were illegal. After release of the codefendants, Noia similarly challenged his illegal confession and sought relief in federal court. New York acknowledged that Noia's conviction was illegal and his confession coerced. Nevertheless, the state argued that because Noia failed to appeal his conviction he was barred under the rules of habeas corpus from any remedy.

Justice Brennan's majority opinion held that Noia was entitled to release or a new trial. The opinion was significant not only because it placed limits on the strict enforcement of state procedural rules that undermined federal constitutional rights. Perhaps more important, in a statement that would shape the law of habeas corpus for decades, Justice Brennan hailed the role of habeas corpus as a crucial protection against unjust convictions.

Justice Brennan's written opinion in *Fay v. Noia* was a remarkable and awesome piece of scholarship and analysis. He first cut through the debates and confusion around the scope of habeas corpus and presented a definitive historical analysis of the Great Writ that drew on cases and writings dating back to seventeenth-century England. Justice Brennan detailed the historic role of habeas corpus as a crucial remedy against unjust convictions and imprisonment and gave meaning and perspective to all of the rhetoric surrounding its greatness. His carefully conceived effort in *Fay* redefined the vitality of habeas corpus in a manner that state procedural rules and obscure formal requirements could not easily reduce to insignificance. By placing habeas corpus in a historical context that confirmed its elevated status and its crucial role, Justice Brennan gave the Great Writ renewed meaning and purpose in preserving the rights of thousands of Americans who had been wrongly convicted of crimes and illegally sent to prison.

Justice Brennan's opinion in *Fay v. Noia* was a major development especially for poor people. The rights of poor people to challenge unconstitutional convictions and death sentences through appointed or state-funded counsel had only recently been secured in 1963. There were consequently thousands of previously convicted prisoners with unconstitutional convictions and sentences. Habeas corpus was their sole remedy. Even state-funded legal assistance secured by the Court's decision in *Gideon v. Wainwright* (1963) was often unable to overcome the challenges created by racial bias, prejudicial pretrial publicity, police and prosecutorial misconduct, and a host of sociopolitical and legal barriers to justice for poor people accused of crimes. Yet habeas corpus, revitalized by Justice Brennan, increasingly became a hope for justice in previously less hopeful territory.

Justice Brennan authored over twenty-five majority opinions in habeas corpus cases. His opinion in *Fay v. Noia* was the basis for dozens of other habeas cases that reaffirmed some of America's most basic rights and procedures in the administration of criminal justice. This was particularly true in death penalty cases. Because resumption of the death penalty in the 1970s led to a steady increase in the number of collateral challenges against death sentences, death penalty law and the law of habeas corpus became inexorably interwoven. Under the principles outlined in *Fay* and further developed in *Townsend v. Sain* (1963), which was handed down the same day, federal courts were identifying scores of illegally imposed convictions and death sentences that would have otherwise resulted in wrongful executions. Mentally retarded men who had been coerced into confessing, defendants whose convictions had been obtained only by gross racial bias in jury selection, and innocent men and women who had wrongly been convicted of crimes all found justice through habeas corpus petitions.

THE POLITICS OF DEATH

As Justice Brennan clearly recognized, the politics of the death penalty made habeas corpus protections crucial. Death row prisoners are the most hated and despised people in our society. In state and local courts where judges are typically elected, sometimes as often as every six years, the politics of crime and punishment fueled by a growing enthusiasm for executions made impartial adherence to constitutional requirements in capital cases risky business. Federal judges, with life appointments insulating them from politics, were often the only hope for justice. It was in the face of capital punishment that the vaunted precedents of habeas corpus were so critical and Justice Brennan's passionate commitment to equal justice and the Constitution so evident.

Yet the politics of death bred greater resistance to the use of habeas corpus (by death row prisoners and others) and the constitutional rights protected by the Great Writ. Legislative initiatives to dissolve the scope of habeas corpus developed and the Supreme Court began to weaken the writ despite Justice Brennan's persistent objections. Political interest in decreasing the time between conviction and execution in death cases mixed with a general increase in habeas filings to create support for limiting the availability of habeas corpus remedies. The dramatic rise in the number of people sent to prison in the 1980s—the total number of prisoners in the United States more than doubled between 1983 and

1993, from 660,800 to 1,408,685—and the increased use of capital punishment with no corresponding increase in legal representation for death row prisoners were the source of most of the frustrations around habeas corpus, but it was habeas corpus itself that became the target of reform.

As early as 1977 in *Wainwright v. Sykes,* the Court, over Justice Brennan's objections, imposed new procedural devices to restrict the scope and power of the Great Writ. By the late 1980s, habeas had become doctrinally complex with a maze of procedural requirements that often seemed indifferent to the substantive demands of the Constitution or even the innocence of a convicted prisoner. (The Court recently ruled, for example, in *Herrera v. Collins* [1993], that a prisoner's failure to raise a claim correctly in the state courts or in his first habeas petition could be fatal—even if the prisoner could prove he was actually innocent.) Expanding concepts of harmless error in habeas corpus law, blocking retroactive application of new criminal decisions clarifying the rights of the accused, reinforcing procedural requirements for raising claims in state courts, barring successive petitions, and restricting the right to an evidentiary hearing in federal habeas all threatened the power and availability of habeas corpus to identify and remedy unjust convictions and sentences. These trends found Justice Brennan's enraged voice dissenting in more and more opinions. By the time he retired in 1990, he had written close to 100 dissenting and concurring opinions in habeas cases.

HOPE FOR JUSTICE

Yet even in dissent there was a ringing hope for justice in Justice Brennan's work that may be his defining legacy in the area of habeas corpus. Justice Brennan restored habeas corpus in American jurisprudence during the early 1960s and then defended its increased power to overcome injustice for imprisoned men and women throughout his tenure on the bench. His opinions literally saved the lives of many unjustly condemned people in death houses across America. As the "fear of too much justice" Justice Brennan described in *McCleskey v. Kemp* (1987) found expression in decisions reducing the scope of habeas corpus, and the Court became less responsive to the demands of a fair trial for the already convicted, there arose a new challenge for Justice Brennan not unlike the challenge confronting the condemned and imprisoned who also value the Great Writ: the struggle against hopelessness.

The great Czech writer and leader Václav Havel has written that "complete skepticism is an understandable consequence of discovering that one's enthusiasms are based on illusion." In the administration of criminal justice there is clearly an emerging rhetorical vision that regards ensuring constitutional protections for the convicted and condemned a goal too illusory to maintain. To many the commitment to fairness and equal justice dictated by the Constitution may be too great an expectation for a nation engaged in a "War on Drugs." Increasingly, judges and political leaders driven by frustration about violent crime and demands of faster executions and more prisons are accepting less and less reliability in the criminal trial process. There is less diligence about meaningfully honoring constitutional guarantees of effective assistance of counsel to all people accused of crimes regardless of their poverty, retreat from fulfilling constitutional prohibitions against race bias, and ambivalence about insisting on compliance with the requirements of criminal procedure where only presumptively guilty defendants are at risk.

It is against this hopelessness that the force of Justice Brennan's scholarship and reasoning may have its greatest influence. In Justice Brennan's dissenting opinions in *Teague v. Lane* (1989) and *Penry v. Lynaugh* (1989), there is the clever, insightful, sharp, and detailed explanation of how the Court has failed to uphold important constitutional values by limiting habeas relief to an arbitrary time line where a criminal law decision's date is more important than its holding. In *McCleskey v. Kemp* (1987), Justice Brennan's dissent powerfully destroys the shameful reasoning of a majority of the Court that tolerates gross racial bias in Georgia's administration of the death penalty.

These opinions and all of Justice Brennan's work in the area of habeas corpus reflect the brilliance of one of the great jurists of the twentieth century. But the value of his work cannot be fully measured by simply assessing the ideas in his mind without also appreciating the conviction in his heart. When Justice Brennan decries the execution of mentally retarded people permitted by *Penry v. Lynaugh* and details the dangers and destructiveness of the Court's prevailing view, his passionate voice urges everyone to recognize that each of us is more than the worst thing that we have done. In *McCleskey* when he describes the sad duty of counsel to explain to a minority defendant that race bias is now acceptable in the administration of criminal justice, he urges America to recognize the psychic harm that attends the tolerance of race bias and its debilitating effect.

Whether in dissent or in the majority, there is in Justice Brennan a vision of justice that is unyielding in its protection of the Constitution and its demands for fairness and equality. It is a vision of justice that hopes for the fulfillment of every constitutional guarantee and insists that we never give up and accept a system of justice that institutionalizes bias, unfairness, prejudice, inequality, and unreliability.

Justice Brennan's perspective on the promise of the Great Writ—to protect the hopes of innocent people in prison and the illegally convicted and unfairly sentenced—will continue to guide the future of this historic remedy against injustice. As Congress passes more drastic restrictions on the availability of habeas remedies, and as statutes of limitation with new standards of review threaten to permanently ban the innocent and wrongly convicted from federal habeas review, the struggle against hopelessness for the unjustly imprisoned will become more difficult.

Regrettably, when it comes to protecting the rights of despised and rejected people like the imprisoned, justice is a constant struggle. Wonderfully, the life and work of Justice Brennan force us to recognize that the balance of this struggle turns not on the fear and skepticism of those who doubt the power of justice but on the hope and spirit of those who believe.

Judicial Redress for Police Misconduct

Stuart Taylor, Jr.

In the early 1920s a Newark politician, popular for his unfailing defense of the interests of workers, embarked on a crusade to rid Newark of public corruption of all varieties. One of his proudest accomplishments as director of public safety was his zero tolerance for police brutality and coerced confessions, which were common instruments of law enforcement in that age. The theme of his 1925 reelection campaign must have been even more curious seventy years ago than it would be today. He touted his success in ensuring that "the use of unnecessary force in making arrests, and violence in any form towards the citizens, has been done away with."

The politician was a gregarious Irishman named William J. Brennan, whose nineteen-year-old son, William J. Brennan, Jr., would rise to become one of the greatest Supreme Court justices in the history of our nation. One can scarcely resist presuming that the father's passion for curbing police misconduct profoundly influenced the son. It can hardly be a coincidence that among Justice Brennan's signal contributions to the rule of law have been his remarkably creative and productive efforts to vindicate the rights of victims of police brutality and other official misconduct—and, in the process, to deter such abuses.

The still-controversial Warren Court precedents excluding unconstitutionally obtained evidence from criminal trials have been the most conspicuous rulings touching on police misconduct. But a succession of less famous decisions, in which Justice Brennan played an even greater part, may well have been more effective as remedies for police brutality and other violations of the Constitution. Those rulings cleared the way for victims to bring lawsuits seeking money damages for injuries caused

The author is a senior writer with American Lawyer Media. He covered the Supreme Court for the *New York Times* from 1985 to 1988.

by such violations of their rights—"constitutional torts," as they have come to be called.

Among the landmark rulings in this area are two written by Justice Brennan: *Bivens v. Six Unknown Named Agents of the Federal Bureau of Narcotics,* in 1971, and *Monell v. New York City Department of Social Services,* in 1978. Victims of unconstitutional government action can now hope to win monetary redress from federal officials under *Bivens* and from local governments under *Monell.*

"*Bivens* and *Monell* are among the most important decisions of our generation—really in American history—in holding government accountable for its wrongdoing," asserts Professor Erwin Chemerinsky of the University of Southern California Law Center, an expert in civil litigation over police misconduct.

Justice Brennan also fleshed out the meaning, and extended the reach, of both decisions in several subsequent opinions for the Court. Indeed, the entire body of law concerning the rights of individuals to seek redress from the courts for violations of constitutional rights bears a distinctive Brennan imprimatur.

The remedies for constitutional violations by police and others are not quite as strong as they would be if Justice Brennan had been able to win four other justices over to his way of thinking in all of the cases that came in the wake of *Bivens* and *Monell.* But such strength as these remedies have and such progress as we have made are a reflection of his leadership.

RAMPANT POLICE BRUTALITY

Police brutality and other official violations of individual rights have long blighted this nation's aspiration to provide liberty and justice for all. And because shocking violations have persisted, it's easy to forget how far we have come since Justice Brennan joined the Court in 1956.

"Prior to the mid-1950s, there were no meaningful legal controls over routine police behavior," according to Professor Samuel Walker of the School of Criminal Justice at the University of Nebraska at Omaha. "By all accounts, American policing in the 19th century was utterly lawless. Physical brutality was rampant and essentially unpunished." And well into this century, searches without warrants or probable cause, coercive "third-degree" interrogations, unjustified beatings and shootings, reckless car chases and the like were still more the rule than the exception.

Meanwhile, it was virtually impossible for a victim of police brutality or other official violation of civil rights—*especially* an innocent victim—to win judicial redress of any kind.

The Fourth Amendment, in particular, was enforced only through the exclusionary rule, which since 1914 had barred the use in federal criminal trials of evidence obtained through unconstitutional searches and seizures. This and other protections for criminal defendants were of course extended to the state courts during the 1960s, by the Warren Court, reflecting what Walker calls "a growing awareness of the depth of police misconduct and the need for a judicial remedy." But these decisions did nothing for most victims of misconduct, in particular those whose prosecution did not depend on use of illegally obtained evidence, and those who were clearly innocent and thus were not prosecuted.

As Justice John Marshall Harlan was later to stress in an opinion concurring in the judgment in *Bivens,* "Assuming Bivens' innocence of the crime charged, the 'exclusionary rule' is simply irrelevant. For people in Bivens' shoes, it is damages or nothing."

Nor could one look to the exclusionary rule to deter the many forms of misconduct that officials engage in for purposes other than obtaining admissible evidence: unwarranted police harassment, beatings, shootings, reckless high-speed chases in which police cars endanger bystanders, racially or politically motivated firings of government workers, and more.

In 1956, a victim of such misconduct—even one with evidence as vivid as the videotape of the Rodney King beating in Los Angeles—would have gotten nowhere with a suit for damages. Whether the suit were brought against local, state, or federal officials, or against the governmental units for which they worked, it would have hit a stone wall of sovereign and official immunities and related doctrines in federal court. State courts were generally no more receptive.

Lying dormant on the statute books, however, was a Reconstruction-era act of Congress that contained the seeds of a doctrinal revolution: the Civil Rights Act of 1871, also known as the Ku Klux Klan Act. Its key provision is now codified as Section 1983 of Title 42 of the U.S. Code:

> Every person who, under color of any statute, ordinance, regulation, custom, or usage, of any State or Territory, subjects . . . any . . . person . . . to the deprivation of any rights . . . secured by the Constitution and laws,

shall be liable to the party injured in an action at law, suit in equity, or other proper proceeding for redress.

On its face, Section 1983 (as it is commonly called) seems a sweeping mandate for courts to award money damages—among other remedies—for injuries caused by all manner of lawless conduct by state and local officials.

But for ninety years after its enactment, Section 1983 was virtually a dead letter. Federal courts allowed some defendants to escape liability on the ground that even if they had violated the Constitution, they had complied with, or acted in good-faith reliance upon, state laws; courts dismissed claims against other defendants on the ground that if they had *violated* state law, then they had not been acting "under color of" such law within the meaning of Section 1983.

This Catch-22 logic blocked off just about every conceivable Section 1983 lawsuit. And, in fact, there were but a handful of such suits before 1960.

Brennan's Doctrinal Revolution

The doctrinal ice began to break in 1961, when the Court decided a case called *Monroe v. Pape.* The complaint, filed by a black Chicago man, his wife, and six children, alleged (in the Court's words) that "13 Chicago police officers broke into [their] home in the early morning, routed them from bed, made them stand naked in the living room, and ransacked every room, emptying drawers and ripping mattress covers"—all without a warrant; they then took Mr. Monroe away and grilled him about a murder case, held him incommunicado for ten hours, and finally released him with no charges.

The Monroe family sued the individual officers and the city under Section 1983. While their case was dismissed by the lower courts, the Supreme Court reversed, reinstating the claims against the individual officers. In an opinion by Justice William O. Douglas (in which Justice Brennan joined), the Court held that the actions of police clothed with official authority are "under color of" state law even when they violate it.

Monroe was a dramatic step toward reviving Section 1983, and has become a fount of thousands of lawsuits. But it was a mixed blessing for victims of unconstitutional action by local officials, because it held that the city itself—on whose behalf the police officers had been acting—could not be sued under Section 1983. The Court held that Congress had not intended to include municipalities within the word "person," which defines the class of defendants suable under the statute.

Another gap in this nascent structure of judicial redress for official misconduct was that Section 1983 applied only to state and local officials. There was no analogous act of Congress authorizing damage suits against *federal* officials who violated constitutional rights.

Justice Brennan filled this gap in 1971, in his seminal opinion in *Bivens.* It was an exercise in constitutional common law making at once so creative in its conception and so well grounded in law and logic that it has stood well the test of time.

The facts were reminiscent of *Monroe v. Pape.* Webster Bivens claimed that six federal narcotics agents had entered his Brooklyn apartment without warrant or probable cause, manacled him in front of his wife and children, threatened to arrest the whole family, searched the entire apartment, arrested him, and subjected him to a strip search at the federal courthouse. Bivens sought $15,000 in damages from each agent for the humiliation and mental suffering inflicted on him by their violation of his Fourth Amendment rights.

The lower courts dismissed the suit, and the Justice Department argued in the Supreme Court that since damage suits for Fourth Amendment violations had not been authorized by Congress, Bivens should be relegated to suing the agents in state court for any violations of state trespassing or privacy laws.

But Justice Brennan held that Bivens "is entitled to recover money damages for any injuries he has suffered as a result of the agents' violation of the [Fourth] Amendment," even though the amendment does not authorize such judicial redress "in so many words." He cited the courts' traditional duty to "adjust their remedies so as to grant the necessary relief" to vindicate federal rights.

Victims of Fourth Amendment violations should not be relegated to state law remedies, Justice Brennan stressed, because state laws were typically conceived with intrusions by private actors in mind, and might be inadequate or hostile to the federal constitutional interest. "An agent acting—albeit unconstitutionally—in the name of the United States possesses a far greater capacity for harm than an individual trespasser exercising no authority other than his own," he explained.

Bivens was the first decision definitively to establish that even when Congress has not created or recognized a right to sue for money damages, federal courts can award such damages for injuries caused by violations of constitutional rights.

In subsequent Brennan opinions the Court extended the *Bivens* damage remedy to cases involving violations of other constitutional provisions: *Davis v. Passman*, in 1979, held that a woman who had been fired by a congressman because of her sex could seek back pay for violation of the Fifth Amendment due process clause, and *Carlson v. Green*, in 1980, held that a federal prisoner could sue prison officials for violating the Eighth Amendment ban on cruel and unusual punishment. In *Carlson*, Justice Brennan cited *Bivens* for the broad proposition that "the victims of a constitutional violation by a federal agent have a right to recover damages against the official in federal court despite the absence of any statute conferring such a right." Lower courts have, accordingly, extended the *Bivens* remedy to virtually the entire panoply of constitutionally protected individual rights.

The *Bivens* opinion itself cautioned, however, that there would not necessarily be a damage remedy for every constitutional tort by a federal official. In particular, Justice Brennan said, the Court might heed "special factors counseling hesitation in the absence of affirmative action by Congress," and might defer to a "congressional declaration" remitting victims of some kinds of constitutional torts to other remedies deemed by Congress to be "equally effective."

In recent years the Court has cited this language in declining to extend the *Bivens* remedy to some new contexts, such as improper denials of Social Security disability benefits. But Justice Brennan's holding in *Bivens* remains the most potent weapon in the arsenal of persons complaining of violations of their constitutional rights by federal officials.

Moreover, the Congress—perhaps prodded by *Bivens*—acted in 1974 (by amending the Federal Tort Claims Act) to provide a complementary remedy in damages against the federal government itself for certain types of misconduct by federal law enforcement officials. Such suits had previously been barred by the federal government's sovereign immunity.

MUNICIPAL LIABILITY

But the problem of police brutality and misconduct is most acute at the local government level, where the vast majority of police officers work.

And the theoretical right to monetary redress that victims of such misconduct had enjoyed under Section 1983 since *Monroe v. Pape* was often hollow in practice.

The obstacles to recovering damages from individual police officers and other local government officials are difficult even for the most appealing plaintiffs to surmount: Sometimes it's impossible to identify the responsible officials; juries will often be reluctant to hold them personally liable for excesses of zeal in the cause of fighting crime; and officials are cloaked with a "qualified immunity" for official acts undertaken in the good-faith belief that they were lawful, and by absolute immunity in the cases of judges and prosecutors.

A vivid example of the sometimes illusory nature of the Section 1983 remedy against individual officials came in the lawsuits growing out of a bloody barrage of police gunfire at a dormitory at virtually all-black Jackson State College, in Jackson, Mississippi, in May 1970. After student disturbances that had included rock-throwing, police responded to shots from a lone sniper by raking the dorm with gunfire, killing two people and wounding twelve others. Injured students and survivors of the dead students sued sixty-nine individual state and city police officers and their superiors, the state, and the city for damages under Section 1983.

The U.S. Court of Appeals for the Fifth Circuit held (in *Burton v. Waller* [1974]) that the police barrage had "far exceeded the response that was appropriate." But the court nonetheless upheld a jury verdict for all defendants. The individual officers were absolved on the grounds that the conduct of some was not so flagrant as to strip them of their privilege of self-defense, and that those who had fired the most unjustifiable fatal and wounding shots could not be identified. The state was immune under the Eleventh Amendment. And the city was effectively immunized by *Monroe v. Pape*.

Even in cases in which easily identifiable officers have committed flagrant and indefensible constitutional violations, victims often find that suing them is a costly exercise in futility that few lawyers will take on. The reason is that almost all police officers and other local officials lack the means to pay substantial monetary awards.

For all these reasons, the inability of victims to sue local governments under Section 1983 after *Monroe v. Pape* was a source of great frustration to civil rights lawyers and lower courts seeking to vindicate constitutional rights; scholars subjected this aspect of *Monroe* to cogent criticism, and urged the Court to reconsider it.

The Court finally did so in 1978, in a Brennan opinion that overruled *Monroe's* preclusion of Section 1983 suits against municipalities. The facts of the case, *Monell v. New York City Department of Social Services,* had nothing to do with police misconduct. But the *Monell* precedent has become a major weapon against such misconduct.

Monell was a Section 1983 suit against New York City by a class of social workers and schoolteachers who had been forced by a city policy to take unpaid leaves of absence starting early in their pregnancies. In allowing the claim against the city to proceed, Justice Brennan held that *Monroe* had misread the legislative history of the Ku Klux Klan Act, and in particular of Congress's rejection of a proposal called the Sherman Amendment.

That amendment would have subjected municipalities to sweeping liability, regardless of fault, for all injuries to persons and property within their borders that might be caused by private groups like the Klan. The *Monroe* Court inferred from the rejection of this amendment a congressional intention to exempt municipalities altogether from Section 1983. But Justice Brennan held in *Monell,* after painstaking analysis of the legislative history, that Congress's unwillingness to impose such sweeping liability on local governments for private violence did not imply any intention to immunize them from liability for their *own* unconstitutional actions.

Rather, Justice Brennan held, Section 1983's language and legislative history manifested an intent "to provide a remedy, to be broadly construed, against all forms of official violation of federally protected rights," and to include "municipalities and other local government units . . . among those persons to whom section 1983 applies." ("Person" is often used in the law in a broad enough sense to encompass corporations and other impersonal entities including municipal corporations, and indeed Justice Brennan pointed out that only months before the passage of Section 1983, Congress passed a law declaring that the word "person" in any federal statute "may extend . . . to bodies politic and corporate" unless the context suggests otherwise.)

Monell stopped well short, however, of allowing the victim of every constitutional tort by a police officer or other municipal employee to win damages from the municipal treasury. Rather, Justice Brennan specified, "It is when execution of a government's policy or custom, whether made by its lawmakers or by those whose edicts or acts may fairly be said to represent official policy, inflicts the injury that the government as an entity is responsible under section 1983."

This requirement of proving that the unconstitutional act was brought about by an official "policy or custom" has produced considerable confusion and tripped up some deserving plaintiffs. But *Monell* lawsuits have nonetheless proven a potent remedy for many victims of police and other official misconduct.

For one thing, *Monell* lawsuits are not subject to the defense of good faith that so often defeats suits against individual officials. The Court made this clear in 1980, in *Owen v. City of Independence,* also written by Justice Brennan. Stressing that "a damages remedy against the offending party is a vital component of any scheme for vindicating cherished constitutional guarantees," Brennan provided a detailed articulation of the underlying policy goals:

> Section 1983 was intended not only to provide compensation to the victims of past abuses, but to serve as a deterrent against future constitutional deprivations as well. . . . The knowledge that a municipality will be liable for all of its injurious conduct, whether committed in good faith or not, should create an incentive for officials who may harbor doubts about the lawfulness of their intended actions to err on the side of protecting citizens' constitutional rights. Furthermore, the threat that damages might be levied against the city may encourage those in a policymaking position to institute internal rules and programs designed to minimize the likelihood of unintentional infringements of constitutional rights.

The availability of municipal defendants unprotected by good-faith immunity cleared the way for such decisions as *Tennessee v. Garner,* in 1985, in which the Court ruled that the Fourth Amendment bars police from using deadly force to stop fleeing felons unless they appear to pose "a significant threat of death or serious physical injury to the officer or others."

The *Garner* decision (written by Justice Byron R. White) grew out of a Memphis police officer's fatal shooting of an unarmed, 110-pound, fifteen-year-old black boy as he tried to escape over a fence after burglarizing an empty house. The boy's parents sued, but the officer successfully invoked the defense of good faith, since he had fired in accordance with a state law authorizing police to shoot any fleeing felon.

Before *Monell,* that would have been the end of the case. But *Monell* and *Owen* meant that the parents' suit could proceed against the city. This provided the occasion for the Court to reach the Fourth Amendment question, and to issue a ruling with considerable practical and symbolic importance as a restraint on unwarranted use of deadly force.

In 1986, another Brennan opinion for the Court, *Pembaur v. City of Cincinnati,* made it clear that a single decision by a single official could establish municipal "policy" for purposes of *Monell.* It held that the city could be sued for violating a physician's Fourth Amendment rights when a deputy prosecutor told police to break down the door to the doctor's office (which they did) to serve court papers on employees who had refused to open the door or come out.

This line of Brennan opinions set the stage for the Court's holding in 1989, in *City of Canton v. Harris,* that a municipality is liable for any misconduct that can be attributed to inadequacies in its police training program, if they are glaring enough to indicate "deliberate indifference to the rights of persons with whom the police come into contact." Justice White wrote the opinion, in which Justice Brennan joined.

Lower courts have built on this foundation by holding that "deliberate indifference" can be established by such evidence as a city's failure to act in response to repeated complaints of police misconduct or to teach restraint in the use of force, car chases, strip searches, and other activities impinging on individual liberty.

Lasting Influence

"The results of *Monell,* evidence suggests, have included a boom in civil rights litigation against the police," according to *Above the Law: Police and the Excessive Use of Force,* a 1993 book by two leading experts, Jerome H. Skolnick and James J. Fyfe. "In 1971, for example, Los Angeles paid settlements and judgments of about $11,000 to people who had sued the police. In 1980, lawsuits against the LAPD cost about $890,000 in verdicts and settlements; by 1986, about $4 million; by 1989, $6.5 million; in 1990, $11.3 million."

And as Professor Walker has written, "There is in most cities today a local civil rights bar, which includes private attorneys whose practice includes police misconduct cases [and which] barely existed thirty years ago"; this means that "someone who has a claim of injustice has access to a potential advocate."

While plaintiffs prevail in only a minority of such lawsuits, the costs and risks of Section 1983 litigation have become an important part of the calculus of police executives and other local officials responsible for police training and other policies that implicate constitutional rights.

Has all this had the desired effects in the real world? Do victims of police misconduct have a reasonable shot at compensation, at long last? Has police brutality been deterred?

There is no simple answer. Police brutality and misconduct are obviously still very much with us, as we have been reminded by the Rodney King videotape, the Mark Fuhrman audiotapes, the shocking police scandals in cities like Philadelphia and New Orleans, and other recent events.

But it also seems likely that police in most parts of the country are less brutal, less quick to shoot their guns, less reckless in situations like car chases, and better trained than they were in the 1950s—and that some of this improvement is attributable to Justice Brennan's work, especially in the *Monell* line of cases.

Such propositions cannot be proven with empirical rigor; they implicate too many variables that are not susceptible to objective measurement. The best one can do is to consult the insights of seasoned observers like Skolnick and Fyfe.

In their 1993 book—perhaps the leading work on police brutality—they assert that *Monell* suits "serve as the most significant form of judicial oversight of the police" and have "reduced police violence significantly," largely because "many police departments and professional police organizations have responded to the liability problem by codifying and implementing carefully crafted policies and directives [and training programs that] decrease the chance of spontaneous brutality during such high-risk activities as car chases and use of force."

The authors add, "It is likely that *Monell,* a decision . . . in a civil matter that most directly affected a social worker's employer, has had, and will continue to have, as broad an effect on police operations as any criminal case decided by the liberal Warren Court. *Mapp* affected police searches, and *Miranda* affected police interrogations, but *Monell* offers a remedy for wrongful conduct in virtually every sphere of police activity, including brutality and use of force."

Justice Brennan's work in *Monell, Bivens,* and their progeny also continues to have incalculable symbolic importance, with a far-reaching impact on our entire way of thinking about relationships between citizen and government at all levels: These cases stand for the proposition that the police, and the government, are not above the law. Justice Brennan secured for the nation the legacy on which his father campaigned seventy years ago in Newark: "Nightsticks should last a long time. The police have been made the servants of the people and not their masters."

© Chip Bok, Akron Beacon Journal

Equality

Court Architect of Gender Equality: Setting a Firm Foundation for the Equal Stature of Men and Women

RUTH BADER GINSBURG AND
WENDY WEBSTER WILLIAMS

William Joseph Brennan joined the Supreme Court in October of 1956, the very pinnacle of the *Ozzie and Harriet* era. The Court he joined showed no eagerness to unsettle women's traditional place in the law, no greater inclination to intervene than was shown by the brethren of 1873, the Court that tersely turned away Myra Bradwell when she sought admission to her state's bar. Concurring Justice Bradley elaborated in *Bradwell v. Illinois* (1873): "The constitution of the family organization, which is founded in the divine ordinance, as well as in the nature of things, indicates the domestic sphere as that which properly belongs to the domain and functions of womanhood."

Nearly nine decades later, as evidenced by Gwendolyn Hoyt's case, the Court's perception of women had scarcely changed. Convicted of murdering her husband, Hoyt pursued constitutional challenges to the statutory and administrative mechanisms that produced the all-male jury empaneled to decide her case. The Court, in *Hoyt v. Florida* (1961), rejected her equal protection and due process pleas. Recalling that "woman is still regarded as the center of home and family life," the Court reasoned: "We cannot say that it is constitutionally impermissible for a

Ruth Bader Ginsburg is an associate justice of the Supreme Court of the United States. A founder of the Women's Rights Project of the American Civil Liberties Union in 1971, she litigated a series of cases throughout the 1970s solidifying a constitutional principle against gender-based discrimination. Wendy Webster Williams is a professor of law at Georgetown University Law Center. She has written numerous articles and litigated numerous cases on gender discrimination and equal rights and served for many years as the chair of the advisory board of the ACLU's Women's Rights Project.

State, acting in pursuit of the general welfare, to conclude that a woman should be relieved from the civic duty of jury service unless she herself determines that such service is consistent with her own special responsibilities."

The junior justice, signaling no discontent with the age-old tradition, signed on to the opinion that left undisturbed the twelve-man verdict against Gwendolyn Hoyt. No one would have predicted, after this inauspicious beginning, that Justice Brennan would emerge, a little over a decade later, as the great builder of a new tradition, a tradition of respect for women's claims to equality under the Constitution. Yet those who knew him and followed his budding career on the Court would not have been surprised. No one on the Court was more suited by judicial philosophy and personal generosity to respond to emerging claims of human dignity and equal stature than Bill Brennan. As Stephen Wermiel wrote, "Brennan always maintained that the role of law and the courts was to better the lot of mankind. The judge, he said, should always function with 'a sparkling vision of the supremacy of the human dignity of every individual.' "[1]

Justice Brennan's Constitution was one of enduring principles, capable of governing through changing times, interpreted to address new understandings. When women's voices joined with those of African Americans seeking justice and equality, Justice Brennan was poised to listen.

The revolution in the Court's treatment of women began quietly. On November 22, 1971, a unanimous Court, in a brief opinion written by Chief Justice Burger, struck down an Idaho law that preferred males over females for appointment as estate administrators. The case was *Reed v. Reed.* The Court did not say it was marking a new path. It was apparent, however, that the Court had scrutinized the sex-based Idaho law with unprecedented vigor. And the outcome spoke volumes. For the first time since ratification of the Fourteenth Amendment, the Court had used the equal protection clause to invalidate a law that treated women differently and less favorably than men.

A year and some months after *Reed,* Justice Brennan stepped forward as the Court's clearest, most constant speaker for women's equality. *Frontiero v. Richardson* (1973) was the occasion for his bold stroke.

---

1. Clare Cushman, *The Supreme Court Justices, Illustrated Biographies, 1789–1995,* at 450 (2d ed. 1995).

The plaintiff, Sharron Frontiero, an air force lieutenant, challenged federal laws that automatically accorded married male officers increased housing allowances and medical benefits for their wives, but denied those benefits to female officers absent proof that they provided over three-quarters of the family's income. Eight justices agreed that this military pay scheme denied Lieutenant Frontiero the laws' equal protection. But Justice Brennan's plurality opinion went further, bringing the Court within one vote of declaring sex classifications "inherently suspect, and . . . therefore . . . subject . . . to strict judicial scrutiny." To this day, his *Frontiero* opinion stands as the high-water mark for constitutional review of sex-based classifications.

WWW: *Of course, the position in the plurality opinion did not come out of the blue. A certain Professor Ruth Ginsburg, who had co-authored Sally Reed's brief to the Court, followed that contribution with a lengthy and learned "Brandeis brief" in support of Sharron Frontiero. Ceded argument time by Sharron Frontiero's attorneys, your debut on behalf of the American Civil Liberties Union as an oral advocate for sex equality coincided with Justice Brennan's as Court architect of gender equality principles.*

RBG: *Prompted by my students, and by a parade of brave women like Sally Reed and Sharron Frontiero, I had the great good fortune to be "in the right place at the right time." Bill Brennan's opinion in* Frontiero *seemed to me the highest compliment a lawyer can receive: He grasped and developed the arguments made in the brief, putting to good use the statistics and historical sources provided there.*

Justice Brennan understood what had escaped legions of jurists who viewed as protective and benign all manner of laws that "spared" women from jury service, public office, the vote, "unsuitable" work, educational opportunities, and even, if they were married, ownership of the fruits of their own labors: "There can be no doubt that our Nation has had a long and unfortunate history of sex discrimination," he wrote in *Frontiero*; "such discrimination was rationalized by an attitude of 'romantic paternalism' which, in practical effect, put women, not on a pedestal, but in a cage."

As recounted by Diana Gribbon Motz, Justice Marshall's papers document Justice Brennan's role in producing *Frontiero*'s plurality position. In conference, the justices had agreed that they would hold the statutes unconstitutional without reaching the question whether sex qualifies as a suspect classification. Justice Brennan, true to the agreement, drafted an opinion as low key as *Reed*. But he attached a note to the draft, gently probing whether he could say more: "I do feel . . . that this case would provide an appropriate vehicle for us to recognize sex as a suspect criterion . . . perhaps there is a court for such an approach." Justice Douglas responded favorably. So did Justice Marshall. Justice White followed Marshall, commenting: "Thurgood is right about this."

When Justice Powell declined to join the redrafted opinion on the ground that the Court should take no great stride while the Equal Rights Amendment (ERA) was before the states for ratification, Brennan urged his colleagues not to count on passage of the ERA. Failing to change Justice Powell's mind, the Court's "great conciliator" could have retreated to his original draft. Had he done so, his majority opinion would have been supported by eight justices. Instead, he chose to go forward with a plurality opinion, stating in pages of the *United States Reports* the position that sex classifications, like race classifications, should be subject to the strictest scrutiny.

If *Frontiero* raised expectations, hope dimmed as the Court upheld official sex lines in its next three encounters with laws treating men one way, women a different way.[2]

In each, Justice Brennan dissented, applying the strict-scrutiny standard he had formulated in *Frontiero*. Then came *Weinberger v. Wiesenfeld*, argued in the late fall of 1974 and decided in 1975.

WWW: *This was your third appearance before the Court. I came all the way from the West Coast for the argument. I remember being moved by your opening words: With stark lucidity you put the facts before the Court, explaining that the statute created a threefold discrimination— against the bereaved husband whose wife had died in childbirth, the infant who needed a parent's care, and the wage-earning woman, whose Social Security tax payments (unlike a man's) did not yield the benefits*

---

2. Those cases were, in order, *Kahn v. Shevin* (1974), *Geduldig v. Aiello* (1974), and *Schlesinger v. Ballard* (1975), all discussed below.

that would allow her spouse to tend to the child. Justice Brennan, characteristically, listened quietly and attentively to the advocates before him.

RBG: *My client, Stephen Wiesenfeld, was determined to rear his infant son personally after his wife's unanticipated death. He sought Social Security benefits as caretaker of a deceased wage earner's child, but he was told he could not even apply. The law provided child-in-care benefits for widowed mothers but not for widowed fathers. The stereotyping was plain: Men were preferred as wage earners, women as caregivers. And the system did not accommodate people who refused to fit into the mold.*

Justice Brennan wrote for seven justices. "It is no less important," he explained, "for a child to be cared for by its sole surviving parent when that parent is male rather than female." But this was his main theme: "The notion that men are more likely than women to be the primary supporters of their spouses and children is not entirely without empirical support. . . . But such a gender-based generalization cannot suffice to justify the denigration of the efforts of women who do work and whose earnings contribute significantly to their families' support."

Wiesenfeld was a turning point in Justice Brennan's pursuit of gender justice. Speaking for a clear majority, he did not label sex a "suspect criterion," he simply demonstrated why the classification in *Wiesenfeld* was indistinguishable from the one invalidated in *Frontiero.* A year later, Justice Brennan bound up *Reed's* pronouncement that sex classifications are "subject to scrutiny," with the teachings of *Frontiero, Wiesenfeld,* and *Stanton v. Stanton* (1975),[3] a post-*Wiesenfeld* decision written by Justice Blackmun. In *Craig v. Boren* (1976), Justice Brennan described an "intermediate" but distinctly elevated standard of review for sex discrimination cases. "To withstand constitutional challenge," Brennan wrote, "previous cases establish that classifications by gender must serve important governmental objectives and must be substantially related to achievement of those objectives."

---

3. In *Stanton,* the Court held that setting the age of adulthood at eighteen for women and twenty-one for men for child support purposes discriminated against young women. Justice Blackmun acknowledged changing times and values when he proclaimed: "No longer is the female destined solely for the home and the rearing of the family, and only the male for the marketplace and the world of ideas."

From *Craig* forward, Justice Brennan's elevated standard became the Court's standard. His well-presented opinions, for the Court and in dissent, comprehensively explained what the *Craig* standard should mean. As he declared in *Craig*, no longer would gender be permitted to serve "as an inaccurate proxy for other, more germane bases of classification." Legislatures, he said, must "either . . . realign their substantive laws in a gender-neutral fashion, or . . . adopt procedures for identifying those instances where the sex-centered generalization actually comport[s] with fact."

By the start of the 1980s, it had become the Court's repeated instruction that parties who seek to defend gender-based government action carry a heavy burden of persuasion, the burden of demonstrating an "exceedingly persuasive justification" for that action.[4]

Without equating gender classifications to racial classifications for all purposes, the Court effectively "presum[ed] that gender classifications are invalid."[5]

It insisted upon justifications that are genuine, not invented in response to litigation. Mindful of Justice Brennan's patient exposition in *Wiesenfeld*, the Court refused to rely on overbroad generalizations about the different talents, capacities, or preferences of males and females.

The point first developed in *Wiesenfeld*, that classifications apparently disfavoring men could mask a certain way of thinking about women—a way that devalued women's work and worth—soon received reinforcement. The issue resurfaced the term following *Craig* in *Califano v. Goldfarb* (1977). At issue in *Goldfarb* was a Social Security provision that qualified a widow for survivor benefits automatically, but a widower only upon proof that his wife supplied three-fourths of the couple's support (all of hers and half of his).

WWW: Goldfarb *was your case, too—your fifth appearance before the Court in a gender case.*

RBG: *I have described* Goldfarb *as* Frontiero *revisited or* Wiesenfeld *without the baby—once again the government had ordered social insurance so that a wage-earning woman's efforts yielded less for her family than the efforts of a wage-earning man.* Goldfarb, *in contrast to*

4. E.g., *Mississippi University for Women v. Hogan* (1982); *Kirchberg v. Feenstra* (1981).
5. *J.E.B. v. Alabama ex rel. T.B.* (1994) (Kennedy, J., concurring in the judgment).

Frontiero *and* Wiesenfeld, *was an uneasy case for the Court. The judgment striking the gender line gained the support of a bare (5–4) majority. The reason, largely this:* Goldfarb *carried a high price tag. If the complainant prevailed, many more people would qualify for spousal benefits. It was not at all certain that the justices would be willing to impose the added cost.*

Justice Brennan wrote for a plurality of four justices in *Goldfarb*; as in *Wiesenfeld,* he emphasized the law's discrimination against the wage-earning female: "Covered employees and their employers pay taxes into a fund . . . to purchase protection against the economic consequences of old age, disability, and death. But under [the statute] female insureds receive less protection for their spouses solely because of their sex. Mrs. Goldfarb worked and paid Social Security taxes for 25 years at the same rate as her male colleagues, but because of [the statute] the insurance protection received by the males was broader than hers." The next time round, when the issue repeated in the context of state workers' compensation survivor benefits, Justice Brennan's view met little resistance. The Court struck down the gender-based distinction and held in favor of the widower 8–1.[6]

Another strand in Justice Brennan's gender jurisprudence was one he pursued simultaneously in the context of race—the constitutionality of remedial or compensatory government action on behalf of groups traditionally burdened by discrimination. In contrast to the race classifications the Court encountered in the 1950s and 1960s, in which legislation ostensibly intended to benefit minorities was hardly the pervasive pattern, women had long been considered beneficiaries of "protect[ive]" legislation—provisions designed to shelter the "dependent" sex, "to compensate [woman] for some of the burdens which rest upon her."[7] What would become of that constitutional tradition in the wake of *Reed* and *Frontiero?*

Kahn v. Shevin (1974), the Court's third gender classification case of the 1970s, provided an early and unsatisfactory answer. *Kahn* upheld a

6. *Wengler v. Druggists Mutual Insurance Company* (1980). See also *Califano v. Westcott* (1979) (AFDC-UF program, providing benefits to families whose dependent children had been deprived of parental support because of the unemployment of their father, but not of their mother, violates equal protection).

7. *Muller v. Oregon* (1908).

nineteenth-century Florida real property tax exemption law that provided a small tax break for widows, the blind, and the totally disabled.
Mel Kahn, a widower, had sought and was refused an exemption because of his sex. The Court's majority, in an opinion written by Justice
Douglas, upheld the law; Douglas said that the exemption was "reasonably designed to further the state policy of cushioning the financial
impact of spousal loss upon the sex for which that loss imposes a dis-
proportionately heavy burden."

RBG: *Widower Kahn's case was not what one would call a "good vehicle" and it came to the Court too soon. To make a bad case worse, Kahn
was argued the very day the Court heard* DeFunis v. Odegaard *(1974),
a white applicant's challenge to the University of Washington Law School's
affirmative-action program.*

WWW: *Called upon to distinguish* DeFunis, *you argued that the
law school's program was "designed to open doors to equal opportunity,
to assure a law student body with diverse backgrounds and experience,
and to rectify the conspicuous absence of minority groups from the profession." In contrast, you said,* Kahn *involved a law of general application, where there could be no justification for labeling any group—racial,
ethnic, or sexual—as needy persons when an income test was readily
available.*

In startling contrast to his majority opinion in *Kahn*, Justice Douglas, dissenting from the Court's disposition of *DeFunis* as moot, addressed the merits, declaring: "There is no superior person by
constitutional standards. A DeFunis who is white is entitled to no advantage by reason of that fact; nor is he subject to any disability, no matter what his race or color." Justice Brennan, who was not attracted to
this profoundly divided vision of race and sex discrimination, wrote a
dissent in *Kahn* that forecast his approach to racial affirmative action.
Joined by Justice Marshall, he concluded that "alleviating the effects of
past economic discrimination against women" is a proper, indeed, a compelling, goal. But the state had not shown a close connection between
that goal and the means the statute employed. Florida held the exemption equally available to "a financially independent heiress" and "an
unemployed widow with dependent children." That, in Justice Brennan's judgment, would not do. By excluding "widows who earn annual

incomes, or possess assets, in excess of specified amounts," he said, Florida might have "narrow[ed] the class of beneficiaries to those . . . for whom . . . economic discrimination . . . ha[d] been a practical reality." Such an approach would be fatal to laws based on notions of women's inevitable dependency upon men, but it would leave room for genuinely compensatory classifications.

Following *Kahn, Schlesinger v. Ballard* (1975) again upheld legislation on the ground that it compensated women for disadvantages they faced. Lieutenant Ballard, a male officer, challenged a scheme that gave women naval officers thirteen years to achieve promotion. Men, however, were obliged to leave service when twice passed over for promotion. In practice, that meant male officers faced discharge in eight or nine years. The majority saw the promotion scheme as compensating women for the limited opportunities they had to gain advancement. Categorically excluded from sea duty, women faced large shoals when they endeavored to achieve leadership posts. Congress, the Court thought, could respond to women's diminished chances for promotion by allowing them to remain in service—albeit on land and not at sea— longer than men. Justice Brennan dissented. He did not comprehend how one discrimination could justify another. Why not even out the opportunities, he suggested, if Congress really wanted to secure for women fair and equitable treatment.

As we have seen, Justice Brennan paved the way for the Court's demand for an "exceedingly persuasive justification" for most gender classifications, and he approached compensatory rationalizations with care. Benign or compensatory reasons alleged in support of differential treatment, he cautioned, warrant close inspection for genuineness. In *Califano v. Webster,* a 1977 per curiam decision bearing signs of Brennan's mind, the Court offered a synthesis:

> "Classifications by gender must serve important governmental objectives and must be substantially related to achievement of those objectives." . . . Reduction of the disparity in economic condition between men and women caused by the long history of discrimination against women has been recognized as such an important governmental objective. . . . But "the mere recitation of a benign, compensatory purpose is not an automatic shield which protects against any inquiry into the actual purposes underlying a statutory scheme." . . . Accordingly, we have rejected attempts to justify gender classifications as compensation for past discrimination against women when the classifications in fact penalized women wage earn-

ers, . . . or when the statutory structure and its legislative history revealed that the classification was not enacted as compensation for past discrimination.

Guided by this restatement, the Court upheld a Social Security Act transitional provision that gave women a slightly more favorable formula for computing old-age benefits. Legislative history confirmed that Congress sought to alleviate the lingering effects of rank discrimination against women in the labor market. "Deliberately enacted to compensate for particular economic disabilities suffered by women," the statute survived the Court's review.

Justice Brennan again confronted an allegedly benign or compensatory classification in *Orr v. Orr* (1979), a case from Alabama about a once common law, a prescription that alimony is for men (and never women) to pay, women (and never men) to receive. The specific case hearings the state already provided for parties in divorce proceedings "can determine which women were in fact discriminated against vis-à-vis their husbands, as well as which family units defied the stereotype and left the husband dependent on the wife"; through hearings focused on the individuals affected, Justice Brennan observed, "Alabama's alleged compensatory purpose may be effectuated without placing burdens solely on husbands." Hence, the gender-based distinction was "gratuitous." Bringing to bear an insight deepened by race cases,[8] Justice Brennan warned that even genuinely compensatory and ameliorative gender-based legislation carried "the inherent risk of reinforcing stereotypes about the 'proper place' of women and their need for special protection." Such legislation must be trimly crafted, he observed, and, as in *Orr* itself, avoided altogether if a gender-neutral approach would serve as well.

Justice Brennan's most basic contributions to the Court's sex discrimination equal protection jurisprudence are the heightened review standard he developed and nurtured, and the caring attention he gave to the compensatory legislation question. He deserves large credit, too, for two notable dissents. Both cases involved pregnancy, a condition unique to women. The Court's majority saw the law's different treat-

---

8. See *United Jewish Organizations v. Carey* (1977) (Brennan, J., concurring in part). Notably, in *Regents of the University of California v. Bakke* (1978), Justice Brennan borrowed from his sex discrimination analyses; he maintained that the elevated, but not rigid, standard used in sex discrimination cases should also govern racial affirmative-action cases.

---

ment of men and women in that regard as unchallengeable, not based on sex at all. First to come before the Court, and first to prompt a Brennan dissent, was *Geduldig v. Aiello* (1974). Unlike the majority, Justice Brennan comprehended without doubt that the case fundamentally involved sex discrimination.

The plaintiffs in *Geduldig* challenged a provision of California's comprehensive disability insurance program. The provision excluded disabilities caused by or arising in connection with pregnancy. The majority said this: "The lack of identity between the excluded disability and gender as such under this insurance program becomes clear upon the most cursory analysis. The program divides potential recipients into two groups—pregnant women and nonpregnant persons." Accordingly, the Court applied traditional rational basis review—then an almost "anything goes" approach—and upheld the exclusion. Astute observer of the human condition, Justice Brennan discerned sex discrimination where the majority found none:

> The State has created a double standard for disability compensation: a limitation is imposed upon the disabilities for which women workers may recover, while men receive full compensation for all disabilities suffered, including those that affect only or primarily their sex, such as prostatectomies, circumcision, hemophilia, and gout. In effect, one set of rules is applied to females and another to males. Such dissimilar treatment of men and women, on the basis of physical characteristics inextricably linked to one sex, inevitably constitutes sex discrimination.

RBG: Geduldig *was your day (more precisely, half hour) before the Supreme Court.*

WWW: *Yes, as fate would have it. Your pregnancy case,* Struck v. Secretary of Defense *(1972), would, I think, have been the better vehicle for educating the Court and the public about the link between reproduction and discrimination against women.[9] In that case, Air Force Captain Struck, an exemplary officer, challenged a rule that required a woman officer's discharge "with the least practicable delay" once she was determined to be pregnant. In contrast to the* Geduldig *plaintiffs, who sought benefits during pregnancy-related disabilities, Captain Struck sought nothing save the preservation of her career in military service. The air force decided to*

9. See Ruth Bader Ginsburg, "Speaking in a Judicial Voice," 67 *N.Y.U. L. Rev.* 1185, 1200–02 (1992).

switch rather than fight in the High Court, and waived Captain Struck's discharge. That made her case moot. In Geduldig, *only Justice Brennan, speaking for himself, Justice Marshall, and Justice Douglas, saw the link that seemed so palpable to me. How could discrimination on the basis of a sex-linked characteristic not be considered as suspicious as other gender-based distinctions?*

When the question of pregnancy discrimination as sex discrimination came up under Title VII a few years later, in *General Electric Co. v. Gilbert* (1976), the Court replayed *Geduldig,* and Justice Brennan again dissented. This time, however, instead of defining equal protection under the Constitution, the Court was interpreting a federal law. Justice Brennan lost the fray in Court, but his understanding prevailed. Congress soon "overruled" *Gilbert.* The lawmakers amended Title VII to provide a definition: Discrimination on the basis of sex, Congress instructed, includes discrimination on the basis of pregnancy. Meanwhile, the California legislature also had changed its law, to include pregnancy-related disabilities within the compass of the state's insurance program.

Pregnancy figured in yet another case, yielding yet another Brennan dissent. In *Michael M. v. Superior Court* (1981), California's venerable statutory rape law, first enacted in 1850, received the Court's attention. Under that most traditional prescription, minor males but not females could be indicted for engaging in sexual intercourse. The statute was concededly sex-based, but the plurality and concurring justices accepted a newly pressed justification for the vintage law. California defended the statute as a pregnancy prevention measure, and the Court found the defense satisfactory. Impressed by the magnitude of California's teen pregnancy problem (and perhaps by seventeen-and-a-half-year-old Michael's sexual aggressiveness), the plurality and concurring opinions paid little attention to the legislature's design. Did the lawmakers have teen pregnancy in mind when they enacted and reenacted the statute? Did they at any time consider whether the statutory sex classification would in fact work to prevent pregnancy? The plurality regarded the measure as one that promoted equality: While young females were deterred from sexual intercourse by the risk of pregnancy, young males, lacking such "natural sanctions," required the equalizing inhibition of the criminal law.

Justice Brennan, in dissent, adhered to principle and precedent.

Under the *Craig* standard, it was the state's burden to show that the male-only statutory rape law could deter minor females from sexual intercourse more effectively than would a gender-neutral law. That burden the state manifestly failed to carry. Perhaps, Justice Brennan suggested, this failure related to the statute's real design—to protect the chastity of young girls rather than to reduce the incidence of teenage pregnancies. Some years later, his dissenting view again influenced the legislators. In 1993, the California legislature amended the *Michael M.* statute, converting it to a sex-neutral illegal intercourse law.

Over the years, Justice Brennan seemed barely aware of the frequent commentary on his opinions in the press and in academic journals. Nor was he anxious about academic or editorial writers' appraisals of him. What Justice Brennan *did* care about became apparent to one set of his law clerks on a midmorning in March 1977, when he dashed into their office, waving the *New York Times.*[10] What had caught his eye was not the front-page article on the just-announced decision in *Califano v. Goldfarb,* for which he had written the plurality opinion. Rather, he fastened on a small report following the tag end of the Goldfarb article, a piece inconspicuously placed on page nineteen. The article featured the victorious litigant before the Court. Written by Anna Quindlen, the item was headlined "Leon Goldfarb Doubly Happy with Decision."[11] "I'm glad I'm here, I'm glad I'm alive, I have two beautiful children, and now this—this will help me enjoy the years I have left," the seventy-two-year-old widower was quoted as saying. Goldfarb described his dismay when he applied for Social Security survivor benefits on his wage-earner wife's account after she died: "I knew it wasn't fair. We earned that money, we gave it in every month, there shouldn't have been strings tied to it." He praised his lawyers. "These ladies presented their cases beautifully," he said. "I hope I don't sound mushy," Goldfarb continued, "but I've been waiting to see what our good judges would decide for a long time. And they decided right. I really believe this country is looking the right way for all of us." "See," Justice Brennan exulted to his clerks, "this is what it's all about. This is what we're here for."

This is the way Bill Brennan saw his mission, the mission of the High Court—for him, the Court had done its job when every day citizens

10. We thank Gerard Lynch, professor of law at Columbia Law School and former Brennan clerk, for this anecdote.

11. Anna Quindlen, "Leon Goldfarb Doubly Happy with Decision," *New York Times,* March 3, 1977, at 19.

like Leon Goldfarb could see it as the place where justice is served. Under Justice Brennan's skilled and sympathetic guidance the Supreme Court was at last becoming a place where the women of the country—and men like Stephen Wiesenfeld and Leon Goldfarb who valued their life partners' work—could seek and expect gender justice.

WWW: *You ended a tribute to Justice Brennan last summer with a 1987 quote from Robert McKay on the occasion of Justice Brennan's Cardozo Lecture at the Association of the Bar of the City of New York. Reflecting on the magnitude of his contribution to constitutional jurisprudence on gender, I can't think of a more appropriate way to end.*

RBG: *This is what Robert McKay said: Bill Brennan "is a hero, he is our hero of the Constitution of the United States."*

Racial Realism in Retrospect

Derrick Bell

Reviewing Justice William J. Brennan's opinions in race cases, I felt like a military historian returning to the scenes of great battles and assessing the significance of those conflicts many years after the events. From time's advantaged perspective, victories and defeats tend to recede in importance. What remains, besides the debris-scarred landscape, is a question. How could those who fought so hard for civil rights have won so many campaigns and yet, somehow, allowed the hoped-for outcome of the war to slip away?

Even as we honor one who did much to aid our struggles, we can hardly deny that, despite all our efforts and the efforts of those who sided with us, we face as many—albeit different—barriers to racial equality today as we did when the decision in *Brown v. Board of Education* (1954) launched the equal opportunity phase of black people's three-centuries-long war for recognition first as human beings and then as equal citizens of this country.

Surely, some who fought the battles in the courts should have seen darkly then what is so apparent now: that the hated policies of segregation were only the exposed tentacles of the evil we fought, and that even when, at great cost, we managed to lop off many, perhaps most, of those tentacles, the true evil, the deeply felt need of so many whites to maintain priority status over blacks, would manifest itself in a myriad of new forms—many of them immune from the laws and policies so carefully wrought to end segregation.

In our defense, perhaps we can plead that our perceptions were weakened by idealism. We might strengthen this defense by asserting that, befuddled by our idealistic state, we were victimized by a kind of "precedential entrapment," a serious mental delusion unintentionally

The author, visiting professor of law at New York University, has written several books, including *Confronting Authority: Reflections of an Ardent Protester* and *Faces at the Bottom of the Well: The Permanence of Racism*.

brought on by that small band of judges who read our briefs, understood our arguments, and pushed the boundaries of existing law to find in our favor. On the Supreme Court, there was Chief Justice Warren, Justices Douglas and Marshall, and, later, Justice Blackmun.

For thirty-four years, there was also Justice Brennan. These liberal judges stood against the tide of both hostile public opinion and the ambivalence and outright opposition of so many of their judicial brethren. Were they any more aware than we of the true nature of our enemy—the depths of its resources, its resiliency under our persistent attacks, and its ability when seemingly vanquished to recast itself in guises that appeared benign but were no less insidious? The late Yale professor Alexander Bickel warned that the critics of *Brown* read that decision more carefully than those who hailed it. In the decisions affirming our rights, was there a subtext of caution that we were too busy celebrating to notice?

While Justice Brennan sat on the Court, the nation underwent a major transformation in its relationship with its African-American minority. Much of the change was resisted bitterly, and the courts were called on to resolve many of the challenged laws and policies that could be formulated in legal terms. Civil rights proponents, lacking economic power or political clout, turned to the courts with more faith in their cause than optimism based on past experience.

During most of our history, American courts were not very supportive of efforts by racial justice advocates to use law and litigation to protect the basic rights of people of color. Time after time, petitions for judicial relief were met with responses ranging from uncaring rejection to callous prejudice. In the three decades or so following World War II, however, the courts played a more positive role in moving the society beyond the Jim Crow era and toward a future we hoped would be characterized by equal opportunity. Justice Brennan, as much as any other judicial figure, played a prominent role in this racial transition.

Gifted with what we might call "racial realism," Justice Brennan was usually a welcome vote for the civil rights position—whether that placed him with the majority or in dissent. His work on the Court reflected a simple truth that most in the society refuse to acknowledge—even understand. Racial discrimination causes harm to blacks and creates benefits for whites. As a consequence, real racial remedies require whites to relinquish their race-based advantages and their presumptions of priority to economic and political resources. In the remedial process, Justice

Brennan was not burdened by the stifling baggage of politics and prejudice that led so many jurists to deny civil rights claims for reasons of procedure or prudence. He was not deterred by the barriers imposed by "neutral rules," particularly when their neutral character served as a screen for discriminatory intent. Most important, Brennan seemed to possess a keen sense honed by long experience that the remedies blacks sought against racial injustices offered reforms needed by most whites.

Relatively early in his tenure, Justice Brennan, writing for the Court in *NAACP v. Button* (1963), acknowledged Virginia's authority to enact laws barring practicing lawyers from engaging in solicitation and other unethical practices. But he found that Virginia's effort to use this authority to hamstring civil rights lawyers' efforts to gain clients willing to challenge the state's segregation laws was a violation of the plaintiffs' rights to political expression and association. Nor was he unaware that the state's laws were enacted as part of a package of measures intended to bar desegregation of the state's public schools. Justice Brennan wrote:

> We cannot close our eyes to the fact that the militant Negro civil rights movement has engendered the intense resentment and opposition of the politically dominant white community of Virginia; litigation assisted by the NAACP has been bitterly fought. In such circumstances, a statute broadly curtailing group activity leading to litigation may easily become a weapon of oppression, however evenhanded its terms appear. Its mere existence could well freeze out of existence all such activity on behalf of the civil rights of Negro citizens.

Not only was Justice Brennan unwilling to examine the Virginia statutes in a political vacuum, he also noted that the result was not based on the fact that petitioners were proponents of civil rights. The entitlement to association and advocacy was no less available to other groups, including those with views quite the opposite of the petitioners. Based on this precedent, unions and other groups, freed by the decision from encumbrances imposed by local bar rules, were able to establish lawyering groups for the benefit of their members.

In a similarly pathbreaking decision, Justice Brennan's decision in *New York Times v. Sullivan* (1964), while of crucial importance to the civil rights movement, also broadened the free speech rights of those wishing to criticize persons in official positions. The suit, initiated by two Alabama officials, charged that erroneous facts in a pro–civil rights advertisement published in the *New York Times* constituted actionable libel entitling them to substantial money damages. If granted, the judgment would bankrupt the civil rights groups who placed the ad, and would make the media vulnerable to litigation, a status likely to make the media reluctant to cover civil rights news. Noting the national commitment to "uninhibited, robust, and wide-open" debate on public issues, debate that may well include vehement, caustic, and sometimes unpleasantly sharp attacks on government officials, Justice Brennan characterized the *New York Times* advertisement "as an expression of grievances and protest on one of the major public issues of our time," and within the gambit of constitutional protection. This protection, he held, was not lost in the absence of proof that the erroneous statements were made with actual malice—that is, with knowledge that they were false or with reckless disregard of whether they were false or not. Developed further in later decisions, the *New York Times* precedent opened the way for constitutionally protected criticism of both public officials and private persons in the public eye.

Actions against civil rights lawyers for soliciting clients and potentially crushing libel suits were only two of the tactics civil rights opponents adopted to frustrate compliance with *Brown v. Board of Education*'s mandate for the elimination of segregated schools. Justice Brennan joined the Court in rejecting blatant refusals to comply, and later made it clear that "Road to Damascus" conversions to racial neutrality by school officials who had been operating racially segregated schools were insufficient without more. Many southern school boards began adopting "freedom-of-choice" plans that gave each student a choice of whether to attend a previously all-black or all-white school. School officials viewed the plans as formal compliance with *Brown*. They also expected that social pressures and economic coercion would limit the number of black parents who would choose to send their children to white schools. Justice Brennan, in *Green v. County School Board* (1968), speaking for a unanimous Court that by then had tired of school board evasions, held that freedom-of-choice plans would be acceptable only if they worked to disestablish the dual school system, a function the plan was not fulfilling in the county's schools.

When school desegregation litigation moved to northern districts, the Court at first refused to review decisions refusing relief where there was no history of state-ordered segregation. Finally, in *Keyes v. School District No. 1, Denver, Colorado* (1973), Justice Brennan, writing for the Court, held that "where plaintiffs prove that the school authorities have carried out a systematic program of segregation affecting a substantial portion of the students, . . . it is only common sense to conclude that there exists a predicate for a finding of the existence of a dual school system." The beginning of the end of school desegregation came with the 5–4 decision in *Milliken v. Bradley* (1974), the civil rights effort to require integration of the predominantly black Detroit school system with its more than fifty suburban counterparts. Justice Brennan joined Justice White, whose dissent bemoaned the effect of the Court's decision: "The education of children of different races in a desegregated environment has unhappily been lost, along with the social, economic, and political advantages which accompany a desegregated school system as compared with an unconstitutionally segregated system."

Justice Brennan was also a rigorous defender of blacks' right to vote. He construed civil rights statutes expansively in order to maximize their value in the fight to undo generations of discriminatory patterns. Thus, in *Katzenbach v. Morgan* (1966), he found Congress had the authority in enacting the Voting Rights Act to prohibit the use of English literacy tests as prerequisites for registering to vote, even though the Supreme Court had not found such barriers in violation of the equal protection clause. Later, he dissented in *City of Mobile v. Bolden* (1980), where the majority held that plaintiffs challenging a voting plan under civil rights laws must show that the plan was enacted with a discriminatory purpose. Acting upon Justice Brennan's dissent, in which he stated that proof of discriminatory impact alone is sufficient, Congress passed the Voting Rights Act Amendments of 1982, which provided that proof of discriminatory intent was not required when voting plans are challenged. Later, he wrote for the majority in *Thornburg v. Gingles* (1986), providing an expansive reading of the 1982 amendments.

Had he remained on the Court, Justice Brennan would have almost certainly dissented in the 1992 decision in *Pressley v. Etowah County Commission,* where a majority found no Voting Rights Act violation when an Alabama county commission redistributed its powers so as to deny a first-ever black commissioner control over spending traditionally held by commission members. He would probably have also dissented in *Shaw v. Reno,* the 1993 decision where the bare majority found an oddly shaped North Carolina congressional district, created to provide black voters with a second majority-black district, would have to meet strict scrutiny standards to avoid a violation of the equal protection rights of white voters.

Throughout his tenure, Justice Brennan recognized the value of affirmative steps by employers to reverse settled patterns of job discrimination. In *United Steelworkers of America v. Weber,* an early affirmative-action case that came to the Court in 1979, Justice Brennan's opinion for the majority rejected the reverse discrimination claim of a white worker who was not admitted to an apprenticeship training program established by the company in which half the positions were assigned to whites based on seniority and half were assigned to blacks based on their seniority. Weber lacked the seniority needed to win a place in the white program. Despite the fact that some blacks in the black program had less seniority, but for the blacks' efforts, there would have been no program at all. Weber took his case all the way to the Supreme Court to have the whole program struck down as a violation of Title VII, the federal statute that prohibits employment discrimination.

Justice Brennan, noting that Congress had enacted fair employment legislation out of its concern about the serious disparity in unemployment rates between white and black workers, interpreted the law as permitting private employers to voluntarily adopt affirmative-action plans as a means of qualifying black workers for positions from which they had long been excluded. He also wrote opinions broadening the scope of Title VII. In *Sheet Metal Workers v. EEOC* (1986) and *Firefighters v. Cleveland* (1986), he ruled that the law authorized a court to issue relief benefiting those who were not identified victims of unlawful discrimination. In effect, this was a form of affirmative action.

Several years later, the affirmative-action debate continued to spark contentious debate and numerous legal challenges. Justice Brennan cut through all the pained lamentations of "reverse discrimination" by reminding the nation in the *Bakke* case that "race . . . too often [has] been inexcusably utilized to stereotype and stigmatize politically powerless segments of society." Reviewing the positive values of these programs, he distinguished any harm that might befall whites from the discrimination long suffered by blacks by explaining:

Unlike discrimination against racial minorities, the use of racial preferences for remedial purposes does not inflict a pervasive injury upon individual whites in the sense that wherever they go or whatever they do there is a significant likelihood that they will be treated as second-class citizens because of their color. This distinction does not mean that the exclusion of a white resulting from the preferential use of race is not sufficiently serious to require justification; but it does mean that the injury inflicted by such a policy is not distinguishable from disadvantages caused by a wide range of government actions, none of which has ever been thought impermissible for that reason alone.

Here was the ultimate key to effective remediation of generations of blatant discrimination, a history that the Court and the country wish to ignore in a tardy and suspect commitment to constitutional color blindness, a visual defect raised to virtuous status. Brennan's position failed to convince a majority of the *Bakke* Court that struck down the minority quota for minority students, but the case did approve the use of race as one of several factors that could be considered in the admissions process.

Justice Brennan had an opportunity to reiterate his racial remediation theme while responding to challenges to the FCC's policies designed to increase minority ownership of broadcasting facilities.

> In the context of broadcasting licenses, the burden on nonminorities is slight. . . . Applicants have no settled expectations that their applications will be granted without consideration of public interest factors such as minority ownership. Award of a preference in a comparative hearing or transfer of a station in a distress sale thus contravenes "no legitimate firmly rooted expectation[s]" of competing applications.

What Justice Brennan said implicitly is that the broadcasters had no more reason to complain about the policies utilized to help long-excluded minorities break into the system than they did about any of the myriad other rules that might frustrate their bids. Race, having long been a basis for exclusion, could serve as a basis of entrance. In his last years on the Court, Justice Brennan dissented vigorously or joined the dissents of others as a slim majority of the Court began narrowing the scope of Title VII, and requiring even moderate affirmative-action policies to meet the same strict standards as the most invidious discriminatory practices. He agreed with Justice Marshall, who dissented in *City of Richmond v. Croson* (1989), that "a profound difference separates governmental actions that themselves are racist, and governmental actions that seek to remedy the effects of prior racism or to prevent neutral governmental activity from perpetuating the effects of such racism."

Sadly, the current Court has undermined, even dismantled, the precedential protections Justice Brennan's opinions erected to protect black rights. It is thus appropriate to inquire: Is there any meaning or message in his long and earnest efforts? The answer for him, no less than those whose cause he sought to advance, is a resounding yes. There is meaning in struggle for righteous causes even when—especially when—those causes are frustrated and overwhelmed.

Justice Brennan's written opinions, whether in the majority or in dissent, contain a message that the nation ignores at its peril. It is this: The constitutional rights that black people seek are also the rights a great many white people need. His labors sought to illuminate this obvious truth in the face of its rejection by so many whites who fear that racial equality would diminish rather than enrich their lives.

For these whites, Justice Brennan was quite like the wise elder in an ancient time whose sagacity and commitment to truth and justice earned him more envy than respect, more enmity than fame. Rather than cater to their fears or comfort them in their prejudices, the elder counseled reform and required the abandonment of long-practiced customs. His statements challenged accepted conventions and made the comfortable uneasy.

Unable to question his integrity, two young usurpers sought to humiliate him before a large gathering of his followers. "Wise man," they called out. "Use your wisdom to tell us whether the bird we hold in our hands is alive or dead."

There was a prolonged silence. One youth, almost tasting their victory, interpreted the silence as confusion. If the wise man claimed the bird was alive, they planned to crush it to death, and if he said it was dead, they were going to open their hands and let the bird fly free—and very much alive.

What the usurpers saw as an unsolvable riddle, an ultimate dilemma, was readily apparent to the wise man, who cared more for truth than for show. Even though hidden, the correct answer was obvious to one not blinded by personal interests, settled conventions, and comforting beliefs. The wise elder confounded his challengers without glorifying himself or humiliating them.

"Well, old man," they taunted him. "Tell us if you can. Is the bird alive or dead?"

"The answer," the wise man replied, "the answer is in your hands."

The Majoritarian Difficulty: One Person, One Vote

Lani Guinier and Pamela S. Karlan

Ask the average person on the street what democracy means and she is likely to reply "majority rule." Ask her what political equality means and she is likely to reply "one person, one vote." But neither majority rule nor one person, one vote has quite the historical pedigree that most people assume. Indeed, until the 1960s, small elites had managed to entrench themselves in state legislatures and congressional delegations where they frustrated the will of a majority for decades. The new requirement of one person, one vote broke the logjam by requiring America's legislatures to undergo decennial reapportionment, with at least some reallocation of political power toward growing constituencies.

Justice Brennan was a key player in producing that shift—the Supreme Court's most successful modern-day effort at fundamental legal and political change. Many of the Court's other transformative ventures—*Roe v. Wade* (1973), *Furman v. Georgia* (1972), *Miranda v. Arizona* (1966), and *Brown v. Board of Education* (1954)—triggered widespread resistance or revisionism. By contrast, the "reapportionment revolution" launched by the Justice's opinion in *Baker v. Carr* (which Chief Justice Warren called "the most important case of my tenure on the Court") has been a smashing popular and judicial success.

In this essay, we explore both the landscape from which Justice Brennan embarked on his trek into the "political thicket" of apportionment and the harvest his odyssey has borne. *Baker's* holding that

Lani Guinier, a professor of law at the University of Pennsylvania, was special assistant to Assistant Attorney General Drew Days at the Civil Rights Division from 1977 to 1980 and directed the Voting Rights Project at the NAACP Legal Defense and Educational Fund in the 1980s. Pamela S. Karlan is a professor of law and the Roy L. and Rosamond Woodruff Morgan Research Professor at the University of Virginia School of Law. She served as assistant counsel at the NAACP Legal Defense and Educational Fund where she specialized in voting rights and employment discrimination litigation.

courts may require legislatures to reapportion is rooted both in a desire to secure majority control of the political system and in Justice Brennan's profound concerns about the ability of all individuals to participate fully and effectively in self-governance. One person, one vote, however, is not an end in itself or an equation of democracy and simple majority rule, as many members of the current, post-Brennan Court believe. Equating democracy with simple, winner-take-all majority rule denies the minority a voice and fuels the activist impulses of a conservative judiciary that uses its power to narrow, rather than to expand, the meaning of political equality.

ORIGINS OF ONE PERSON, ONE VOTE

Baker v. Carr challenged Tennessee's state legislative apportionment. Crafted in 1901—and resistant to revision ever since—the plan had created legislative districts that by midcentury had wildly different populations. One house member was elected by Moore County's 2,340 citizens; another was chosen by Sullivan County's 55,712. The multimember legislative delegation from Shelby County had one member for every 39,043 voters; the multimember delegation from Gibson County had one for every 14,916. The interaction of Tennessee's initial bias against urban areas with population growth and movement over the intervening sixty years resulted in what Justice Tom Clark colorfully described as "a topsy-turvical of gigantic proportions. . . . a crazy quilt."

Previous attempts to challenge such glaring population disparities among legislative districts had failed, largely because the Court had viewed them as raising "political questions" that are "nonjusticiable"—not amenable to judicial resolution. Justice Brennan accepted the vitality of precedent constraining any judicial role in enforcing the "guaranty clause"—the Constitution's guarantee "to every State in this Union [of] a Republican Form of Government." He resorted instead to a different constitutional tool—the equal protection clause of the Fourteenth Amendment. That amendment, he explained, protects the "right to a vote free of arbitrary impairment by state action." And "well developed and familiar" principles, already applied by judges in a variety of circumstances, would now govern the courts' review of districting stalemate.

Justice Brennan found his most powerful precedent in favor of judicial review in a case decided only the term before, *Gomillion v. Light-*

foot. There, the Court had unanimously struck down Alabama's re-drawing of Tuskegee's municipal boundaries as a violation of the Fifteenth Amendment, which secured the right to vote regardless of race. Justice Brennan used *Gomillion* to overcome the judicial blockage that had until then embargoed any excursions into so-called political territory. In Tuskegee, blacks were a population majority, but politically powerless. Whites outnumbered blacks in voter registration three to two. Using simple majority rule to hoard *all* political power, the white electorate refused to share *any* power with the black citizens of Tuskegee. Whites in Tuskegee worried that blacks might eventually realize registration parity. If blacks followed the example set by whites, the black electorate might eventually increase to the point where it would play a meaningful, even decisive, role. When the black community began to sponsor candidates for city office (who lost by about the margin by which white voters outnumbered black ones), the malapportioned Alabama legislature, controlled by a white rural population minority, redrew the city boundaries to exclude all but four or five black voters while keeping all white voters within the new municipality.

To the Warren Court, these statistics showed that the gerrymander was a transparent subterfuge. The basis for the Court's willingness to intervene was its recognition that "the inescapable human effect of [Alabama's] essay in geometry and geography" was to deny the constitutional rights of particular individuals, in that case the still largely disenfranchised black majority in Tuskegee. Though the constitutional deprivation came in the *form* of a statute that drew political boundaries, its *effect* was every bit as bad as a law flatly singling out blacks for diminished voting rights. The conclusion was irresistible, "tantamount to a mathematical demonstration," that the purpose of the gerrymander was to keep political power firmly and exclusively in white hands. Thus was born the Court's impulse toward precise mathematical standards, as a manageable guide through the political thicket. And thus was born its faith that protection of individual rights would protect the fairness of the political system more broadly.

Gomillion, however, had not forced the Court to think very deeply about questions of governance. The motivation behind the Tuskegee gerrymander had been to enable the city's numerical white minority to perpetuate its monopoly control over the government by fencing out the black majority (who, incidentally, remained subject to municipal regulations and police powers). Thus, white minority control was assured in the city proper, where it had been most threatened. But despite their numerical population potential, the goal of the black citizens of Tuskegee was not to substitute black control for white control. As Charles Gomillion, the lead plaintiff, explained, "We didn't wish to control, merely to share" political power. *Gomillion* was thus one of those rare instances in which individual rights, the interests of a traditionally excluded group, and the principle of majority rule were perfectly aligned. The pathology that confronted the Court in *Gomillion* could be cured simply by enabling each citizen to participate fully in the electoral process. As the succeeding decades would show, however, many political maladies were resistant to such straightforward remedies.

The substitution of the equal protection clause for the guaranty clause had several long-term consequences for judicial oversight of the political process, not all of them readily apparent at the time. First, it situated apportionment claims within an individual rights framework: Within two years, the Court had identified the core equal protection concept governing reapportionment as "one *person,* one vote." The guaranty clause, by contrast, might have focused attention on electoral and governmental structures. Interestingly, in *Wesberry v. Sanders,* decided in 1964, the Court located the one person, one vote requirement for congressional districts (as opposed to state and local electoral districts) in Article I, Section 2's requirement that members of the House be chosen "by the People of the several States." This textual anchor, with its collective noun, might have suggested a richer view of the electoral process, one that focused on democratic and pluralistic structures for sharing or dispersing power. In fact, congressional cases engendered an even more rigidly individualistic or atomized vision, as we shall see in a moment.

Second, the new doctrine was procedural; it focused on voting, rather than on the fairness of political outcomes. The anonymity of the voting booth perhaps encouraged the Court to treat claimants as atomized abstractions, rather than as members of communities with distinctive, affiliative interests. By focusing on the mathematical weight of individual voters' ballots, the Court avoided the murkier political thicket in which questions regarding the allocation of political power lurked. Nonetheless, the *goal* of one person, one vote was quite ambitious. As Chief Justice Warren explained in his memoirs, "Henceforth elections would reflect the collective public interest—embodied in the 'one-man, one-vote' standard—rather than the machinations of special interests."

Third, the Fourteenth Amendment's role in redefining the relationship among individual citizens, the states, and the national government created a more hospitable climate for national regulation of local political processes more generally. The Court's resurrection of the Reconstruction Amendments' protection of the political process raised the question of how those amendments would be used to regain the voting rights of their original intended beneficiaries—blacks in the South. Once the Court recognized that disenfranchisement and dilution were two sides of the same debased coin, the nation was at least poised to begin to address the exclusion of black citizens from full participation.

Fourth, reliance on the equal protection clause brought the notion of *equality* to the forefront of the judicial conversation about politics. One person, one vote was a means of assuring not just the collective public interest, but individual dignity and equality as well. As Justice Douglas declared in *Gray v. Sanders* (1963), "The conception of political equality from the Declaration of Independence, to Lincoln's Gettysburg Address, to the Fifteenth, Seventeenth, and Nineteenth Amendments can mean only one thing—one person, one vote." But although equality was now a central political imperative, the Court's one person, one vote cases left open, or offered only a partial definition of, the meaning of full political equality.

One person, one vote captured overwhelming, and immediate, public and political acceptance. As Justice Brennan noted in his dissent in *White v. Regester* (1974), perhaps contrasting the Court's experience here with its forays into school desegregation and criminal procedure, there "has been a truly extraordinary record of compliance with the constitutional mandate." In the early 1960s, forty-eight of the fifty states had state legislative bodies with total population variances (meaning the difference between the size of the largest and smallest districts) of greater than 15 percent; after the 1970 census and reapportionment, only fourteen states had such large variances.

REFINEMENTS OF ONE PERSON, ONE VOTE

Although many justices were involved in the original articulation of one person, one vote, Justice Brennan became its most enduring partisan. Perhaps Justice Brennan's warmest embrace of a purely majoritarian vision of one person, one vote came in *Gordon v. Lance* (1971). The West Virginia constitution required that local governing bodies hold referenda and obtain the approval of at least 60 percent of the voters before issuing bonds. A majority of the voters in Roane County had voted in favor of permitting the school board to issue bonds to alleviate overcrowding, remove fire hazards, build vocational education facilities, and meet the special needs of disadvantaged children. But the vote in favor—like all votes in the preceding quarter century—fell short of the 60 percent mark.

A group of voters claimed that the 60 percent rule violated one person, one vote, because it debased or diluted the value of an affirmative vote when considered in relation to the value of a negative vote: If, for example, forty-five voters voted against the bond issue, their votes would carry more weight than the votes of the fifty-five voters who had voted in favor. Chief Justice Burger's opinion for the Court rejected their claim. Unlike apportionment schemes that disadvantaged suburban voters or gerrymanders that fenced out black citizens, the West Virginia requirement did not single out voters on the basis of an irrelevant characteristic such as residence or race: "We can discern no independently identifiable group or category that favors bonded indebtedness over other forms of financing. Consequently no sector of the population may be said to be 'fenced out' from the franchise because of the way they will vote." The Court acknowledged that "any departure from strict majority rule gives disproportionate power to the minority. But there is nothing in the language of the Constitution, our history, or our cases that requires that a majority always prevail on every issue."

Justice Brennan, joined by Justice Marshall, indicated simply that he would have struck down the West Virginia provision "for the reasons expressed in the opinion of the West Virginia Supreme Court of Appeals." Those reasons centered around a populist, majoritarian view of democratic self-governance. The West Virginia court had explained that bond elections were one of "the very few instances in which the individual voter is permitted to have a direct and wholly effective voice in government." One person, one vote was not merely a principle of legislative redistricting; rather, it was the very bedrock of *all* political equality: The principle of one person, one vote "could not in reason and logic be restricted to the mere right to vote for representatives in government":

> The right of the voter to equal protection, the right to protection against the dilution or debasement of the weight or force of an individual's vote, is fully as sound, sacred and important when he is voting on issues in-

volving taxation, public revenue and the promotion of an adequate public school system, as when he is voting for the nomination or election of a constable, a state senator, a governor or any other public official to represent the voter in government.

For the West Virginia court, the evil in the 60 percent rule was that it undervalued the weight of votes in favor of bond issues, thus thwarting majority preferences. The individual bond proponents were denied their "democratic" right, as a numerical majority, to decide the outcome for everyone. Thus, the position that Brennan implicitly embraced in *Gordon* saw one person, one vote as a key element of direct democratic majoritarianism—a communitarian, rather than a classic liberal individualistic, approach. As we shall see, however, the latter perspective soon came to dominate the field.

With Brennan dissenting in *Gordon,* the Court retreated from an essentially majoritarian rationale for one person, one vote. Instead, a new Court majority focused again on the individualism of the right to vote. Justice Brennan, indefatigable in his support of popular democracy, also found the individualistic rationale persuasive. Indeed, Justice Brennan will best be remembered, in the annals of one person, one vote, for his successful championship of a particularly stringent adherence to absolute population equality among districts. He was successful in achieving his goal for congressional apportionments: His opinions for the Court in *Kirkpatrick v. Preisler,* decided in 1969, and *Karcher v. Daggett,* decided in 1983, adopted a rule that any avoidable deviation from "precise mathematical equality," no matter how small, required the state to show that the population disparity was necessary to the achievement of some permissible state goal. But he was less successful regarding state and local apportionment. There, over his strenuous objection, the Court gave the states substantial leeway: As long as the total percentage deviation was less than 10 percent, no justification was required.

The Justice's most extensive discussion of his reasons for insisting on absolute population equality came in his separate opinion in *White v. Regester* (1973):

> It is important to understand that the demand for precise mathematical equality rests neither on a scholastic obsession with abstract numbers nor a rigid insensitivity to the political realities of the reapportionment process. Our paramount concern has remained an individual and personal right— the right to an equal vote. "While the result of a court decision in a state

legislative apportionment controversy may be to require the restructuring of the geographical distribution of seats in a state legislature, the judicial focus must be concentrated upon ascertaining whether there has been any discrimination against certain of the State's citizens which constitutes an impermissible impairment of their constitutionally protected right to vote." We have demanded equality in district population precisely to insure that the weight of a person's vote will not depend on the district in which he lives. The conclusion that a State may, without any articulated justification, deliberately weight some persons' votes more heavily than others, seems to me fundamentally at odds with the purpose and rationale of our reapportionment decisions.

But it is important not to oversimplify the Justice's commitment to voting as an individual right. Significantly, the Justice's opinion in *White v. Regester* treated one person, one vote as part of a larger arsenal for securing political equality. He concurred with the Court's alternative reason for striking down Texas's legislative apportionment: that it diluted the group voting strength of blacks in Dallas and Hispanics in San Antonio. Although the Justice spoke in the language of individual and personal rights, his ultimate goal was a political system in which voters enjoyed equal opportunities to share political power by participating fully in the political process broadly understood.

This larger goal can be seen in an evolution in Justice Brennan's thinking from *Kirkpatrick* to *Karcher*. *Kirkpatrick* struck down a Missouri plan in which the total percentage deviation between the largest and smallest districts was slightly less than 6 percent. Such a deviation, the Court held, rendered the plan presumptively unconstitutional, unless the state could justify the variance. On this question, Justice Brennan took an exceptionally hard line:

> Missouri contends that variances were necessary to avoid fragmenting areas with distinctive economic and social interests and thereby diluting the effective representation of those interests in Congress. But to accept population variances, large or small, in order to create districts with specific interest orientations is antithetical to the basic premise of the constitutional command to provide equal representation for equal numbers of people.

Karcher v. Daggett, which invalidated New Jersey's post-1980 congressional plan, was the high-water mark, both doctrinally and practically, of the absolute approach to one person, one vote. The total population deviation between the state's largest and smallest congressional districts was tiny: only 0.6984 percent. Whatever the problems with New Jersey's plan, they bore little overt resemblance to the malapportionments of pre-*Baker* days. But there was a similar entrenchment problem beneath the New Jersey plan. Advances in districting technology had enabled New Jersey's Democrats, who controlled the reapportionment process, to concoct a fierce partisan gerrymander while coming quite close to absolute population equality. The plan was signed into law by the Democratic governor the day before his Republican successor's inauguration. Not only did Justice Brennan's account of the facts refer repeatedly to the various political machinations and rationalizations that had produced the deviations at issue in *Karcher;* it also recognized that one person, one vote had become a weapon in the partisan battle: The *Karcher* lawsuit had been brought by "a group of individuals with varying interests, including all incumbent Republican Members of Congress from New Jersey." Whatever the doctrinal pigeonhole into which the litigants forced their lawsuit, the real issue was the allocation of political power among groups. Given both Justice Brennan's lifelong familiarity with New Jersey politics and his general aversion to political entrenchment, it is easy to imagine his finding renewed enthusiasm for absolute adherence to one person, one vote in its potential for attacking this more group-driven problem of power allocation as well as its original target of individual vote degradation. By clamping down hard on any deviation, perhaps at least some group dilution could be prevented.

Thus, although New Jersey's population deviations were minuscule, they were not legally negligible. Because they could have been reduced even further, the Court held that New Jersey's plan was presumptively unconstitutional. In Justice Brennan's piquant phrase, "As between two standards—equality or something less than equality—only the former reflects the aspirations of" the Constitution.

Interestingly, when it came to the question of justifying population deviations, Justice Brennan's opinion took a decidedly less severe tack:

Any number of consistently applied legislative policies might justify some variance, including, for instance, making districts compact, respecting municipal boundaries, preserving the cores of prior districts, and avoiding contests between incumbent Representatives.

And, consistent with his views in the Court's racial vote dilution cases, he suggested that "preserving the voting strength of racial minority groups" could also provide a justification for some deviations. But he agreed with the district court that none of these potentially legitimate interests justified New Jersey's deviations.

In *Brown v. Thomson* (1983), a case decided the same day as *Karcher,* in which the Court upheld a Wyoming state apportionment that, because it accorded a seat to tiny Niobrara County, had a total population deviation of 89 percent, Justice Brennan dissented. Once again, he relied on one person, one vote to attack group-based political allocations in which power was not fairly dispersed. He worried most about the voting power of individual voters whose votes were devalued by deviations from absolute population equality, but he was equally concerned that exaggerating the power of small groups violates the "principle of equal representation":

> Severe dilution of the votes of a relatively small number of voters is perhaps the most disturbing result that may attend invalid apportionments, because those unfortunate victims may be virtually disfranchised. It is not the sole evil to be combated, however. It is equally illegal to enact a scheme under which a *small group is greatly overrepresented,* at the expense of all other voters in the State. . . . It is the principle of equal representation, as well as the votes of individual plaintiffs, that a State may not dilute.

Karcher and *Brown v. Thomson* firmly established the dual principles that all avoidable deviations from absolute population equality in congressional districting and all deviations of over 10 percent in state and local apportionments require the defendants to show that the deviations are necessary to achieve a permissible governmental purpose. But the same technology on which Justice Brennan remarked in *Karcher* has essentially overtaken one person, one vote. The principle still serves its function of requiring decennial reapportionment since population growth and shifts will almost always render the last decade's plan presumptively unconstitutional. But its broader ambition of ensuring that elections will "reflect the collective public interest . . . rather than the machinations of special interests" has fallen victim to the incredible sophistication of contemporary line-drawing techniques which permit the most grotesque sorts of political gerrymandering with absolute population equality.

The activist impulse behind Justice Brennan's reapportionment revolution was guided by three ideas: (a) an embrace of precise arithmetic standards; (2) an equation of majority rule with democracy; and (3) a commitment to individual rights. Justice Brennan understood that the second and third ideas were in tension: A majority that ruled on behalf of everyone might be at odds with a "discrete and insular" minority that might never become part of the governing majority; even worse, a majority enjoying monopoly power might directly target that minority. He used the first idea, therefore, to mediate between the second and the third. That is, he thought that judicially manageable standards—as evidenced in an insistence on absolute population equality among districts—would ensure majority rule while protecting minority rights. While population majorities should control a majority of the legislative seats, this still left room for population minorities to gain representation too. For Justice Brennan, the rule of strict population equality resolved both his commitment to minority representation and the majoritarian impulse behind one person, one vote.

Brennan's View in Retrospect

Looking back at thirty-five years of judicial regulation of apportionment, it turns out that one person, one vote, by itself, offered only a partial definition of equality. Justice Brennan's optimism about "well developed and familiar" standards was perhaps premature. The political theorist Jonathan Still has identified six potential aspects of political equality:

- *Equal suffrage* means that everyone is allowed to vote (and casts the same number of votes).
- *Equal shares* means that each elected official represents the same number of voters; put slightly differently, each voter enjoys an equal "piece" of a representative.
- *Equal probabilities* means that, in the abstract, each vote is equally likely to determine the outcome of the election.
- *Anonymity* means that changing the structure of the election system—for example, redrawing the various district boundaries—will not change election outcomes.
- *Majority rule* means that the outcome preferred by the majority will prevail.
- *Proportional group representation* means that each group of voters

receives a proportion of the legislative seats equal to its proportion of the total electorate.

One person, one vote presupposes equal suffrage—an unwarranted assumption in the South of *Baker* and *Wesberry* and *Reynolds,* to be sure, although as other contributors to this volume have pointed out, Justice Brennan was in the forefront of judicial solicitude for the right to participate. By definition, one person, one vote achieves equal shares; indeed, that is its animating vision. Arguably, as a matter of abstract political theory in which the unit of voting is the atomized individual and elections are conducted in equipopulous single-member districts, it satisfies equal probabilities. But as for anonymity, majority rule, or proportional group representation—the three more expansive and functional definitions of equality—one person, one vote has been at most only intermittently successful. As we have seen, absolute population equality imposes only a mild constraint on partisan or racial gerrymandering, and thus does little to achieve anonymity; similarly, creative line drawing can embolden a numerical minority that controls the reapportionment machinery to award itself a majority of the seats. And perhaps most profoundly, one person, one vote, with its individualistic and majoritarian rhetoric, has done little to ensure proportionality in the legislative process: As Justice Stewart noted in dissenting from one of the companion cases to *Reynolds,* if our paramount constitutional goal were solely to ensure that all voters' votes were absolutely equal, and that the majority would rule, we would use at-large elections, with their winner-take-all consequences. If, however, democracy requires both majority rule and a minority role, we need to modify the winner-take-all consequences of our present voting systems by adopting more candidly proportionate or semi-proportionate voting rules.

THE PARODY OF BRENNAN'S VISION

Baker v. Carr was decided in 1962, the same year that Alexander Bickel published perhaps the most influential book in modern constitutional law, *The Least Dangerous Branch.* Bickel identified the now-famous "countermajoritarian difficulty" with judicial review. Judicial review, he argued, was profoundly antidemocratic; when a court strikes down leg-

islative actions, it "thwarts the will of representatives of the actual people of the here and now; it exercises control, not in behalf of the prevailing majority, but against it."

Bickel and others targeted liberal and activist justices, like Justice
Brennan, for frustrating majority rule. But there was a deep irony in
Bickel's analysis. At the time he wrote, sitting legislators consistently refused to reapportion their districts and most legislatures had become
backwater relics of past political deals. Many state legislatures were controlled by lawmakers from rural hamlets in decline; their reactionary politics stymied the interests of voters in the burgeoning cities and suburbs
as well as progressive policies more generally. Particularly in the area of
civil rights, where extremist politicians from underpopulated and disenfranchised "Black Belt" regions were at the forefront of massive resistance, much of the Supreme Court's workload was an indirect
consequence of malapportionment's hold on state political processes.
Legislatures were not representing the current majority; they were club-
bish excuses for majority rule in name only. But Justice Brennan's commitment to one person, one vote helped to unseat the bogus *legislative*
"majorities" that had represented only a fraction of the actual population, in favor of a system in which a majority of the population actually controlled a majority of the legislative seats.

One upshot of Justice Brennan's malapportionment jurisprudence—
which Bickel had wrongly disparaged—has been to strengthen the argument against judicial activism, which is now often practiced by judges
with conservative views on social policy. The countermajoritarian difficulty seems more troubling now, because legislative majorities, thanks
to Justice Brennan, are more often acting on behalf of population majorities. Thus, Bickel's opprobrium seems misdirected at Justice Brennan, who in the area of one person, one vote was a genuine majoritarian.

But some of Bickel's fears were well founded. His insight about the
countermajoritarian difficulty is now being borne out in the bold practices of a so-called conservative Court. Today, an activist judiciary is
thwarting a pluralistic and egalitarian democratic vision. In an unprincipled fashion, the current Supreme Court recklessly wields a pseudo-
majoritarian club. On the one hand, the Court has shown itself quite
hostile to claims by racial minority groups that they have been excluded
from full participation; in those cases, the Court denies minorities an

opportunity to share political power because it equates democracy with simple majority rule. On the other hand, when a fairly elected white majority embraces a different, and richer, vision of democracy—one in which the majority shares power with traditionally excluded groups— the Court has embarked on a determined countermajoritarian offensive that threatens to halt the progress.

Slogging his way through the underbrush of race and voting, Justice Brennan tried to clear a more democratic space. It was there, relying on judicial precedents like *Gomillion* and the White Primary Cases, that he discovered a rationale to overcome the then-traditional judicial inclination to abstain. Yet it is in this very arena that a new form of individual activism has taken root. Justice Brennan's vision of reforming the political process to make it fundamentally more participatory has gotten lost in a conservative judicial, not political, thicket.

Tragically, the current Court has recast majority rule as a formidable barrier to power sharing, particularly with the racial minorities whose earlier struggles for the right to full participation had served as the opening wedge to judicial oversight. In a cruel parody of Justice Brennan's noble vision, majority rule now becomes majority monopolization. By this Court's new logic, the numerical majority is entitled not to a majority of the seats, but to *all* of them.

In a peculiar twist of Professor Bickel's admonition, the Court now intervenes to prohibit a white majority from recognizing, sharing power with, or even being self-conscious about underrepresented nonwhite minorities. The new Court majority "thwarts the will of representatives of the actual people of the here and now." But unlike the activist judicial majority in *Baker* that was the object of Bickel's opprobrium, this Court presumes to know better than a political majority itself what democracy means. It is "protecting" a majority not from minority control, but from self-governance. The architects of the reapportionment revolution could point in 1962 to profound pathologies in the political process to justify their intervention. The Court today, however, intervenes not to protect individual or majority rights, but to impose its own, quite controversial, view of what democracy means onto a political process that has reached a far more inclusive conclusion. The original, democracy-reinforcing incursion into the political thicket has now engineered judicial activism with a vengeance.

In *Shaw v. Reno* (1993 and 1996), the Supreme Court rebuffed North Carolina's decision to draw two congressional districts in which, for the first time in this century, black voters had a realistic chance to elect candidates of their choice. As it had in the malapportionment cases, the Court invoked the rhetoric of individual rights. The Court suggested that somehow white voters had been denied a newly discovered right to participate in a color-blind electoral process. Once again, that rhetoric masked the fact that, in reality, the Court was determining how political power should be allocated among identifiable voting blocs. The Court's preoccupation with the shape of the newly created districts reflected the recognition that absolute population equality does virtually nothing to prevent oddly shaped districts designed to produce particular outcomes. At the same time, it elevated compactness to a constitutionally significant position in disregard of Justice Brennan's warning in *Kirkpatrick* that the "preference for pleasingly shaped districts" should not be used to justify denials of political equality. Even worse, unlike the categorical rules in the one person, one vote cases, the Court's new rule as to what should trigger constitutional scrutiny is biased against traditionally excluded groups: An unusual district shape produces judicial skepticism only when black voters are in the majority. *Gomillion* has now come full circle. In *Baker v. Carr*, it served as the springboard for Justice Brennan's aspiration of increasing the responsiveness of the political system; in *Shaw*, it serves as a limit on black aspirations to meaningful participation.

In *Miller v. Johnson* (1995), the Court struck down a Georgia congressional apportionment that gave black rural voters their first realistic opportunity to elect representatives to Congress. The Court propounded a "predominant factor" test—districting is constitutionally suspect if race is the predominant factor explaining the district lines— that is as opaque and subject to exploitation by a partisan federal judiciary as one person, one vote was transparent and easy to apply. And although *Miller* purports to be about the individual right to vote that Justice Brennan championed, it ignores completely his broader aspiration: to assure "equal representation for equal numbers of people," a principle designed, he explained in *Kirkpatrick*, "to prevent debasement of voting power and diminution of access to elected representatives." *Miller* overlooks completely the enduring dilution of black citizens' voting power that previous apportionments had produced. It professes no concern at all with the continuing denial of meaningful access to responsive representatives that black citizens have suffered. *Wesberry v. Sanders*, the first one person, one vote case, has now come full circle as well. Thirty years after the Warren Court struck down Georgia's congressional apportionment because it denied many of Georgia's citizens an equal "voice in the election of those who make the laws under which, as good citizens, we must live," the Rehnquist Court has reintroduced precisely that possibility by foreclosing Georgia's black citizens from having an effective voice in selecting the state's congressional delegation.

In sum, the present Court has aggressively campaigned for a new, phony, majoritarian vision. Whereas Justice Brennan intervened to prevent legislative minorities from exercising *dis*proportionate power, the present Court intervenes to thwart legislative majorities from exercising *proportionate* power. This Court acts not to protect discrete and insular minorities, but to disable them. It denies the majority the political freedom to act in its perceived best interests. In the name of *Gomillion* and *Baker,* the Court repudiates the very vision Charles Gomillion articulated in bringing his lawsuit: the desire of the real population majority "to share power."

This is not to say that one person, one vote was trivial. In fact, it formed the opening wedge in the contemporary understanding that the right to vote "can be denied by a debasement or dilution of the weight of a citizen's vote just as effectively as by wholly prohibiting the free exercise of the franchise." That understanding turned out to be critical to guaranteeing that the right to participate secured by the Voting Rights Act of 1965 provided more than merely a formal, deracinated form of opportunity to traditionally excluded groups. But most of the heavy lifting in the struggle for political equality, although it was made possible by Justice Brennan's assertions of justiciability in *Baker v. Carr,* awaited and continues to await more sophisticated and sensitive tools than one person, one vote. "You are not required," the *Pirkei Avot* reminds us, "to complete the work, but neither are you at liberty to abstain from it." Justice Brennan's work in *Baker* and its progeny offered the Court and the nation a good starting point for a journey that without his leadership remains incomplete.

The "Right that Is Preservative of All Rights": Voting Rights Act Enforcement

Deval L. Patrick

Justice Brennan was a central figure in the development of modern voting rights law. In the previous essay, Lani Guinier and Pam Karlan describe the impact of the one person, one vote decisions—cases that would never have been decided if Justice Brennan had not written his masterful opinion for the Court in *Baker v. Carr.* I shall focus on another aspect of Justice Brennan's voting rights jurisprudence—his contributions to the enforcement and application of the Voting Rights Act. The Justice's opinions in Voting Rights Act cases represent many of the same qualities as his jurisprudence generally: a keen technical legal acumen, a deep respect for the role of Congress in enforcing civil rights, an incisive understanding of the practical realities of discrimination, and a pronounced preference for relatively formal rules over general standards. Through his opinions, Justice Brennan served an essential role in assuring the success of the Voting Rights Act—from the statute's earliest days to the end of his tenure on the Court. Justice Brennan's impact in this area continues to be felt today.

The Voting Rights Act has been called the most effective civil rights statute, and for good reason. When Congress passed the act in 1965, it targeted several "covered jurisdictions" (largely corresponding to the Deep South) for special treatment. In those jurisdictions, black voter registration lagged behind white voter registration by nearly 45 percent. In Mississippi, one of the original covered states, the situation was particularly extreme—less than 7 percent of eligible black citizens were reg-

The author is assistant attorney general in charge of the Civil Rights Division of the United States Department of Justice. He served as staff attorney at the NAACP Legal Defense and Educational Fund where he litigated a variety of civil rights cases, specializing in capital punishment and voting rights.

istered to vote. The Voting Rights Act changed all that. In one fell swoop, the act eliminated many of the discriminatory barriers that had kept minorities from registering to vote in those states: literacy tests in all their pernicious variants, moral character requirements, "voucher" rules. The act also included an extraordinary provision—Section 5—designed to assure that the covered states, which had a long history of evading federal court decrees, could not easily circumvent Congress's new prohibitions. Jurisdictions subject to Section 5 may not enforce a change in *any* "voting qualification or prerequisite to voting, or standard, practice, or procedure with respect to voting," *unless and until* the attorney general or a federal court certifies that the change has neither a discriminatory purpose nor a discriminatory effect. That procedure for federal approval is called the "preclearance" process.

Thanks to vigorous enforcement of these provisions, the Voting Rights Act has had a dramatic effect. Within three years, the gap between black and white registration rates in the seven covered states closed by almost half. In Mississippi, black voter registration soared by over 700 percent. Throughout the nation, barriers to registration and voting came tumbling down.

Justice Brennan played a crucial role in the early days of the Voting Rights Act. In his opinion for the Court in *Katzenbach v. Morgan* (1966), Justice Brennan upheld a key provision of the act that barred New York from enforcing its English-language literacy requirement to disenfranchise large portions of the state's Puerto Rican population. In an opinion that is as important for its broad conception of Congress's power to enforce the Fourteenth Amendment as it is for the specific provision it upheld, the Court squarely rejected New York's argument that Congress could do no more than simply prohibit practices that are judicially determined to violate equal protection. Justice Brennan's opinion reflects an essential belief in both the ability and the responsibility of the national legislature to assure the protection of civil rights. He wrote, "A construction of § 5 [of the Fourteenth Amendment] that would require a judicial determination that the enforcement of the state law precluded by Congress violated the Amendment, as a condition of sustaining the congressional enactment, would depreciate both congressional resourcefulness and congressional responsibility for implementing the Amendment."

Justice Brennan's respect for congressional competence, as well as his intensely practical understanding of the real-world effects of the legislation, is evident in his analysis of Congress's justifications for adopting the provision at issue in *Morgan*. Although "the practical effect of [the provision was] to prohibit New York from denying the right to vote to large segments of its Puerto Rican community," Justice Brennan did not rest its constitutionality solely—or even principally—on its effect of expanding the right to vote. He focused instead on an important secondary effect of the provision—enhancing the political power of the Puerto Rican community. "This enhanced political power" serves the purposes of the equal protection clause because it "will be helpful in gaining nondiscriminatory treatment in public services for the entire Puerto Rican community."

In that passage, Justice Brennan recognized precisely what was at stake in the entire voting rights debate. It was not simply the right to go to the ballot box and participate in a civic ritual—important as that is. Justice Brennan's *Morgan* opinion recognized that the right to vote, while fundamental in itself, is the linchpin—"the right that is 'preservative of all rights,' " the Justice called it. Where disfavored persons and groups are denied the vote, they have little recourse against oppressive and discriminatory laws and practices. That is why, when the enemies of Reconstruction were consolidating their power across the South at the turn of the century, they chose disenfranchisement as a principal tool. It is to Justice Brennan's credit that he had the vision to understand precisely why the right to vote is so important. It is to his greater credit that he had the legal skill and the determination to incorporate that insight into constitutional doctrine.

In another early Voting Rights Act case, *Perkins v. Matthews* (1971), Justice Brennan once again demonstrated his keen understanding of the subtle ways in which discrimination can occur. *Perkins* involved the question of what constitutes a change in a "standard, practice, or procedure with respect to voting" that a covered jurisdiction (in that case the city of Canton, Mississippi) must submit for federal approval under Section 5 of the act. The plaintiffs argued that the city violated the act by changing the locations of polling places for local elections without obtaining preclearance. Over Justice Black's vigorous dissent arguing that these changes could not possibly have been motivated by a discriminatory animus, Justice Brennan's opinion for the Court concluded that "there inheres in the determination of the location of polling places an obvious potential for 'denying or abridging the right to vote on account of race or color.' " Accordingly, the city was barred from enforcing its changes in polling place locations unless and until it obtained preclearance.

Justice Brennan's elaboration of this conclusion places his acute awareness of practical reality into sharp focus. "The abstract right to vote means little unless the right becomes a reality at the polling place on election day," he wrote. "The accessibility, prominence, facilities, and prior notice of the polling place's location all have an effect on a person's ability to exercise his franchise." As a result, Justice Brennan recognized, a potential for abuse inheres in every decision to move a polling place: "Locations at distances remote from black communities or at places calculated to intimidate blacks from entering, or failure to publicize changes adequately might well have [a discriminatory] effect." In those jurisdictions in which Congress found pervasive and unremitting voting discrimination, Justice Brennan held, decisions with such a clear discriminatory potential must be submitted to federal authorities for preclearance.

Justice Brennan's majority opinions in *Morgan* and *Perkins* were second only to Chief Justice Warren's opinions for the Court in *South Carolina v. Katzenbach* (1966) and *Allen v. Board of Elections* (1969) in their importance for the original Voting Rights Act. Taken together, these four decisions firmly established the constitutionality of the act, and they made clear that Section 5 was to be enforced broadly, as Congress intended. Without such clear, early statements from the Supreme Court, the phenomenal successes of the first decade of the Voting Rights Act might never have occurred.

As the Voting Rights Act moved into its second decade, Justice Brennan continued to be a principal champion of the act's purposes. His voting rights opinions during this period once again exhibited the two tendencies apparent in his early voting cases: a deep respect for the authority and responsibility of Congress, and a keen understanding of the practical dynamics of discrimination. These tendencies are evident in Justice Brennan's forceful dissenting opinion in *City of Richmond v. United States* (1975). *City of Richmond* involved the city's decision to annex a large portion of adjoining land. As Justice Brennan explained, this annexation "represented a clear victory for Richmond's entrenched white political establishment: the city realized a net gain of 44,000 white citizens, its black population was reduced from 52% to 42% of the total population, and the predominantly white Richmond Forward organization retained its 6–3 majority on the city council." A three-judge federal district court had refused to preclear this annexation under Section 5, finding that it had both a discriminatory purpose and a discriminatory effect. The Supreme Court vacated that decision.

In his dissent, Justice Brennan argued powerfully for upholding the denial of preclearance. The annexation, in his view, had the basic motivation of avoiding "a transfer of political control to what was fast becoming a black-population majority." The city could not "purge the taint of its impermissible purpose by dredging up supposed objective justifications and by replacing its practice of at-large councilmanic elections with a ward-voting system." The Court's decision to accept these post hoc justifications, Justice Brennan argued, directly undermined the purposes of Section 5: "To hold that an annexation agreement reached under such circumstances can be validated by objective economic justifications offered many years after the fact, in my view, wholly negates the prophylactic purpose of § 5."

In *City of Richmond,* the Court also held that an annexation that significantly reduces the black voting percentage in a city does not have a discriminatory effect under Section 5 so long as the city's electoral system "fairly reflects the strength of the Negro community as it exists after the annexation." Thus, because black voters could control three of the nine seats on the city council after the Richmond annexation, the Court found no discriminatory effect. Justice Brennan sharply criticized that holding as well. The Court's rule, Justice Brennan explained, "would support a plan which added far greater concentrations of whites to the city and reduced black voting strength to the equivalent of three seats, two seats, or even fractions of a seat." It thus affords covered municipalities an obvious stratagem for evading the substantive prohibitions of Section 5: "Municipal politicians who are fearful of losing their political control to emerging black voting majorities are today placed on notice that their control can be made secure as long as they can find concentrations of white citizens into which to expand their municipal boundaries." Justice Brennan expressed a similar determination to guard against possible loopholes in Section 5 coverage in his majority opinion in *United States v. Board of Commissioners of Sheffield, Alabama* (1978), in which the Court rejected a rule that "would invite States to circumvent the Act . . . by allowing local entities that do not conduct voter registration to control critical aspects of the electoral process."

Both *Sheffield* and *City of Richmond* exemplify Justice Brennan's respect for congressional authority and responsibility to enforce civil rights. In both cases, the Justice rejected policy arguments against a broad interpretation of the statute and instead sought to implement Congress's intent that Section 5 exist as a "broad, prophylactic rule." He resisted interpretations that would contravene Congress's purpose by "plac[ing] the advantages of time and inertia back on the perpetrators of the discrimination." Even if these interpretations might be reasonable as a matter of policy, they were contrary to the balance Congress struck.

Justice Brennan's respect for congressional authority is perhaps most apparent in his concurring opinion in *United Jewish Organizations v. Carey* (1977). *United Jewish Organizations* was in many respects a precursor to *Shaw v. Reno* (1993). In 1974, the state of New York, in an attempt to comply with its responsibilities under the Voting Rights Act, drew ten state legislative districts in Brooklyn with minority populations of at least 65 percent. Under the previous redistricting plan, the Hasidic community in the Williamsburgh area of Brooklyn had been largely contained within a single house district and a single state senate district; the new plan split the community between two house districts and two senate districts. A group of Hasidic voters sued, claiming that they had been assigned to districts solely on the basis of race in violation of the Constitution. In voting with the Court to reject that claim, Justice Brennan relied principally on the fact that the districting had been impelled by the requirements of the Voting Rights Act. After canvassing all of the reasons why the Court should be particularly cautious in upholding "benign" or "remedial" uses of race, Justice Brennan concluded that the role of Congress in enacting the Voting Rights Act made the case before him an easy one: "However the Court ultimately decides the constitutional legitimacy of 'reverse discrimination' pure and simple," he was convinced that Congress had "adequately struck [the] balance" between the risks and benefits of "benign racial sorting" when it enacted "the carefully crafted remedial scheme embodied in the Voting Rights Act." (Justice Brennan's final opinion for the Court, in *Metro Broadcasting v. FCC* [1990], rested on an identical deference to congressional competence.)

In all of these cases, Justice Brennan demonstrated his commitment to the goals of the Voting Rights Act, an incisive understanding of the subtle stratagems of discrimination, and a deep respect for the role of Congress in enforcing voting rights. The Justice's opinions in the first two decades of the Voting Rights Act resolved important issues in the act's application, and helped assure the act's success. But Justice Brennan's greatest contribution to the enforcement of the Voting Rights Act came in the statute's third decade, in *Thornburg v. Gingles* (1986).

While Justice Brennan's earlier Voting Rights Act opinions had focused on Section 5 and its preclearance procedure, *Gingles* involved Section 2 of the act—which authorizes affirmative suits against voting practices that deny the right to vote. Section 2 had been the subject of political controversy since the Court's decision in *City of Mobile v. Bolden* (1980). *Bolden* was a vote dilution case. The claim was not that minority voters were denied the right to cast ballots, but that the use of at-large elections effectively disenfranchised minority voters by submerging them within a larger white electorate. The concept of minority vote dilution, of course, owes much to the intellectual leap that took place in the one person, one vote cases that Justice Brennan did so much to bring about—for both rest on the principle that the right to vote can be effectively denied by the way in which votes are counted, just as surely as it is denied by the failure to count someone's vote at all. Indeed, Justice Brennan foreshadowed the Court's subsequent doctrine on minority vote dilution in his 1965 opinion for the Court in *Fortson v. Dorsey*—which was essentially a one person, one vote case. In a passage at the end of the *Fortson* opinion, Justice Brennan recognized that "it might well be that, designedly or otherwise, a multi-member constituency apportionment scheme, under the circumstances of a particular case, would operate to minimize or cancel out the voting strength of racial or political elements of the voting population."

In a series of cases during the 1970s, the Supreme Court and lower courts had built on Justice Brennan's *Fortson* language and held that at-large or multimember districting schemes violate the Constitution if they result in denying minority voters an equal opportunity to elect the candidates of their choice. This so-called results test found its clearest expression in the Court's opinion in *White v. Regester* (1973). But *Bolden* marked a sharp turn away from a pure focus on "results." There, the Court held (over Justice Brennan's dissent) that the Constitution prohibited vote dilution only when it resulted from an intentional decision to weaken minority voting strength.

The political response to *Bolden* was swift and furious. Almost immediately, efforts to overturn its holding began in Congress. Opponents of *Bolden*'s intent requirement argued that the standard required plaintiffs to bear an unreasonable burden of proof, entailed a divisive inquiry into whether public officials were racist, and simply "asks the wrong question"—the "right" question being whether minority voters in fact had a full and equal opportunity to participate in electoral politics. Those who advocated retaining the intent requirement argued that the "results test" would mandate proportional representation by race and that it would put in jeopardy at-large election systems in many jurisdictions where they had been adopted for legitimate reasons.

In 1982, Congress amended Section 2 to incorporate the "results test." Amended Section 2 prohibits states from imposing any voting practice "in a manner which results in a denial or abridgement of the right of any citizen of the United States to vote on account of race or color." A violation is established if, in "the totality of circumstances," minority group members "have less opportunity than other members of the electorate to participate in the political process and to elect representatives of their choice." In a carefully drafted compromise brokered by Senator Dole, the amendment states that "the extent to which members of a protected class have been elected to office in the State or political subdivision is one circumstance which may be considered: *Provided,* That nothing in this section establishes a right to have members of a protected class elected in numbers equal to their proportion in the population."

Gingles was the first case in which the Court undertook to apply the broad, amorphous terms of the 1982 amendment to Section 2. Given the statute's reference to the "totality of circumstances" and the accompanying Senate report's identification of no less than nine "typical factors" that might be relevant to a finding of vote dilution, the Court could easily have reverted to a relatively standardless deference to the district court. But in an opinion by Justice Brennan, the Court did just the opposite. While recognizing that the vote dilution inquiry "requires an intensely local appraisal of the design and impact of the contested electoral scheme," and that the district court's findings on the issue could not be disturbed absent clear error, Justice Brennan's opinion set forth clear standards by which lower courts should weigh the evidence before them.

In particular, courts adjudicating vote dilution cases must be guided by the "essence of a § 2 claim"—"that a certain electoral law, practice, or structure interacts with social and historical conditions to cause an inequality in the opportunities enjoyed by black and white voters to elect their preferred representatives." And courts must not make this determination in the abstract. Rather than simply throwing all of the indicia of past and present discrimination into a hopper and declaring that, "in the totality of circumstances," the evidence either demonstrates or fails to demonstrate vote dilution, they must focus on the evidence most relevant to deciding whether a practice impairs minority voting strength: "Stated succinctly, a bloc voting majority must *usually* be able to defeat candidates supported by a politically cohesive, geographically insular minority group." If minority plaintiffs do not establish these elements, Justice Brennan wrote, they have not proved vote dilution.

Justice Brennan's *Gingles* opinion is of surpassing importance, for several reasons. On a methodological level, *Gingles* superimposed a relatively straightforward and clear framework of proof on a statute that was drafted in broad terms. Of course, the very nature of the issues involved in a vote dilution case guarantees that proof will be complex. But *Gingles* at least established a definite, intelligible basic rule of liability. After Justice Brennan's opinion, states and localities could no longer claim that their responsibilities under Section 2 were uncertain, and lower courts would no longer be left at sea in determining whether vote dilution occurred. Nor would unprincipled trial court decisions be entitled to deference as some generalized finding "in the totality of circumstances."

On a doctrinal level, *Gingles* made clear that the essence of vote dilution is that a particular election system facilitates consistent bloc voting majority efforts to prevent a cohesive minority group from electing its chosen candidates. Justice Brennan's formulation did not require proportional representation, and it reserved federal intervention for those states and localities in which racially polarized voting is persistent and severe. But it correctly rejected the proposed standard, offered by Justice O'Connor in *Gingles,* that would have required minority plaintiffs to show not only that they lacked the opportunity to elect their chosen candidates, but also that they lacked access to or influence on the representatives who were elected. As Justice Brennan's opinion recognized, minority voters suffer a distinct harm—one that Congress intended to remedy—when their chosen candidates consistently lose because white voters refuse to cast ballots for them. This is true even if minority voters can still participate in the political process in other ways.

But *Gingles* is most important on a practical, empirical level. For there can be no doubt that Justice Brennan's opinion deserves primary credit for the recent, dramatic increase in minority representation in

Congress and the state legislatures. Thanks to vigorous enforcement of the Voting Rights Act after the 1990 census—the first decennial redistricting to occur since Justice Brennan's opinion in *Gingles*—more black and Hispanic representatives serve in Congress than ever before. And in the decade since *Gingles,* jurisdictions throughout the South—indeed, throughout the nation—have abandoned dilutive multimember districting and at-large electoral systems in favor of procedures that provide minority voters a fair chance to elect their chosen candidates. In many if not most cases, these jurisdictions have done so as a result of a suit or a threatened suit under Section 2.

In recent years, the Voting Rights Act as interpreted in *Gingles* has come under attack from a variety of quarters. Some have argued that the act has been a vehicle for partisan manipulation of the redistricting process. Others claim that the act's imperative of race consciousness is inconsistent with our nation's constitutional traditions. In response, the Court has offered a range of opinions, inconsistent from case to case and reflecting a tendency to reason any sense of practical justice out of the act. It is unfortunate that Justice Brennan has not had the opportunity to serve on the Court while it has grappled with these issues. For while he would have surely stood firm against any abuse of the Voting Rights Act, he would have also made clear precisely why the act remains so important: In too many parts of this nation, race or national origin is still the most important factor in politics. In such places, the Voting Rights Act is necessary to assure everyone a fair opportunity to influence the political process. Thanks to Justice Brennan's long and consistent efforts to advance the goals of the act, minority voters throughout the country now enjoy that opportunity. Let us hope the present Court respects that milestone.

Fair Hearing: Legacy to the Poor

Tony Mauro

In a drab hearing room on the eighth floor of the District of Columbia's main city office building, Justice Brennan's legacy to the poor lives on.

This is where recipients of public assistance, food stamps, and more than fifty other benefit and entitlement programs go to object when a government agency wants to terminate those benefits.

Here the recipient can tell his or her side of the story, with sworn witnesses, a transcribed record, and a guaranteed right of appeal. If the recipient has no lawyer, then the agency can't be represented by a lawyer either. As much as possible, in this room, the playing field is level; here, more than 100 times a year, the recipients of government benefits avail themselves of a process that gives them a voice that must be heard.

Brennan's Enduring Impact on Poverty Law

The fact that welfare recipients, viewed with disdain in many quarters, are treated with dignity in this room and hundreds like it around the country is a direct result of Justice Brennan's advocacy for the poor in *Goldberg v. Kelly. Goldberg*, a 1970 decision that required government to give welfare recipients a fair hearing and due process before their benefits could be terminated, revolutionized welfare and government benefit programs forever.

"*Goldberg v. Kelly* is our Bible here, our Ten Commandments," says Holloway Wooten, who presides over the hearing room as chief of an

The author is the legal affairs correspondent for *USA Today* and a columnist for the *Legal Times*. Research assistance was provided by the Freedom Forum and by the Center on Social Welfare Policy and Law. The author also wishes to thank Holloway Wooten and Santo Fleres of the Washington, D.C., Office of Fair Hearing, Professor Martin Schwartz of Touro College Law Center, Professor Susan Bennett of the American University, Washington College of Law, Professor Jeffrey Gutman of George Washington University Law Center, Professor Laura Macklin of the Georgetown University Law Center, and Professor Gay Gellhorn of the District of Columbia School of Law.

office whose very name honors Justice Brennan: the Office of Fair Hearing. "And our First Commandment for the agencies we deal with is to do nothing that violates *Goldberg* because if you do, you're not going to win."

Into the hearing room come families fighting to keep their food stamps, single mothers pleading to keep Aid for Families with Dependent Children (AFDC) payments coming, citizens battling over foster care benefits or emergency shelter, all arguing against an adverse government determination. All of them, because of Justice Brennan, were given adequate notice and, now, a chance to be heard.

Goldberg was a 7–2 decision that could have dealt mundanely with the welfare procedures of New York State. But instead, Justice Brennan took the Court on an impassioned journey into the real-world plight of the poor nationwide to join his conclusion: that welfare recipients are entitled to a hearing before—not after—their benefits are terminated. The dignity of those on welfare, as well as the real-life predicaments they face, requires no less, Brennan said.

"From its founding the nation's basic commitment has been to foster the dignity and well-being of all persons within its borders," Brennan wrote. "The same governmental interests that counsel the provision of welfare, counsel as well its uninterrupted provision to those eligible to receive it; pre-termination evidentiary hearings are indispensable to that end."

In a single stroke, Justice Brennan's opinion replaced stingy, bureaucratic neglect for the poor with procedure and fairness. Welfare was no longer a government gift that could be withdrawn arbitrarily; now it was an entitlement, whose recipients had rights.

Though *Goldberg*'s force has been weakened somewhat in rulings since, its precepts of fairness have informed virtually every area of government benefit—from Social Security to special education, from child support enforcement to housing.

As a judge, Brennan could not solve the problems of the poor that he saw since his childhood in Newark, New Jersey. He could not increase welfare payments to the poor. As only one of nine Supreme Court justices, he could not elevate welfare or subsistence to the level of a constitutional right, as the poverty law movement of the 1960s and 1970s had so fervently wished. As a jurist apart from the political fray, he could do little as the tide turned against the Great Society and the welfare state in recent years.

But through *Goldberg* and other crucial decisions, Justice Brennan could ensure that the poor would be heard, that their needs and rights would not be ignored by an indifferent state.

"He was the most important Supreme Court justice in this area, bar none," says Henry Freedman, longtime executive director of the Center on Social Welfare Policy and Law. "He set out the due process and equal protection standards that have shaped welfare policy in this country. He made the field." The center dedicated its twenty-fifth anniversary report in 1990 to Justice Brennan.

Even as the national government speeds toward "welfare reform" that is criticized as indifferent to the poor, most observers believe that Brennan's principles of fairness as enunciated in *Goldberg* are too deeply ingrained to be swept aside. The National Governors Association in its proposal speaks of "fair and equitable treatment" of recipients.

"It's inconceivable to me that recipients of welfare wouldn't have some recourse before their benefits are cut off, even under the new system," says American University law professor Susan Bennett.

"*Goldberg* is even more vital today than when issued in 1970," declared Alan Houseman of the Center for Law and Social Policy in a 1990 law review article. "*Goldberg* will be used . . . to assist the poor in gaining greater control over the environment in which they work and reside."

THE WELFARE RIGHTS MOVEMENT

Before *Goldberg*, public assistance programs were governed by a wide range of arbitrary policies and procedures. When caseworkers decided that welfare recipients no longer qualified for benefits, hearings of any kind were rare—and when they occurred, they often did not stop the state from cutting off benefits while a decision was pending. Few recipients had lawyers, and neither the recipients nor most lawyers knew about appeals procedures—even in New York City, where procedures were fairly well developed.

Seeking to require that welfare recipients be given a fair hearing before their benefits were cut off became the "central prong" of the legal strategy adopted by the fledgling welfare rights movement in the 1960s, according to Martha F. Davis in her 1993 history of the campaign entitled *Brutal Need*. Poverty lawyers, drawing strength from the popular movement, had begun peppering the courts with lawsuits to expand and vindicate the rights of welfare recipients. The legal effort was patterned after the litigation strategy of the NAACP Legal Defense Fund in the area of desegregation, and by 1966 had gained the Legal Defense Fund's blessing: "We are moving into an era of poverty law which is in some sense comparable to the civil rights law of the mid-1930s," said the fund's Jack Greenberg.

As with any movement, there was division over goals and strategies. But several ambitious legal, even philosophical, objectives were behind much of the poverty and welfare litigation.

In addition to winning specific battles over unfair procedure, the movement sought to prod the courts into regarding the poor as a specially protected class in the same way that racial minorities had won special care in the eyes of the law. The result of such treatment would be that laws and policies resulting in unequal treatment for poor people would be struck down under a "strict scrutiny" standard, just as surely as Jim Crow laws had fallen. As early as 1949, Jacobus tenBroek of the University of California at Berkeley had made this argument, asserting that "the mere state of being without funds should be a neutral fact," as was a person's race or national origin.

Edward Sparer, viewed as the "guru" of welfare law, also had a grander goal in mind in the early welfare litigation—to fashion a constitutionally protected "right to live," which included a right to a minimum income or welfare. He urged in 1969 that equal protection principles be applied to welfare litigation as a strategy to expand benefits and establish a minimum income. Rather than viewing welfare as a gift to the poor, he sought to have the courts view welfare as a right inherent in a civilized, humanitarian society.

But the most influential works came from onetime Supreme Court law clerk and Yale law professor Charles Reich, who argued in a pair of law review articles in 1964 and 1965—later cited by Brennan in *Goldberg*—that welfare should be regarded as a form of "property" that could not be withdrawn easily by government. Welfare recipients had a constitutionally protected property right in their benefits, he suggested.

"A first principle should be that government must have no power to buy up rights guaranteed by the Constitution," wrote Reich. "When individuals have insufficient resources to live under conditions of health and decency, society has obligations to provide support, and the individual is entitled to that support as of right."

Reich's work did not fall on deaf ears at the nation's highest court.

In an interview with author Martha Davis, Brennan said, "I was looking for a 'new property' case. I knew of Charles Reich's work—I remembered him from his clerkship with Justice Black—but I was interested in the issue before that, back in New Jersey. . . . *Goldberg v. Kelly* seemed to be a good vehicle to present the issue."

THE TEST CASE: *Goldberg v. Kelly*

The New York regulations under dispute in *Goldberg v. Kelly* did not seem draconian or overly arbitrary at first glance. Even Justice Brennan called New York's system "a model of rationality" in his now-famous 1987 lecture on reason and passion in the law.

When a caseworker proposed discontinuing benefits, the state required that recipients be notified in writing. Recipients, in turn, had the opportunity to submit a written response, but benefits could be suspended in the meantime. Opportunity was given for a "post-termination" hearing that could lead to reinstatement.

On paper, the procedures seemed fair enough. But Justice Brennan heeded the call of the welfare plaintiffs in the case to go beyond the abstract procedure and look at how it worked in the cases of real people— real poor people.

The plaintiffs' attorneys told of their clients' plight in vivid detail. John Kelly, the named party in the title of the case, was a homeless black man whose benefits had been terminated in a dispute with his caseworker over where he should live. Randolph Young was cut off after he was robbed of $20, which constituted "mismanagement of funds" in the eyes of his caseworker. Pearl Frye was terminated for missing an appointment with her caseworker.

The story of Esther Lett was particularly compelling. She received AFDC benefits for herself and her four nieces until she was terminated in 1968 for "failure to disclose assets." The welfare department had received a totally erroneous report that Esther Lett was employed, earning income that would have made her ineligible for benefits. She and Legal Aid lawyers tried unsuccessfully to correct the error, but in the meantime her benefits had been cut off and she and her nieces were starving. She fainted at the welfare office after waiting all day to see a caseworker. On another day, she and her nieces went to a hospital emergency room after eating spoiled food.

Their narratives proved to Brennan that the paper fairness of New

York's procedures did not suffice. The constitutional command of due process demanded more, and earlier.

"Termination of aid pending resolution of a controversy over eligibility may deprive an eligible recipient of the very means by which to live while he waits," wrote Brennan. "Since he lacks independent resources, his situation becomes immediately desperate. His need to concentrate upon finding the means for daily subsistence, in turn, adversely affects his ability to seek redress from the welfare bureaucracy."

New York's rule allowing recipients to submit a written statement appealing termination was similarly impractical, Brennan said. "The opportunity to be heard must be tailored to the capacities of those who are to be heard," he wrote. "Written submissions are an unrealistic option for most recipients, who lack the educational attainment necessary to write effectively and who cannot obtain professional assistance."

To meet the requirements of due process, Brennan said recipients must be afforded the opportunity, before termination, to appear with or without counsel before an impartial decision-maker to offer evidence orally to counter the agency's determination, and to confront or cross-examine adverse witnesses.

Brennan's writing was not overly indulgent and did not seek to romanticize the plight of the poor. Early drafts that recounted the recipients' predicaments in detail had been excised or drastically pared down. Instead, it was a clear-eyed view of due process, informed by Justice Brennan's passion for the rights of the disadvantaged. For everyday welfare recipients whose needs were urgent and whose resources were meager, the New York system simply did not work.

Indeed, it was the *Goldberg* opinion that Brennan pointed to most often in his 1987 lecture about the role of passion in judicial decision-making. "The decision can be seen as an expression of the importance of passion in governmental conduct, in the sense of attention to the concrete human realities at stake," Brennan said. "From this perspective, *Goldberg* can be seen as injecting passion into a system whose abstract rationality had led it astray."

Through his majority opinion, Brennan said, "The Court . . . realized that the state's procedures lacked one vital element: appreciation of the drastic consequences of terminating a recipient's only means of subsistence."

The *Goldberg* opinion also went as far as Brennan felt it was possible to go in meeting the more theoretical objectives of the welfare rights movement. Earlier drafts with bolder formulations that described poverty as "largely a product of impersonal forces" were eliminated to appease Justices Byron White and John Marshall Harlan, according to Martha Davis's account.

But Brennan was able to declare that welfare benefits "are a matter of statutory entitlement for persons qualified to receive them. Their termination involves state action that adjudicates important rights." Quoting from his own earlier opinion in *Sherbert v. Verner* (1963), involving the denial of unemployment compensation, Brennan added, "This constitutional challenge cannot be answered by an argument that public assistance benefits are a 'privilege' and not a 'right.' "

In a footnote citing Reich's work, Brennan also wrote, "It may be realistic today to regard welfare entitlements as more like 'property' than a 'gratuity.' "

The opinion may not have elevated welfare to a constitutional right, but it did pinpoint welfare's role in the constitutional scheme.

"Welfare, by meeting the basic demands of subsistence, can help bring within the reach of the poor the same opportunities that are available to others to participate meaningfully in the life of the community," wrote Brennan. "Public assistance, then, is not mere charity, but a means to 'promote the general welfare, and secure the blessings of liberty to ourselves and our posterity.' "

Goldberg stands as the most important ruling the Supreme Court has ever handed down on the rights of the poor; it has been described as the opening shot in the modern due process revolution.

And to fair hearing officer Wooten in Washington, D.C., the *Goldberg* decision is without peer. "What *Miranda* did in criminal law, *Goldberg* did in poverty law," he says.

APPROACHING A RIGHT TO WELFARE

But *Goldberg* was not the only opinion in which Justice Brennan addressed the needs of the poor. A year before *Goldberg,* Brennan wrote the majority in *Shapiro v. Thompson* (1969).

In this 6–3 decision, Brennan invoked the equal protection clause of the Fourteenth Amendment and the right to travel (an implied constitutional right that appears nowhere in the Constitution's text) to strike down one-year residency requirements for welfare eligibility in Connecticut, Pennsylvania, and Washington, D.C. Again, Brennan wrote of the poor with respect.

"An indigent who desires to migrate, resettle, find a new job, and start a new life will doubtless hesitate if he knows he must risk making the move without the possibility of falling back on state welfare assistance during the first year of residence, when his need may be most acute," Brennan found. "But the purpose of inhibiting migration by needy persons into the state is constitutionally impermissible."

Fears expressed by states that a flood of new residents would be attracted by high welfare benefits were unjustified, Brennan wrote. "We do not perceive why a mother who is seeking to make a new life for herself and her children should be regarded as less deserving because she considers, among other factors, the level of a state's public assistance," said Brennan. "Surely such a mother is no less deserving than a mother who moves into a particular state in order to take advantage of its better educational facilities."

The residency laws, Brennan said, impermissibly create two classes of needy families, one of which is deprived of "the very means to subsist—food, shelter, and other necessities of life."

If that sounds close to a declaration of a "right to live," and if from *Shapiro* and *Goldberg* it appeared that the Court was on the verge of finding poor people to be a classification deserving of protection under strict-scrutiny standards when laws adversely affected them, then these Brennan opinions went as far as the Court would ever go toward those vaunted goals of the welfare rights movement.

THE COURT SLAMS THE DOOR

Shortly after *Goldberg* was handed down, the Court issued *Dandridge v. Williams* (1970), which dashed all such hopes that the Court would go further. Justice Potter Stewart's opinion seemed to go out of its way to announce that the Court had gone far enough in defining the rights of the poor, and would go no further.

By a 5–3 vote, the Court upheld Maryland's practice of setting a family maximum on welfare benefits. The policy was challenged on equal protection grounds, but the Court was not sympathetic. The Court would not apply strict-scrutiny standards to state welfare regulations, Stewart said. "The intractable economic, social, and even philosophical problems presented by public welfare assistance programs are not the business of this Court," Stewart said.

With that, the litigation strategy of welfare advocates collapsed, and the defeats came almost unrelentingly. In *Wyman v. James* (1971), the Court said welfare recipients could not prevent caseworkers from making unannounced searches of their homes. In *San Antonio Independent School District v. Rodriguez* (1973), the Court found that education was not a fundamental right. *Jefferson v. Hackney* (1972) upheld Texas policies that resulted in unequal payments for whites and blacks in certain categories of aid.

A rare victory for Brennan came nearly a decade later in 1982, when the Court held that undocumented aliens could not be barred from public schools. The 5–4 ruling in *Plyler v. Doe* did not apply strict scrutiny, but under a "heightened-scrutiny" standard, Brennan said the Texas policy violated the equal protection clause. The children of illegal aliens, he said, could not be held to account for their status and be deprived of education's lasting benefits. The decision has been cited in the current debate over popular measures aimed at reducing benefits for aliens.

In his later years on the Court, Brennan's writing on the poor came mainly in dissent—especially during the Reagan years when regard for the poor was at a low legal ebb. One of Brennan's most poignant dissents came in *Bowen v. Gilliard* (1987). The Court upheld regulations that in effect reduced welfare payments to a household when one of the children in that household is supported by child support payments from a noncustodial parent.

To Brennan, those rules posed an unacceptable choice: "The government has told a child who lives with a mother receiving public assistance that it cannot both live with its mother and be supported by its father. The child must either leave the care and custody of the mother, or forgo the support of the father and become a government client."

Again, Brennan was looking not at the rules in the abstract, but in terms of their impact on real people: "The government has thus decreed that a condition of welfare eligibility is that her child surrender a vital connection with either the father or the mother."

After a long and sad look at the importance and the disintegration of families, Brennan concludes that, in many instances, child support payments represent the only tangible bond between father and child.

"The father is not there on a daily basis to wake the child in the morning," Brennan wrote. "Nonetheless, by helping to meet the child's daily material needs, the father can let the child know that the father is committed to participating in the child's upbringing. Meals, clothes, toys and other things made possible by this support represent this commitment. . . . Braces, special shows, lessons—a father may not be able to provide all these things for his child, but he is entitled to try."

Brennan concluded, "No society can assure its children that there will be no unhappy families. It can tell them, however, that their government will not be allowed to contribute to the pain."

In the current political climate, welfare is often viewed as a revenue-devouring nuisance, an unwanted burden on society. Even the word "entitlement" has become a term with negative connotations.

But at a time when American society was prepared to set a baseline for government benefits for the poor, a minimum standard of fairness and dignity, Justice Brennan was at the forefront, injecting passion and real-world sensitivity into the debate.

Even as "welfare as we know it" is dead, that Brennan baseline still stands.

Government

Goldberg v. Kelly: Administrative Law and the New Property

Stephen G. Breyer

The Warren Court focused first and foremost upon the Fourteenth Amendment's equal protection clause, the promise of equal treatment that it held out to all races in principle, and the law's denial of that promise in practice. In carrying out much of its legal work during the 1960s, the Court asked simply whether a particular law or governmental practice was consistent with the constitutional promise that the amendment contained. It repeatedly found that the answer to this question was no; it thereby gradually dismantled the legal apparatus that supported segregation; and, in doing so, it helped to translate the Constitution's words into a practical reality.

This same attitude—comparing basic Fourteenth Amendment legal promises with current practical reality—informs much of the Warren Court's work in other areas of constitutional law, and particularly in Justice Brennan's most important decisions. *Baker v. Carr* (1962), for example, essentially asks why a democracy that promises individuals equal political rights should deny them equal treatment when they vote. *New York Times v. Sullivan* (1964) examines how to make the First and Fourteenth Amendments' promise of a free press a practical reality in the face of libel suits that threaten damages based on statements printed about government officials. No case, however, better illustrates the importance, the challenge, and the difficulty of practically implementing in today's world a basic constitutional protection—here, of procedural fairness—than does *Goldberg v. Kelly* (1970), a groundbreaking case that revolutionized administrative law.

The concept "groundbreaking legal decision" is, in a sense, an oxymoron. Courts as institutions normally apply the law approximately as they find it. And even when courts "create" law, they ordinarily have

The author is an associate justice of the Supreme Court of the United States.

stressed the many connections between new and old. The judicial task requires judges to understand both that they are not democratically elected instruments of change and that too radical a change threatens unfairness through the disruption of settled expectations. Nonetheless, law does change, even aside from changes in the language of statutes or constitutions. As technology changes, as the economy grows, as population increases, society itself may change, and consequently in certain areas of law, legal doctrine designed to serve an important set of human values may no longer adequately do so. Where that is so, judicial interpretation of statutory language, or judicial implementation of prior precedent, may become confused as tension grows between literal application and basic purpose. And, in that context, a judge may write a decision that, in a sense like a prism, casts old legal doctrine in a new light. That decision may force courts to focus on new questions, which, with hindsight, we see must be asked if the law is properly to serve its underlying objectives.

Goldberg v. Kelly is such a case. In that case the Court held unconstitutional New York's procedure for terminating public assistance payments to individuals whom New York considered ineligible. New York's procedure required a caseworker, believing that a recipient was ineligible to receive, say, Aid to Families with Dependent Children, to notify that recipient, to listen to his or her side of the story, and to provide the recipient with an opportunity to present that story, in writing, to a supervisor. At that point, if the supervisor agreed with the caseworker, aid was cut off (though the recipient then could subsequently obtain a post-termination "fair hearing" and restoration of the lost payments if he or she won).

Justice Brennan, writing for the Court, held that this procedure violated the Fourteenth Amendment's due process clause, which says that the state may not deprive a person of "life, liberty, or property without due process of law." The problem that he and five other justices saw in this procedure was its failure to give the AFDC recipient an opportunity to appear personally before the eligibility decision-maker, to present witnesses, or to confront adverse witnesses *before* the state cut off payments. The recipient's likely need for continued payments made the cutoff important; the failure to provide those pre-termination procedures made it unfair.

This deceptively simple decision turned out to be a critically important one. Its holding, based on easily understandable facts, suddenly brought into focus an entire field of administrative law—the field of constitutionally required procedural fairness. It did so by forcing lawyers and judges to ask two basic questions about the due process clause and thereby forcing them to reconceptualize the way in which they understood that area of law.

The first question concerns the nature of the interests that the due process clause protects. Just what is it that the government cannot take from a person ("deprive" that person of) without "due process of law"? In particular, when does a person's interest in a thing become important enough to count as the "property" that the clause procedurally protects? When do the Constitution's due process clause procedural protections come into play?

This question is important because of the major changes in society which, while taking place over centuries, had accelerated in the twentieth century. At least since the time of the Magna Carta, the law had gradually developed categories, such as the category of "property," which called into play a host of complex legal rules, including various procedural protections. Judged by the protections provided and the legal formalities involved, the most important kind of "property" was land, though other forms of property, such as chattels, money, or contract rights, received varying degrees of protection as well. Certain of the rules embodied in this legal structure might have helped protect thirteenth-century barons, unwilling to become Robin Hoods, against a powerful, but willful, monarch's whim of iron. Others would have given a typical landowner, say, John Smith, the owner of seventeenth-century Blackacre, the security he needed to build a house, to harvest crops, and to supply his household and his neighbors with food. In principle, Smith need not have feared dispossession by an arbitrary government, for he would have known that neither the sheriff nor any other government official could take his land and give it to someone else without his having had an opportunity to understand why they were doing so and to contest the validity of their decision under the "law," that is, according to preset rules and standards.

Now, consider Mary Jones, a twentieth-century lawyer. She and ever more men and women like her earn a living not by growing vegetables, but by selling services, and they depend upon the government for a license in order to do so. She may be unable to earn a living without that license. And were the state to take it from her, she may find it as difficult to obtain food or shelter as John Smith would have done without Blackacre.

Finally, think of Angela Velez, Esther Lett, and other individuals mentioned in the brief for the appellees in *Goldberg v. Kelly* itself. They received Aid to Families with Dependent Children and used those welfare payments to buy food and shelter for their families. Justice Brennan later wrote that, after their welfare payments were terminated,

> Angela Velez and her four young children were evicted for nonpayment of rent and all forced to live in one small room of a relative's already crowded apartment. The children had little to eat during the four months it took the Department to correct its [termination] error. Esther Lett and her four children at once began to live on the handouts of impoverished neighbors; within two weeks all five required hospital treatment because of the inadequacy of their diet. Soon after, Esther Lett fainted in a welfare center while seeking an emergency food payment of $15 to feed herself and her family for three days.

In terms of the individual's need for security, can one easily distinguish between landowner John Smith's Blackacre, lawyer Mary Jones's license, and welfare recipient Angela Velez's AFDC payment? Over the course of time, as the number of landowners diminished, as the government's regulatory powers expanded, and as the range of governmental activity increased, members of the legal profession asked these, and similar, questions with ever-increasing frequency.

One way the courts, before *Goldberg v. Kelly,* had tried to answer these questions was through the development of a distinction between "rights" and "privileges." Under this approach, government permissions necessary to engage in certain activities, particularly the practice of a licensed profession such as law or medicine, became "rights" that the government could not remove without "due process" protection. Other, somewhat similar permissions to engage in gainful activities, such as operating a liquor store, a billiard parlor, or a movie theater, were "privileges," which the government could withdraw at will. For the most part, government contracts, government employment, and most government pension, educational, and welfare benefits all fell into the latter category of "privilege." The grounds underlying many of the classification decisions were obscure. A 1965 Texas decision, for example, could not decide whether a license to sell cigarettes was more like a liquor license or a dentist's license. Moreover, the right/privilege categorization did not answer, but only continued to raise, the question of why one should distinguish, for purposes of procedural protection, among items that seemed similarly essential to an individual's basic security.

Another way the courts, particularly the Supreme Court, had tried to deal with the due process clause "applicability" problem was by avoiding any specific decision about whether a particular set of interests did or did not amount to constitutionally protected "property." Rather, the Court might apply a raw balancing approach, in which it considered the importance of the "interests" on both sides of the equation, regardless of whether or not the interest of the private citizen fit a formal definition of "property" that might also apply to Blackacre. In *Cafeteria Workers v. McElroy* (1961), for example, the Court held that the navy could withdraw Rachel Brawner's security clearance, thereby preventing her from practicing her profession as cook on the navy base. And it did so, not by considering whether the security clearance or her employment were "property," but, instead, by balancing the importance of her interest in cooking on the base against the navy's interest in absolute control over its security clearance system. This method of dealing with the applicability problem, however, seemed to make each case unique, thereby requiring the Supreme Court to intervene almost case by case, while still offering no guarantee that the welfare recipient or any other person dependent on predictable government behavior would obtain legal security in any respect like that which the law traditionally granted the owner of Blackacre.

One could not easily find an answer to the "applicability" question in any basic theory that sought to define "property." Certain institutional economists, such as Robert Lee Hale, and philosophers, such as Morris Cohen, had written in the 1920s that traditional legal "property rights" represent no more than a right (by those who possess them) to call upon the state to intervene in disputes over control of land, or certain physical objects, or other instruments defined by other laws. If one views "property" rights through such a "legal realist" lens, the right/privilege distinction simply becomes one way of deciding who has the power to call upon the state for protection. That theory leaves open the question: Who *should* be able to call upon that power? There is nothing, then, in that concept of property that decides that, if the landowner can do so, the welfare mother should (or should not) be able to do the same. And that is to say that calling one thing, but not another, "property" simply continues to raise, but not to answer, the basic question.

One might also look at property rights as a way of encouraging, say, economic development, in that those rights will encourage the owner of a piece of land to fertilize it, plant seed, and harvest crops, which "development" he might forgo were the land "common land" and were any resident of the community free to take, and thereby deprive him of, the fruits of his labor. This characteristic of much "property," however, does not focus directly upon the "procedural protections" that are the subject of the due process clause. Nor does it explain or justify the full range of entitlement that law has surrounded with procedural security, either traditionally or through use of the right/privilege distinction. Neither does it directly take account of the human need for economic security in an administrative state, where the government has become ever more directly connected with the lives of its citizens through regulation, the administration of grants and benefits, and the provision of a host of important services.

This simplified account is meant to draw a picture of pre-*Goldberg* legal uncertainty and "ferment." The role of government had changed, important human needs were at stake, and the relevant law and theory provided no certain answers. In a sense, the realities of the modern mixed economy were bumping up against the conceptual constraints of the legal doctrine of due process in much the same way that, as Thomas Kuhn points out, inconsistent empirical evidence and internal incoherences conflict with and destabilize scientific paradigms, prodding scientists to change the conceptual framework within which they address problems when further work within existing theory falters. Against this background the Court decided *Goldberg v. Kelly*.

Justice Brennan, writing for the Court, decided the "applicability" question by holding that the welfare recipient's right to continued AFDC payments triggered due process clause protections. That holding automatically meant that welfare payments were not "privileges" which the government could simply withdraw at will. And that holding thereby forced reexamination of the legal theories underlying legal procedural protection.

The opinion itself does not develop a theory of "property." Rather, Justice Brennan pointed out that the parties all had assumed that "procedural due process is . . . applicable to the termination of welfare benefits." He added that the benefits are "a matter of statutory entitlement," that their "termination . . . adjudicates important rights," and that their legal status as "a 'privilege' and not a 'right' " was beside the point. Justice Brennan then explained why the Court had to abandon the "privilege/right" distinction. He said, in a footnote:

> It may be realistic today to regard welfare entitlements as more like "property" than a "gratuity." Much of the existing wealth in this country takes the form of rights that do not fall within traditional common-law concepts of property.

And he then quoted a statement from Charles Reich, who had written about what he called "the new property":

> Society today is built around entitlement. The automobile dealer has his franchise, the doctor and lawyer their professional licenses, the worker his union membership, contract, and pension rights, the executive his contract and stock options; all are devices to aid security and independence. Many of the most important entitlements now flow from government: subsidies to farmers and businessmen; routes for airlines and channels for television stations; long term contracts for defense, space, and education; social security pensions for individuals. Such sources of security, whether private or public, are no longer regarded as luxuries or gratuities; to the recipients they are essentials, fully deserved, and in no sense a form of charity. It is only the poor whose entitlements, although recognized by public policy, have not been effectively enforced.

The opinion goes no further in answering the important questions it raises. It does not explain what other matters—aside from welfare benefits—are, or are not, "new property," to which the due process clause grants procedural protection. Like many significant cases in the common-law tradition, it leaves those determinations for the courts to work out in future cases.

The opinion, then, reflects concerns of existing law in ferment; it consciously rejects a prior unsatisfactory legal categorization; it answers a difficult basic question of principle affirmatively (in deciding that, for purposes of procedural protection, welfare rights are similar to Blackacre); and it forces future courts to grapple with the "applicability" question within that critically important constraint.

The second major question *Goldberg v. Kelly* raises concerns the "process due." What kinds of "process" does the due process clause require the government to make available? Judge Henry Friendly, writing a few years after *Goldberg v. Kelly*, identified ten elements of full-fledged judicial due process:

- An unbiased tribunal
- Notice of the proposed action and the grounds asserted for it
- Opportunity to present reasons why the proposed action should not be taken
- The right to present evidence, including the right to call witnesses
- The right to know opposing evidence
- The right to cross-examine adverse witnesses
- Decision based exclusively on the evidence presented
- Right to counsel
- Requirement that the tribunal prepare a record of the evidence presented
- Requirement that the tribunal prepare written findings of fact and reasons for its decision

Which of these elements does the due process clause incorporate as to the "new property"?

Prior to *Goldberg v. Kelly*, courts had on occasion stated that the extent of the process due was tied to the particular interest the process protected. Most cases in which the Supreme Court was called upon to apply the due process clause, however, were raised in context of traditional property rights, and the primary question raised was *when* must a full, trial-like hearing be held, rather than how much of a hearing is appropriate for the particular interest at stake.

In *Goldberg v. Kelly* Justice Brennan makes clear that, in the context of administration and the "new property," the answer to the question "what process is due" is "it depends." It depends, in part, upon the nature of the interest at stake. He writes, for example, that normally due process does not require a *pre*-termination hearing, even when a constitutionally protected interest is at stake. But, in the present context, where the Constitution protects *welfare benefits*, it does require pretermination procedure. That is because the

> crucial factor in this context—a factor not present in the case of the blacklisted government contractor, the discharged government employee, the taxpayer denied a tax exemption, or virtually anyone else whose governmental entitlements are ended—is that termination of aid pending reso-

lution of a controversy over eligibility may deprive an eligible recipient of the very means by which to live while he waits. Since he lacks independent resources, his situation becomes immediately desperate. His need to concentrate upon finding the means for daily subsistence, in turn, adversely affects his ability to seek redress from the welfare bureaucracy.

Justice Brennan's opinion then selects from among the various potential "due process" elements those elements that he believed would likely give the welfare recipient a practical opportunity to convince the decision-maker that a decision to terminate benefits would be erroneous. These include "timely and adequate notice detailing the reasons for a proposed termination," an "effective opportunity to defend by confronting any adverse witnesses and by presenting . . . arguments and evidence orally," the opportunity "to retain counsel," but at the recipient's own expense, and an "impartial decision-maker" who provides "reasons" for a decision that rests "solely on the legal rules and evidence adduced at the hearing."

The opinion thereby answers the "what process" question by emphasizing the importance of the interest at stake and by tailoring the procedures to those practically important in protecting the interest. In doing so, it recognizes the value of face-to-face confrontation and the ability to present and to refute arguments. It also emphasizes the need to decide the question at issue—the termination of benefits—in terms of a reasoned application of preexisting rules and regulations. As in the case of the "applicability question," the opinion illustrates, but does not present a worked-out theory about, the determination of what procedural elements are "due." It leaves the working out of any such theory to future cases.

The Court in later cases began to answer the questions that *Goldberg v. Kelly* left open. Two years after *Goldberg v. Kelly*, the Court formalized the two-step process inherent in Justice Brennan's approach. It held that, in answering procedural due process clause questions, a court should initially ask whether that of which the government had deprived a citizen was "life, liberty, or property." If so, the court would go on to decide what "process" was "due."

It then considered the first question in the context of "property." It held that, when deciding whether to apply the label "property," courts should take account of one important purpose "of the ancient institution of property," namely, "to protect those claims upon which people rely in their daily lives, reliance that must not be arbitrarily undermined." They should therefore look at other, nonconstitutional laws that defined the interest of which the government had "deprive[d]" the private citizen. If those other laws created a legal expectation of security—if, for example, they created a job (with tenure) or a (guaranteed) education or a welfare benefit that the government could remove only for "cause"—then the due process clause insisted upon "procedure" prior to the deprivation decision. If those other laws did not create a legal expectation of security—if, for example, they created a job (such as probationary employment) or a benefit that the government could remove at will—then they did not provide the citizen with a legal expectation of security and the due process clause did not provide procedural protections in case of removal.

The Court worked out an approach to the second problem, the problem of the "process due," six years after *Goldberg*. In *Matthews v. Eldridge* (1976), the Court held that the aim of the constitutionally required process was accuracy. The Court also used an "interest-balancing" approach to determine what particular procedural items the due process clause required. It would weigh (1) the importance of the claimant's interest adjusted by (2) the increased accuracy that the added procedure would likely provide against (3) the increased burden that providing that procedure would impose upon the government.

The Court's answers to *Goldberg's* questions have not worked perfectly. For one thing, defining "property" requires courts properly to interpret the state or other nonconstitutional law that defines the legal interest in question. And those interpretations themselves are often open to argument. For another thing, this approach sometimes provides procedural protections for comparatively trivial items (where the relevant nonconstitutional law closely circumscribes the government's removal powers), while denying those protections to other more important items (where the law gives the government greater discretionary leeway to remove).

Similarly, one can ask a host of questions about the "process due." Do hearings serve only to promote decision-making accuracy? If so, how does a court measure "added accuracy"? How should the court measure the importance of the claimant's interest? Should it distinguish, for example, among different kinds of welfare claimants? How does it balance the importance of the government's interest in avoiding procedures, as, for example, when the government peremptorily removes tenants it finds undesirable from housing projects in order to protect the remaining tenants from undesirably boisterous, violent, or drug-related behavior? Indeed, will the effort to achieve compliance with law, through procedural requirements, simply lead agencies to substitute detailed substantive rules (violations of which it can easily prove) for delegation of discretionary authority? Or will the opposite occur? Will agencies substitute unchecked discretion for substantive rules in order to bring themselves outside the definition of "property," thereby avoiding the Constitution's procedural requirements?

These continuing questions, however, simply show *Goldberg's*, and Justice Brennan's success. That is because the Court, in seeking answers to these questions, has accepted *Goldberg's* basic insights and basic approach as premises. It has found that approach superior to the obvious alternatives—the right/privilege distinction, the "all factors" balancing approach of *Cafeteria Workers,* and the case-by-case effort to decide when reliance is sufficiently important to warrant constitutional protection. And it has found necessary the continued effort to wrestle with the questions posed, if today's law is to protect valuable interests in a manner comparable to the protection that law in the past has offered comparable interests. Thus, administrative law has come to embody, as basic legal premises, that protection of "property," in part, involves protection of human reliance on, and the related human need for, security; that, in the modern administrative state, human security sometimes involves reliance upon government-related benefits; that "new" property and "old" property warrant somewhat similar treatment in this respect; and that certain trial-type procedural protections, including face-to-face contact between individuals and government decision-makers, comprise an important part of any such protection.

The law's acceptance of *Goldberg's* premises and its continued pursuit of the legal questions that it raised make that opinion a seminal opinion. Justice Brennan found the law disorganized, in the sense that basic legal doctrine seemed both confused and divorced from its underlying basic purposes; he forced the courts to reconceptualize that law so that it might better achieve those purposes; and, in doing so, he refocused legal effort and attention upon a new set of important problems and questions. But in raising those particular questions, he did more. He focused upon the fact that, in the eyes of the law, the pension or disability or welfare payment to an individual is as important to that individual as was land, in former times, to those who owned it. He explained the importance of every citizen, whether rich or poor, having the same kind of opportunity to present his or her case to an administrative decision-maker about to make a decision that, in an important way, will affect their lives. He emphasized the need for fair procedures in governmental decision-making. Justice Brennan thereby set forth an important view of how law, in an administrative state, relates to its citizens. He asked a simple practical question: Why shouldn't the Constitution's demand for fair procedures apply in somewhat similar ways to somewhat similar needs of both rich and poor? And in his efforts to answer that question, he did something rare in the law—he created a symbol, a symbol of the need for equality, dignity, and fairness in the individual's relation to the administrative state.

A Fair Shake and a Square Deal: The Role of the Administrative Judiciary

Jeffrey Toobin

Foley Square isn't. A pentagon, perhaps. Maybe octagonish is more like it. It can be said with certainty, however, that Foley Square is the place in lower Manhattan where Broadway, Centre, and Worth Streets collide in a jumble—and where New Yorkers go to find justice. The twin judicial colossi of the city mark the eastern border of the "Square," their matching pillars familiar to moviegoers for generations: the United States Court House, headquarters of the United States District Court for the Southern District of New York and the Court of Appeals for the Second Circuit, and its dingier neighbor, the New York Supreme Court. From Bernie Goetz to Henry Friendly—the "Mayflower Madam" to Learned Hand—the public faces of New York law have passed through their imposing portals (and lately, their metal detectors).

But justice is sought all over Foley Square, in the quintessentially American form of the hearing. On the twenty-third floor of the Municipal Building, the New York City Civil Service Commission conducts hearings three days a week for disgruntled city employees to dispute their firings, hirings, or promotions (or lack of same). Down on the ground floor of the Municipal Building, you'll see hearings at the Bureau of Parking Violations. Aggrieved ticket recipients make their cases before $180-per-day freelance judges, and a good 73 percent of the complaints win reductions or outright dismissals. Along the western edge of Foley Square sits 26 Federal Plaza, a veritable hearing dispensary. The vast bureaucracy of Social Security hearings begins on the thirty-fourth floor. Nationwide, an army of over 1,000 federal administrative law judges handles hear-

The author is a staff writer for *The New Yorker.* His most recent book is *The Run of His Life: The People v. O. J. Simpson.*

ings in federal agencies. (Two of these judges do nothing, full time, except cases from the Coast Guard.) Up one flight, the Department of Housing and Urban Development holds hearings on discrimination in federal housing projects. OSHA does its hearings on the second floor.

At 125 Worth Street, on the north side of Foley Square, you can go to complain if your application to be a mobile food vendor has been turned down. That's also where they held the noisy hearings on the citywide ban on smoking in restaurants.

Not long ago, there was a big statue—a great slab of rusting steel—sitting in the middle of Foley Square. By and large, the people who worked in the nearby buildings thought it was pretty ugly. After (what else?) a hearing, Richard Serra's *Tilted Arc* was evicted and sent to a new home at the General Services Administration's Motor Vehicle Compound (federal-speak for "parking lot") in Brooklyn.

Inevitably, Foley Square is also the place where many New Yorkers go for hearings about their welfare benefits. These hearings are held on the third floor of the state building, at 80 Centre Street. These welfare hearings are the lineal descendants of those mandated by Justice Brennan's opinion in the 1970 case of *Goldberg v. Kelly.* And so, in some profound sense, are all of the hearings held every day in Foley Square and in the hundreds of other Foley Squares around the United States.

Goldberg v. Kelly is one of those cases that is so big, its influence so persuasive, its implications so immense, that it is difficult to get a firm grip on it. To appreciate the case and its significance, it seems appropriate to start with Justice Brennan's own words. His opinion actually begins with a sentence that offers few hints of the enormity of what is to come. It is, rather, a sentence characteristic of the Brennan style: long but not convoluted, crunchy but clear. "The question for decision is whether a State that terminates public assistance payments to a particular recipient without affording him the opportunity for an evidentiary hearing prior to termination denies the recipient procedural due process in violation of the Due Process Clause of the Fourteenth Amendment."

To answer this question, Justice Brennan began with a deadpan review of the regulations governing the termination of welfare benefits in New York City. Two were most relevant. First, the authorities were required to give the recipient notice of the cutoff "at least seven days prior to its effective date." Second, according to the rules, "the recipient may submit, for purposes of the review, a written statement to demonstrate why his grant should not be discontinued or suspended." *One* week's notice? For what is, by definition, essentially the sole financial support for a family? *Written* statement? For a population that is, again by definition, underprivileged and thus probably not accustomed to, or even capable of, advocating for itself on paper? Justice Brennan thus immediately makes clear that whether or not the regulations are constitutional, they are definitely unfair.

Then the Justice turns to the heart of the issue. He asks, in effect, what difference this all makes. The government gave the benefits, why can't the government take them away? Welfare isn't real estate. In the words of the Fourteenth Amendment, is there any actual "property" at issue in this case? Why are the welfare recipients entitled to any "due process"? Why, in short, is the Constitution implicated at all? Justice Brennan observes that welfare "benefits are a matter of statutory entitlement for persons qualified to receive them"—and drops one of the most famous footnotes in Supreme Court history:

> It may be realistic today to regard welfare entitlements as more like "property" than a "gratuity." Much of the existing wealth in this country takes the form of rights that do not fall within traditional common-law concepts of property.

The footnote then quotes at length from an article by Yale law professor Charles Reich:

> Society today is built around entitlement. The automobile dealer has his franchise, the doctor and lawyer their professional licenses, the worker his union membership, contract, and pension rights, the executive his contract and stock options; all are devices to aid security and independence. Many of the most important entitlements now flow from the government: subsidies to farmers and businessmen; routes for airlines and channels for television stations; long term contracts for defense, space, and education; social security pensions for individuals. Such sources of security, whether private or public, are no longer regarded as luxuries or gratuities; to the recipients they are essentials, fully deserved, and in no sense a form of charity. It is only the poor whose entitlements, although recognized by public policy, have not been effectively enforced.

So it came to pass that William Brennan, the great justice, and Charlie Reich, the hippie professor from Yale, came to be joined in history.

Though less familiar, a later passage in Justice Brennan's opinion is today equally striking. "From its founding," he writes, the Nation's basic commitment has been to foster the dignity and well-being of all persons within its borders. We have come to recognize that forces not within the control of the poor contribute to their poverty. This perception, against the background of our traditions, has significantly influenced the development of the contemporary public assistance system. Welfare, by meeting the basic demands of subsistence, can help bring within the reach of the poor the same opportunities that are available to others to participate meaningfully in the life of the community. At the same time, welfare guards against the societal malaise that may flow from a widespread sense of unjustified frustration and insecurity. Public assistance, then, is not mere charity, but a means to "promote the general Welfare, and secure the Blessings of Liberty to ourselves and our Posterity." The same governmental interests that counsel the provision of welfare, counsel as well its uninterrupted provision to those eligible to receive it; pre-termination evidentiary hearings are indispensable to that end.

The passage is nothing less than a hymn to welfare, a summary of the moral, economic, and even constitutional basis for welfare payments to poor people—which is, in the political climate of 1996, a striking thing to encounter anywhere, much less in the pages of the *United States Reports*. This passage also represents the holding of *Goldberg v. Kelly:* No state may cut its citizens off welfare without first giving them evidentiary hearings.

As always in law—and especially with Justice Brennan—the words matter. To Justice Brennan, as he says, welfare is "not mere charity." To Justice Hugo Black, that is exactly what welfare is. "It somewhat strains credulity," Black wrote in his *Goldberg* dissent, "to say that the government's promise of charity to an individual is property belonging to that individual when the government denies that the individual is honestly entitled to receive such a payment." And that, at its core, seems to be what *Goldberg* is about—the nature and extent of a government's obligations to its citizens.

For the word in Justice Brennan's opinion that jumps out today comes from the first line in the Reich quotation: "Society today is built around entitlement." The word "entitlement" is a staple of political discourse in 1996; it wasn't in 1970. Indeed, much of the discussion in *Goldberg* reflects the date that the decision was announced, March 23, 1970. It was less than a year after Neil Armstrong walked on the moon. (Thus, one notices the passing reference to the government's "long term contracts for . . . space.") It was a little more than a month before the first

Earth Day, which prompted the government's first systematic efforts to protect the environment. It was, in short, during the heyday of the presidency of the man who expanded the American welfare state more than any other—Richard Nixon. Though nominally a conservative, Nixon reflected the temper of his time in his commitment to an activist government that not only deigned to help the poor, but legally and permanently committed itself to do so.

In 1996, it is nothing short of breathtaking that Justice Brennan, speaking for the Supreme Court, once conceived of an almost constitutionally mandated welfare state. In the articles by Professor Reich cited by Justice Brennan, the word "entitlement" is accorded nearly the mandate of law. The concept of "property," as defined by the Fourteenth Amendment, is meant to include a panoply of government benefits, including welfare. Justice Brennan, to be sure, does not go that far, but he asserts that once the government guarantees a service like welfare, it must act with the rationality and fairness implicit in the term "due process."

For better or worse, there is much in *Goldberg v. Kelly* that seems almost poignantly dated today. In current political discourse, the word "entitlement" is invariably preceded by the phrase "the need to cut. . . ." Those "long term contracts for . . . space" have probably long since expired. And Justice Brennan did not even allude to a far greater peril to welfare benefits than post-termination hearings. As we have learned in recent years, Congress and state legislatures can simply cut welfare benefits—and the due process clause can offer the beneficiaries no help. In 1970, it was taken for granted that welfare benefits would be going in one direction; the same in 1996—except down instead of up.

It must be said, too, that the so-called due process revolution symbolized by *Goldberg v. Kelly* has received some justified criticism over the past three decades. It is not at all clear that our society as a whole is better for all those hearings held every day in Foley Square. Even some liberals have come to see some virtue in the efficiencies of a patronage-based, as opposed to a hearing-based, system. To the law-abiding citizens of a housing project, the endless hearings and appeals required to evict a disruptive neighbor may seem dubious constitutional grace. Just how elaborate a hearing should the taxpayers stage for those disappointed would-be mobile food vendors? As for welfare itself, even its supporters in recent years may take a more jaundiced view of it than Justice Brennan. As Justice Brennan wrote, welfare "can help bring within the reach of the poor the same opportunities that are available for others." But so, too, may it create a culture of dependency that serves neither its beneficiaries nor the public at large. Justice Brennan's due process revolution has its critics, but my guess is the American people would find only one thing worse than this cumbersome duty of fairness: its absence.

Still, what is most remarkable about *Goldberg v. Kelly*—and *Baker v. Carr* and *New York Times v. Sullivan* and all the other landmarks of Justice Brennan's years on the Court—is its durability. To cite a parochial example of *Goldberg's* influence, I recall that I was assigned to read the case in no fewer than five different classes in law school: Constitutional Law (what does due process mean and who is entitled to it and for what?); Property (do welfare benefits count as property?); Civil Procedure (how much process is "due" process?); Administrative Law (how much process is "due" process—specifically?); and Law of the Social Welfare State (that course was practically about *Goldberg v. Kelly*). Through three decades of political buffeting, *Goldberg* is still, in more ways than one, "good law."

For all that *Goldberg* represents a landmark in the history of judicial activism, there is something old-fashioned about it. Justice Brennan does not suggest that the government, much less the courts, has an affirmative duty to solve every problem. But when the government does wade into people's lives, it has certain immutable constitutional duties: a fair shake and a square deal. One can scarcely imagine a more noble, or more American, legacy for a justice of the United States Supreme Court.

Federalism, the "Great Design," and the Ends of Government

Lyle Denniston

> In the compound republic of America, the power surrendered by the people is first divided between two distinct governments, and then the portion allotted to each subdivided among distinct and separate departments. Hence a double security arises to the rights of the people.
>
> —James Madison in The Federalist 51

> Perhaps our oldest question of constitutional law . . . consists of discerning the proper division of authority between the Federal Government and the States.
>
> —Supreme Court Justice Sandra Day O'Connor (1992)

> I do not think that a credible case for federalism can be made today in this country without a credible theory about the federalism that is embedded in the Constitution as a document of positive law.
>
> —Harvard law professor Paul M. Bator (1982)

Deep down in his judicial heart, William J. Brennan, Jr., has been a practicing federalist, "a devout believer in our concept of federalism," as he told a New Jersey bar gathering in 1976. To many Americans, perhaps, a Supreme Court justice's devotion to the idea of federalism is of no real-world consequence; federalism, the division of powers between the several states and the federal government, might be seen simply as a constitutional abstraction—something for remote scholars to debate,

The author is the Supreme Court reporter for the *Baltimore Sun* and is the author of *Reporter and the Law: Techniques of Covering the Courts.* The dean of the Supreme Court press corps, he began covering the Court during Justice Brennan's second term and has covered one out of every four justices who have ever served on the Court.

not something likely to filter down to human reality in everyday life. But federalism is a key to what the Constitution can mean to ordinary Americans, especially when it is understood as Justice Brennan understood it.

Federalism is a word that does not appear in the Constitution, but it is as much a part of the core of America's constitutional order as is the Bill of Rights. And to Justice Brennan, both constitutional federalism and the Bill of Rights were aimed at the same goal: "to protect individual freedom from repressive governmental action." He believed that, primarily because he embraced an elementary constitutional truth—the truth that "human beings are, of course, the intended beneficiaries of our constitutional scheme," in the Brennan-like words of Harvard law professor Laurence H. Tribe.

Even an ordinary American who has never thought about federalism would very likely have heard about and thought about the universally familiar Fifth Amendment right against self-incrimination. But until the Supreme Court decided a case involving a Connecticut gambler, William Malloy (in an opinion written by Justice Brennan), Americans had no Fifth Amendment shield when they were held by local or state police. Brennan believed that what benefited William Malloy in that case actually served federalism and the Bill of Rights, too.

Still, anyone who accepts that Justice Brennan *was* a federalist has some further explaining to do—especially in an era when a renewed call in Washington for "limited government" (a basic principle of federalism) surely means something different from Justice Brennan's understanding of the concept.

For the second time within a generation, Americans are debating, with great intensity, the nature of American federalism. It is a topic of fevered discussion among Republican conservatives newly in control of Congress as they press their near-revolutionary back-to-the-states agenda, just as it was after Ronald Reagan grandly proposed a "New Federalism" in his State of the Union message in 1982, early in what was to be "the Reagan revolution."

The question now being put, by the Republicans' Contract with America, is: "Isn't it time we got Washington off our backs?" Justice Brennan, too, has championed the idea that government—*all* government—ought to get "off our backs," but that is not the same thing.

A revived national debate over the proper role of governments at all levels reveals afresh that there is no universal definition of "federalism" in our legal or political lexicon, and no shared understanding of what "constitutional federalism," in particular, might mean.

Thus, in recounting Justice Brennan's contribution to the continuing national conversation about "our federalism," one must be careful not to put too much emphasis on the word "our." *His* federalism is not the same as the federalism of, say, Felix Frankfurter, or Raoul Berger, John Marshall Harlan, Newt Gingrich, Sandra Day O'Connor, or even Louis Brandeis. (Even within that group, one finds, of course, significant variations in perceptions of federalism.)

Defining a "true" federalism, in fact, has never been possible, and it would be quite absurd even to try. The very labels "Federalist" and "Anti-Federalist" among those of the Founding generation in the eighteenth century did not clearly convey what they believed the Constitution did or should ordain. Today, after considerable shifting of labels, one finds that a contemporary federalist, at least one identified by membership in the Federalist Society, is very likely to be perceived as one more attuned to "Anti-Federalist" thinking than to the "Federalist" perceptions of those in on the Founding.

Given the enormous deposit of literature on American federalism, it is possible to browse widely these days among competing, and sometimes conflicting, theories about what it is, and about what it must be to claim legitimacy. Even so, all must acknowledge that no one is free simply to conjure up a brand-new theory of federalism, as if any version of it were as acceptable as any other. Sooner or later, any "credible theory about federalism" (in Paul Bator's quite serviceable phrase) must be anchored in the Constitution.

Agreeing that the Constitution ought to be—can alone be—the source, however, is agreement only at the broadest level of generality. A "credible theory about federalism" is related, intimately, as Professor Bator also reminded us, to "a theory of interpretation" of the Constitution.

For example, constitutional historian Raoul Berger, in his ambitious attempt to synthesize one theory of federalism in a 1987 book, *Federalism: The Founder's Design*, told us where he begins: "For a 'proper understanding' of federalism, nowhere mentioned in the Constitution, we must look to the explanation of the Founders, what is characterized as the 'original intention.'"

That approach, of course, does not take us much closer to agreement on the nature of federalism. The interpretive doctrine of "original intent," we recall, was a central tenet of the constitutional philosophy of those who captained the "Reagan revolution," including then–attorney general Edwin Meese; today, it remains the guiding light of Supreme Court Justice Antonin Scalia and of his philosophical fellows in the ranks of the Federalist Society.

It is not at all clear, though, that this approach has ever attracted majority favor, however enthusiastically it may have been promoted. And, most assuredly, it was not Justice Brennan's approach. In remarks to a seminar at Georgetown University in October 1985, the justice said:

> It is arrogant to pretend that from our vantage we can gauge accurately the intent of the Framers on application of principle to specific contemporary questions. We current justices read the Constitution in the only way that we can: as Twentieth Century Americans.

And, in those remarks, Justice Brennan repeated the essence of a thought he had first expressed in an address on federalism to the Conference of Chief Justices in 1964. Said he at Georgetown:

> The genius of the Constitution rests not in any static meaning it might have had in a world that is dead and gone, but in the adaptability of its great principles to cope with current problems and current needs.

This, then, must be the beginning point for any inquiry into Justice Brennan's understanding of "our federalism," an understanding that he believed sincerely to be constitutionally grounded. Parenthetically, it should be noted that the first step on this path of inquiry ought to be the compelling work of one of Justice Brennan's former law clerks, University of California law professor Robert C. Post (especially the professor's "Justice Brennan and Federalism," in *Constitutional Commentary* in 1990).

As with virtually all of Justice Brennan's constitutional jurisprudence, his view of federalism was drawn from what he sees as the Founding document's "great design." Because the Constitution is a tapestry of governance, its "design" is to be found in the ends of government that it expresses, both as ideals and as working principles.

To some, of course, the primary end expressed in constitutional federalism is a structure, a design for the distribution of public authority between the national and state governments. This is the view reflected, for example, in the comment of University of Texas law professor Lino

A. Graglia that "federalism is a technique or attempt to share political power among sovereignties," with assurances of "a measure of local power as opposed to complete centralism."

Justice O'Connor had the same thing in mind when she suggested that the basic interpretive task regarding federalism was "discerning the proper division of authority between the Federal Government and the States" within "a system of dual sovereignty." It was unremarkable, therefore, that Justice O'Connor, in perhaps her most important opinion dealing with a federalism question (*New York v. United States,* in 1992), would borrow from the anti–New Deal Court of 1936 this thought: "The question is not what power the Federal Government ought to have but what powers in fact have been given by the people."

Justice Brennan's federalism has an entirely different emphasis. He has never harbored any doubt that the end of constitutional federalism was the same end of government toward which most if not all core constitutional arrangements had to point: "to protect individual freedom from repressive governmental action." That, he said, was "the great design" that the Constitution would not allow to be frustrated.

He therefore has seen that the structural distribution of powers, the creation of Madison's "compound republic" that would provide "a double security . . . to the rights of the people," was itself a part of that great design. "The federal system's diffusion of governmental power," he said in his 1964 speech on federalism, "has the purpose of securing individual freedom." The Constitution structured a government as it did, he argued, expressly to bring about "a free society."

At least equally important to Brennan, and very likely more important than the structural division of power, was the existence of specific limitations upon governmental power, as articulated especially in the Bill of Rights. "I do not think," he said, "that there can be any challenge to the proposition that the ultimate protection of individual freedom is found in court enforcement of these constitutional guarantees."

"Court enforcement"—that is a very important key to that thought. To Justice Brennan, the judicial safeguard that shielded "individual freedom" was not the antithesis of a federalist regime, because his enthusiasm for "court enforcement," as we shall see later, was not confined to enforcement only by the federal judiciary. The business of maintaining and expanding freedom through adjudication has been, to him, a shared enterprise—anything but a matter committed exclusively to the national courts. "Our federal form of government," with state and federal courts playing different yet shared roles, Justice Brennan said, "is the keystone of our scheme for achieving liberty through law."

Strange to Justice Brennan's ears, and alien to his beliefs, is the complaint of today's "Federalists" about the supposed usurpation by the federal judiciary of authority that belongs elsewhere. And he very likely would not be amused by a Harvard law professor's conspicuous disdain for a generation of lawyers and judges "infused with the romance of rights," as Professor Mary Ann Glendon put it in her 1991 book, *Rights Talk*.

The Brennan brand of federalism was not mere constitutional wordplay, in which a ritualistic incantation of the phrase "our federalism" provides only superficial justification, in lieu of real federalist substance. Three areas of Justice Brennan's jurisprudence best illustrate the kind of substance he was drawing from federalist principle:

- The reapportionment cases
- The full flowering of what is called "the incorporation doctrine"
- The call for a rights-based jurisprudence under *state* constitutions

Immediately, a present-day "Federalist" is wont to recognize the first two not as the outer manifestations of any theory of federalism, but rather as entirely the opposite: clear signs to a "Federalist" of the error of the modern Court's ways during much of Justice Brennan's service, signs to a "Federalist" of today that the Court had gone too far toward centralization of constitutional authority to the detriment of state sovereignty. Thus, those two areas have given rise to the most aggressive arguments that Brennan was not entitled to make *any* claim to being a legitimate federalist.

Justice Brennan, however, matched the theory of federalism that lay behind those criticisms (the theory that states retain an inviolate domain of authority) with a countervailing theory that buttressed his claim to be a federalist, after all.

Consider, for example, the challenge to Justice Brennan as a result of the apportionment cases, and his response anchored in his approach to federalism. The earliest of those decisions was a source of particular discontent for Justice Frankfurter, who often has been considered to be the keeper of a "one-true-faith" catechism of constitutional federalism. Frankfurter flatly accused Brennan of undertaking "to rewrite the Constitution" and of producing "a virulent source of friction and tension in federal-state relations" after Brennan authored *Baker v. Carr* in 1962, opening the federal courts to constitutional challenges to *state* legislative apportionment.

And, when the *Baker* decision led in time to its logical sequel in *Reynolds v. Sims* in 1964, Justice Harlan, a dissenter in *Baker,* assailed Brennan and the majority in the reapportionment cases for having "cut deeply into the fabric of our federalism" and of forcing "a radical alteration in the relationship between the States and the Federal Government." Pronouncing what he deemed to be the unforgivable error in what the Court had done, Justice Harlan called the *Reynolds* decision "nothing less than an exercise of the amending power by this Court."

From Justice Brennan's perspective, however, *Baker* and its sequels "strikingly illustrated" the importance of having explicit guarantees of rights in the Constitution, rights that had to be judicially enforced. In doing so, the justice deployed his own version of an argument that is usually claimed as the rhetorical property of more traditional federalists: the argument that the Constitution intended the states to be left free to function as laboratories, where the citizens might (in the famous words of Justice Brandeis in a 1932 dissent) "try novel social and economic experiments."

Brennan, accepting eagerly the role of states as laboratories, nevertheless argued: "Freedom of a state's citizens to experiment with their own economic and social programs is hardly meaningful if the political processes by which such programs must be achieved are controlled by only *some* of the people. The ideal is government of *all* the people, by *all* the people, and for *all* the people."

Although he was invoking peculiarly American verbal formulations, Justice Brennan was of the view that he was being guided by something that probably transcended the American experiment, perhaps reflecting the very nature of popular sovereignty in a democratic republic. One imagines him freely accepting the sentiment expressed so well by one of the champions of individual freedom in modern Czechoslovakia, Václav Havel, who wrote in a magazine article in 1968: "Democracy is not a matter of faith, but of guarantees."

To Justice Brennan, a formalistic sovereignty in the people, based on a pretense of democratic representation, meant very little in a state where politics was practiced in "rotten boroughs." And, to him, there was no guarantee that power at the polls would be made real without a constitutional guarantee of equal participation, fully enforced—by the courts, if necessary.

The principle guarantee at stake there, he suggested, was the citizen's "equal voice in his government," embedded in the Fourteenth Amendment's equal protection clause. "Our decisions . . . have reinforced this guarantee," he said, "and the result should be, not the return of discredited judicial intrusion into the field of political judgment, but a more effective operation of the processes by which political judgments are reached."

Justice Brennan thus supplied his own illustration of Robert Post's thesis: "Brennan's philosophy of federalism cannot be understood except as an outgrowth of his concern for individual rights." Post also has taught us precisely why Justice Brennan's view has been so starkly different from that of more traditional federalists: Brennan was unwilling to allow doctrines of structural federalism to act as a check upon the judicial enforcement of individual rights.

As Post put it, the reapportionment decisions showed Brennan's determined focus on "individualism," a focus which the professor said "means the death knell for federalism as a source of limitations on civil rights and liberties. . . . [F]or Brennan and the dominant members of the Warren Court, it was incomprehensible to appeal to federalism as a reason not to protect individual rights."

And, for Justice Brennan, it was equally incomprehensible to use considerations of traditional federalism to inhibit the growth of national rights under the Fourteenth Amendment. Here, too, Brennan has been met by critics with pained cries of constitutional illegitimacy; and, again, he has answered those critics.

His strong devotion to the doctrine of "incorporation"—by which he meant the selective absorption of the Bill of Rights into the Fourteenth Amendment, thus making them applicable to states—is well known. And while he hardly originated that idea (it can be traced back at least to the first Justice John Marshall Harlan in 1892, and perhaps back to Justice Stephen J. Field in 1873, and the sentiment underlying it may even be a legacy of Founding Father James Madison), Justice

Brennan became one of its most ardent champions during the years when the Court was led by Chief Justice Earl Warren.

By 1976, the year in which Justice Brennan pronounced himself to be "a devout believer" in federalism, the Warren Court—with Brennan enthusiastically providing internal leadership on the issue—had drawn most of the specifics of the Bill of Rights into the Fourteenth Amendment, giving very explicit meaning to that amendment's broadly worded promises.

The effort was idealistic in aspiration, yet thoroughly pragmatic in its effect. In an interview on the occasion of his eightieth birthday, in 1986, he repeated the idealism he saw behind the doctrine of incorporation: "There are certain fundamentals without which a society, civilized society like ours, could not survive." But, in the same interview, he defined its practical effect on the development of individual rights, especially the rights of those accused of crime.

He recalled that, when he was a state court judge in New Jersey, "there was never a federal question involved because none of the federal provisions of the Constitution applied to state prosecutions." After the process of incorporation, he went on, "then every state judge had to address federal questions, almost in every criminal case that he had to deal with."

He was then asked: "Is it your perception that the society is any less safe as a result of that?" He replied: "No, I do not think it is. . . . The very reason that we have the Bill of Rights and those protections of those accused of crime [is] that this is the way you measure a civilized society, how it treats those who offend against its laws."

There is no question that the "incorporation" process did change the face and substance of federalism for Americans. The process, according to the *Oxford Companion to the Supreme Court,* "has been the most important single transforming force in American federalism in the last half century."

And, of course, precisely because of this transformation, "incorporation" has drawn vociferous criticism. Historian Raoul Berger, for example, railed against what the Court had done with the Fourteenth Amendment, calling it derisively in a 1977 book *Government by Judiciary.* This process, Berger argued, amounted to "warping the Constitution," "undermining the rule of law," and engaging in a "continuing revision of the Constitution under the guise of interpretation." And the later efforts, by both President Ronald Reagan and President George Bush, to remake the entire federal judiciary were driven by a stubborn determination to take the federal judiciary off center stage in the resolution of the major social and political conflicts of the American polity.

Justice Brennan, however, has never blinked from the acknowledgment that the process of "incorporation" *was* a process of nationalization, a process that put the Bill of Rights clearly near the top of the national agenda—especially the agenda of the national court. In 1986, in the second of his James Madison Lectures, he conceded that the process had "radically altered" the work of the Supreme Court, causing modern constitutional law to "revolve around questions of civil and political liberty."

At the same time, Justice Brennan has seen no contradiction between the "incorporation" doctrine and constitutional federalism. In his first James Madison Lecture, in 1961, he argued that the absorption in the Fourteenth Amendment of specifics of the Bill of Rights *enhanced,* rather than diminished, the role that federalism played in the "preservation of our freedoms." It is clear from that assessment, of course, that he did not regard constitutional federalism and states' rights to be coextensive, as many traditional federalists tend to do. Justice Brennan regarded "excess emphasis upon states' rights" to be a threat to individual freedoms, including those expressed in the Bill of Rights. He did not regard federalism to be such a threat—provided that a federalist structure was not erected by judges as a barrier to the ever-expanding concept of individualism and the rights necessary to preserve it and make it grow.

In one of the clearest statements he has ever made to illustrate his hostility to a judiciary cowed by notions of state sovereignty, Justice Brennan said in that 1961 lecture: "Judicial self-restraint which defers too much to the sovereign powers of the states and reserves judicial intervention for only the most revolting cases will not serve to enhance Madison's priceless gift of 'the great rights of mankind secured under this Constitution.' "

While his primary commitment to "judicial intervention" grew out of his devotion to the "great rights" secured by the federal Constitution, Justice Brennan has long accepted that individuals' rights under state constitutions had to be nurtured, too. In the first James Madison Lecture, after mounting a full-scale defense of the "incorporation" decisions, Brennan turned to a project that he pursued thereafter with increasing vigor and urgency: encouraging the states to preserve rights under their own state constitutions, just as the Supreme Court was then doing increasingly under the national document.

"It is reason for deep satisfaction," he said in 1961, "that many of the states effectively enforce the counterparts in state constitutions of the specifics of the Bill of Rights. Indeed, some have been applied by states to an extent beyond that required of the national government by the corresponding federal guarantees."

This project has had a distinctly federalist cast to it. Justice Brennan was seeking to fashion a partnership of federal and state judiciaries, in the common enterprise of shielding the individual from repressive government action. Since the state judiciaries had virtually the last word on the meaning of their state constitutions' guarantees, any expansion of rights under those guarantees would be an autonomous act of state interpretation, largely if not entirely insulated from compromise or outright rejection even by the highest national court.

If one accepts Justice Brennan's premise, that "the only end and aim of government was to secure the people in their natural and civil rights," as he once put it, then there is no reason to see a different "end and aim" when the particular government exercising authority happens to be a *state* government. "Under our federal system," he said in 1976, "state courts no less than federal are and ought to be the guardians of our liberties."

As time went on, this project took on a strategic significance for Justice Brennan. As the post-Warren Supreme Court began hesitating to expand further the "great rights" under the U.S. Constitution, or actually engaged in curtailment of some of those rights, the Justice saw the state constitutions and the states' judiciary as a refuge.

"It isn't easy to pinpoint why state courts are beginning to emphasize the protections of their States' own Bill of Rights," he said in 1976. "It may not be wide of the mark, however, to suppose that these state courts discern in recent opinions of the United States Supreme Court, and disagree with, a pulling back from, or at least, a suspension for the time being of the enforcement" of the federal Bill of Rights through the Fourteenth Amendment.

The development of state constitutions as guardians of individual rights, he obviously believed, was a triumph of federalist principle. "Federalism," he said, "must necessarily be furthered significantly when state courts thrust themselves into a position of prominence in the struggle to protect the people of our nation from governmental intrusions on their freedoms."

And, in a kind of ultimate benediction on this development, Justice Brennan added: "We can confidently conjecture that James Madison, Father of the Bill of Rights, would have approved."

Opening the Courthouse Door

Herman Schwartz

Behind Justice William J. Brennan's twinkling eyes and unfailing good humor has lain a fervent passion for social justice and individual freedom. That passion, coupled with a shrewd instinct for the possible, has made him, in the eyes of many of us, the greatest Supreme Court justice of our time.

Because his arena was the law and his vehicle a court, he often dealt in what non-lawyers may consider mere technicalities. But these can be crucial. Disagreements over "mere technicalities" often reflect profound differences of philosophy and approach.

Nowhere is this more true than in the matter of citizen access to the courts, a seemingly hyper-technical area overgrown with concepts and doctrines so arcane that even judges, lawyers, and law professors find them bewildering. Even the polysyllabic formal name attached to this body of the law—"justiciability"—is both forbidding and unpronounceable. Yet a court obviously cannot promote justice and freedom if the victims of injustice and oppression cannot get into it. For this reason, Justice Brennan devoted much of his effort during his thirty-four years on the Court to making the federal courts more accessible to ordinary people seeking justice for their grievances.

Access to the courts involves a wide range of issues and topics. Considerations of space allow discussion of only a few in this essay: the political-question doctrine, the subject of Justice Brennan's first major contribution; the right to solicit civil rights lawsuits; and the nature of the interest needed to get into a federal court, what lawyers call "standing."

POLITICAL QUESTIONS: *Baker v. Carr*

In his memoirs, Chief Justice Earl Warren wrote that *Baker v. Carr* (1962), the decision authorizing the federal courts to decide challenges

The author is professor of law at Washington College of Law, the American University.

to the unfair apportionment of legislatures, "was the most important case of my tenure on the Court." It was the first major opinion enlarging access to the federal courts written by Justice Brennan (who had joined the Court six years earlier), and its impact is still being felt.

Those who expect to find in *Baker* a ringing endorsement of the principle of one person, one vote may be surprised to learn that, on its face, the opinion was a technical analysis of the political-question doctrine. The doctrine is a purely judge-made construct designed to exclude from the courts "questions in their nature political," as Chief Justice John Marshall put it. Just a few years before *Baker*, in *Colegrove v. Green* (1946), the Court invoked the doctrine in a 4–3 decision to dismiss a suit challenging the malapportionment of Illinois congressional districts. Writing for three of the four, Justice Felix Frankfurter, who had become the high priest of judicial passivity, explained that "this controversy concerns matters that bring courts into immediate and active relations with party contests. [It] is hostile to a democratic system to involve the judiciary in the politics of the people. [Courts] ought not to enter this political thicket." Under this view, the Court could not remedy even the most shocking disparities that severely diluted the votes of urban residents.

Nor was the problem a small one. In a classic 1957 article, *New York Times* columnist Anthony Lewis, then a Nieman Fellow at Harvard, reported that although

> the constitutions of 40 states require reapportionment of one or both Houses of the legislature every ten years or more frequently and three other state constitutions authorized decennial redistricting, . . . 23 of the 48 states have not been reapportioned for 10, 20, 50 years or more. For example, Alabama's legislature is constitutionally obligated to reapportion every ten years but last did so in 1901.

This inaction affected congressional districts as much as those of the state legislatures. Only seventeen states had made general changes in their congressional districts since World War II.

Lewis also noted some of the results of malapportionment:

> In Florida . . . about 17 percent of the population elects a majority of each House. In Oklahoma, entirely as a result of legislative inaction, a majority of the upper House is elected by 29 percent of the population and a majority of the lower House by 33 percent. . . . Malapportionment has an almost universal rural bias. One estimate is that in 1947 residents of urban

areas made up 59 percent of the United States population but elected only about 25 percent of the state legislators in the country.

A political system that systematically and unfairly favors some people or groups at the expense of others distorts and weakens the democratic process. To prevent the courts from checking such systematic unfairness because politics is a "thicket" is both disingenuous and pernicious. It is disingenuous because the Court has been enmeshed in "political thickets" of one kind or another since its inception, whether they be land deals in the early days, social welfare legislation in the nineteenth and early twentieth centuries, or civil rights litigation, abortion, and much more today. The Court has developed a skin thick enough to come out quite unscathed from the barbs and thorns of such "thickets."

The withdrawal of the federal courts from these issues was also pernicious for there really was no other realistic way to remedy the malapportionment. Justice Frankfurter's call for reliance on "an aroused popular conscience that sears the conscience of the people's representatives" is patently absurd. It relies on legislators' "seared consciences" to get them to commit political suicide, for if they reapportioned the legislature fairly, it would throw many of them out of their malapportioned districts. Politicians are not notable for political suicide on behalf of conscience, "seared" or otherwise.

The discovery that the only remedy lay in the courts made Justice Tom Clark switch his vote late in the course of the Court's consideration of *Baker*. At the conference at which the case was discussed, he was against the Court's getting into these matters, and had voted with Justice Frankfurter. At the latter's suggestion, he looked into other ways of dealing with the malapportionment problem. To his surprise, he found none.

The case was argued and reargued, and, on the first ballot, a bare 5–4 majority voted to allow the suit. Chief Justice Warren turned to Justice Brennan to hold together the shaky majority, as he frequently did. Justice Brennan not only held it together but wrote persuasively enough to secure Justice Clark's vote, ultimately producing a 6–2 decision, with only Justices Frankfurter and John Marshall Harlan dissenting and Charles E. Whittaker taking an abstention.

Justice Brennan's opinion went far beyond the apportionment issue. Reviewing all the precedents since *Luther v. Borden* (1849), the first "political-question" case, he analyzed the nature of political questions and why the Court avoided such issues. In order not to lose Justice Potter Stewart's support, he chose not to get into whether the Tennessee apportionment scheme itself violated the Constitution, leaving that to the lower courts.

What the Court did decide, however, was of far greater significance than the specific Tennessee case: From now on, citizens could get a federal forum for their demand that their votes be treated with the same weight as all others.

Unlike other groundbreaking decisions, it met with immediate approbation. As the late Dean Robert B. McKay reported in 1963,

> Before the end of 1962 at least a dozen legislatures had met in regular or special session to propose constitutional change where necessary and to enact statutory modification where permissible within the local framework; more than sixty lawsuits had been initiated in state and federal courts challenging existing apportionment formulas in at least thirty-five states; and public acceptance of the decision continued on the whole to be enthusiastic.

The impact of *Baker v. Carr* was immense—a reshaping of the electoral map as Americans moved quickly to use the judicial forum that Justice Brennan and his colleagues had made available. Rural dominance in an increasingly urbanized nation was reduced, and the exercise of the franchise was made much fairer. A few years later, Justice Brennan's analysis of the political-question doctrine was used to allow a unanimous Court to prevent the House of Representatives from excluding black congressman Adam Clayton Powell, Jr., of Harlem, against a claim that the issue involved a political question not for the courts to decide.

Access to a Lawyer: *NAACP v. Button*

Justice Brennan's second great contribution to the access issue, *NAACP v. Button,* came a year after *Baker v. Carr,* and grew out of the civil rights movement, one of the primary sources of Court business during Justice Brennan's tenure on the Court.

The legal assault on southern segregation was led by the NAACP and the lawyers it recruited and financed. Just as American business had used the pre–New Deal federal courts to blunt governmental efforts to control the economy, so the NAACP turned to the federal courts to blunt the southern defense of segregation. Despite their vastly differing goals, both the business interests and the civil rights movement acted on the understanding that the federal courts are more than passive observers or ratifiers of decisions by others—they are and always have been active participants in the great social and political issues of their time.

As part of the southern counterattack against the NAACP, in 1956 Virginia passed a statute barring lawyers from soliciting litigation. Six other southern states passed similar legislation. Though the laws were ostensibly race neutral, they were aimed directly at the NAACP, which solicited school desegregation cases and financed and generally controlled the resulting litigation.

The legislation was clearly intended to close the courthouse doors to the efforts to enforce *Brown* by crippling the activities of the only entity then willing and able to take civil rights cases to court. Because of threats, economic pressure, outright violence, and simple ignorance, few southern blacks were about to hunt up a lawyer to file desegregation suits. If they tried, few lawyers were available. As Justice Brennan noted with some irony, "Lawsuits attacking racial discrimination, at least in Virginia, are neither very popular, nor very profitable. They are not an object of general competition among Virginia lawyers." Unless someone actively recruited such litigation and compensated lawyers for their work on these cases, the courthouse doors were effectively shut and the constitutional promise of equality would remain a dead letter.

Nevertheless, the case was not an easy one. It was argued twice, first in November 1961, when Justices Frankfurter and Whittaker were on the Court. At that time, the Frankfurter-led conservatives produced a 5–4 vote to uphold the law. Before the decision was announced, however, Justices Frankfurter and Whittaker retired and the case was set for reargument. Justices Byron White and Arthur Goldberg joined the Court, and the vote switched to 6–3 for reversal, the two new justices joining the four former dissenters. There were different views about the proper ground of decision among the six, and again Chief Justice Warren turned to Justice Brennan to reconcile the differences.

He came close. In a landmark opinion for five members, with Justice White dissenting in one relatively minor respect, he established the principle that litigation was an exercise of the rights of expression and association protected by the First Amendment:

> In the context of NAACP objectives, litigation is not a technique of re-solving private differences; it is a means for achieving the lawful objectives of equality of treatment by all government, federal, state, and local, for the members of the Negro community in this country. It is thus a form of political expression. Groups which find themselves unable to achieve their objectives through the ballot frequently turn to the courts. . . . And under the conditions of modern government, litigation may well be the sole practicable avenue open to a minority to petition for redress of griev-ances.

Even the dissenters were persuaded by Justice Brennan's argument on this score. They, however, preferred to ignore the reasons this statute was passed, and treated it as if it were nothing more than a race-neutral conventional regulation of legal ethics, entitled to the presumption of good faith such rules would ordinarily get. The majority rejected so patently unrealistic a fiction, refusing to be comforted with Justice Harlan's soothing assurance that the NAACP could later challenge the law if it were being enforced discriminatorily against the organization.

Access to a lawyer is obviously the key to access to the courts, and the impact of the decision was very great. The First Amendment rights to initiate litigation that were recognized in Justice Brennan's path-breaking opinion in *Button* provided the constitutional basis for making such access a realistic possibility for the ordinary person. And not just in civil rights cases. In reliance on *Button,* a few years later the Court struck down a series of efforts to prevent labor unions from helping their members obtain legal help. Today, lawyers can advertise and even solicit litigation, especially for nonprofit organizations, and even for profit if there is no likelihood of fraud, misrepresentation, or other adverse consequences in the process.

STANDING

In one area, Justice Brennan's efforts to make the federal courts available to the ordinary person failed consistently: cases that deal with whether a litigant has the kind of interest in a controversy necessary to get into federal court as a party to that dispute, what lawyers call "standing." This is an area of the law that the Court's conservative bloc has made so convoluted as to fully deserve Hamlet's gibe at lawyers' "quiddities and quillities."

The purpose underlying the development of this conceptual morass has been made quite clear: to keep the courts out of the business of forc-ing public officials to honor constitutional principles and ideals of so-cial justice. This was the exact opposite of the goal of the Warren Court, as the *Baker* and *Button* decisions show. But those decisions were in the early 1960s, and after Chief Justice Warren Burger and his fellow con-servatives took over in 1972, things changed drastically.

Chief Justice Burger made his intentions quite clear in an interview with *New York Times* reporter Fred Graham published on July 4, 1971. There, he cautioned young people against becoming lawyers in order to seek social change through the courts, promising them "some disap-pointments" if they tried. Although the Burger Court did not wholly succeed in making good on this promise in most matters, thanks in no small part to Justice Brennan, with respect to enabling ordinary people to get into federal court it was quite successful.

The standard justification for a standing requirement, stated by Jus-tice Brennan in *Baker v. Carr*, is fairly simple and quite sensible: "to as-sure that concrete adverseness which sharpens the presentation of issues upon which the court so largely depends for illumination of difficult constitutional questions." The requirement is supposed to focus on the party, not the issue, on *who* can sue, not on *what* the case is about.

The first most important standing case of the modern era came in 1968, one of the last decisions of the Warren Court. The case involved a challenge by a federal taxpayer to a congressional enactment for vio-lating the constitutional requirement of church-state separation.

Taxpayer suits in state courts against state and local officials are com-mon; the Supreme Court had also allowed federal court suits by mu-nicipal taxpayers against municipalities since at least 1880. In 1923, however, in a very confusing decision, *Frothingham v. Mellon,* the Supreme Court refused to permit federal taxpayers to sue federal offi-cials.

In *Flast v. Cohen* (1968), an 8–1 majority changed course and opened the door to taxpayer suits challenging federal expenditures for parochial schools as a violation of the First Amendment's ban on an establishment of religion. The violation, of course, caused no direct economic or tan-gible harm to any one taxpayer. The harm was entirely psychic. Never-theless, Chief Justice Warren, who wrote for the Court, and at least some of his brethren, obviously intended to begin the process of allowing tax-payer and citizen challenges to governmental action that violated the Constitution. Two years later, a unanimous Court under Chief Justice

Burger followed up *Flast* with a decision giving standing to anyone who claimed an actual injury to some recognized interest—economic, environmental, aesthetic, or other.

With the arrival of Justices Lewis Powell and William Rehnquist in 1972, the climate changed drastically. For the rest of Justice Brennan's tenure, the Court worked steadily at reducing access to the federal courts, in the process developing a maze of confusing, conflicting decisions that make little sense. Again and again, vague notions of separation of powers were invoked. The only discernible rule seemed to be that plaintiffs in cases challenging official action lose—unless for some reason the Court wanted to hear the case.

Throughout this period, Justice Brennan consistently protested, almost always in vain. As early as 1972, a 5–4 majority threw out a challenge to the army's surveillance of lawful civilian political activity by subjects of the surveillance. The Court ruled they had not shown in their initial papers how their speech was inhibited. Justice Brennan dissented, saying that the aggrieved citizens "may or may not be able to prove the case they allege. But . . . they are entitled to try."

In 1974, a 5–4 majority refused to allow a constitutional challenge to the secrecy of the CIA budget, in violation of Article I, Section 9 of the Constitution, and another suit to prevent members of the military from serving in Congress, which clearly violated Article I, Section 6 of the Constitution. Again, Justice Brennan wrote the main dissents.

A year later a 5–4 majority systematically threw out every constitutional challenge under the equal protection clause to an ordinance barring low-income housing in a Rochester, New York, suburb. The plaintiffs included poor people seeking housing in the suburb, prospective builders and their organizations, taxpayer associations, and residents of both the suburb and Rochester. Every single claim was thrown out at the initial stage. Not one plaintiff was allowed a chance to try to prove his case. For example, a builder who had applied for a permit to build in 1969, and was denied, had his claim dismissed because he didn't try again in 1972, despite the obvious expense and inevitable futility of such an effort. Again Justice Brennan protested:

> While the Court gives lip service to the principle, oft repeated in recent years, that "standing in no way depends on the merits of the plaintiff's contention, that particular conduct is illegal," in fact, the opinion, which tosses out of court almost every conceivable kind of plaintiff who could

be injured by the activity claimed to be unconstitutional, can be explained only by an indefensible hostility to the claim on the merits.

There were other such cases. The Court reached a particularly low point in 1982, when a 5–4 majority refused to allow a taxpayer to challenge a gift by the federal government of certain property to a church. The property at issue had initially been purchased with tax funds and involved some $10 million in federal improvements. As the Court had held in the 1968 *Flast* case, if the government had given the *money* to the church, the federal courthouse door would have been open to the challenge that it is unconstitutional to expend federal funds to support a church. Since the government gave *property* which it had already bought, however, the Court reasoned that the transfer was not an "expenditure" and the courthouse door was shut. Again, Justice Brennan complained:

> It can make no constitutional difference in the case before us whether the donation [to the church] was in the form of a cash grant to build a facility . . . or in the nature of a gift of property including a facility already built.

Civil rights did not escape the Court's scythe. In *Allen v. Wright* (1984), two years after the church gift case, the majority threw out a challenge by black parents to a Reagan administration IRS policy that allegedly supported private segregated schools and made desegregation more difficult. The Court bluntly stated that its reason was a reluctance to monitor executive action and a concern for separation of powers, an amorphous and yet far-reaching criterion. As Justice Brennan wrote:

> [The] Court focuses on "the idea of separation of powers" . . . as if the mere incantation of that phrase provides an obvious solution to the difficult questions presented by these cases.

Justice Brennan went on to show how the policy could indeed harm the plaintiffs and justified allowing them to at least try to prove their case. But to no avail.

Professor Laurence Tribe has described the doctrinal progression, as follows:

> The Burger Court dramatically altered the constitutional focus of standing inquiry through its reassessment of how separation of powers concerns guide and shape the doctrine. Two decades ago [1968] these concerns ap-

peared relevant only by insuring that federal courts do not exceed their
. . . powers by entertaining claims of litigants pressing solely abstract interests founded on ill-defined facts, creating a danger that a judicial pronouncement could constitute a prohibited "advisory opinion". . . . [In 1984,
the Burger Court] announced that standing doctrine now was "built on
a single basic idea—the idea of separation of powers. . . ."

And he commented dryly, "Precisely how separation of powers
analysis advances doctrinal application of the standing inquiry may be
difficult to fathom."

Justice Brennan's inability to prevent the Court from erecting this
barrier to public interest litigation was probably inevitable. Once judicial conservatives took over the Court, the one sure thing was that they
would try to shut the courthouse door, for that was the key to everything else. His dissents, however, exposed this effort for what it was: a
deliberate campaign to exclude complaints, the substance of which the
conservative justices do not favor. It is far from accidental that virtually
all of these cases involve actions by individuals or groups on the liberal
side of the political and social spectrum.

CONCLUSION

Some judges fall into the habit of referring to the court as "my court,"
and treating it as their private property. Justice Brennan has always
known better. He knows that "we the people" had created a judicial system "to establish justice . . . and to ensure the blessings of liberty."
Thanks to him, we have a chance to approximate that ideal.

Universal Values and International Law

Jerome J. Shestack

The greatest contribution of modern international law to civilization is recognition of the inviolability of the individual. That universal principle is the bedrock of a just world order. And that principle—hallowing human worth and dignity—infuses the jurisprudence of Justice William J. Brennan, Jr.

THE INTERNATIONAL REACH OF OUR CHARTER OF LIBERTIES

Speaking at the Columbia Law School Bicentennial Celebration in 1987, Justice Brennan said:

> The vision of human dignity embodied in our Constitution throughout most of its interpretive history is, at least for me, deeply moving. It is timeless. It has inspired citizens of this country and others for two centuries. If we are to continue to be an example to the nations of the world, it will be because of our ceaseless pursuit of the constitutional ideal of human dignity.
> . . . The Constitution with its Bill of Rights, thus has a bright future, as well as a glorious past, for its spirit inheres in the aspiration not only of all Americans, but all of the people throughout the world who yearn for dignity and freedom.

Justice Brennan's view of the international outreach of our charter of liberties, with its vision of human dignity, would not have surprised our Founding Fathers. From the start, they were confident their vision

The author, a partner at Wolf, Block, Schorr & Solis-Cohen in Philadelphia, is the president-elect of the American Bar Association. He served as the ambassador to the United Nations Human Rights Commission from 1979 through 1980.

would travel beyond American shores. "That the world may know, in all present and future generations," said John Adams. And, in his Paris letters to Madison, the incomparable Jefferson described a bill of rights as "what the people are entitled to against every government on earth, general or particular and what no just government should refuse or leave to inference." Some thirty years later, writing to John Adams, Jefferson exulted that our example would serve as "a ralliance for the reason and freedom of the globe."

To be sure, the Constitution did have early impact beyond our shores. Even before its ratification was complete, the French Declaration of the Rights of Man paralleled our charter of rights. And in the century that followed, our Constitution served as inspiration and aspiration for a variety of liberal and revolutionary movements that arose in the wake of the Enlightenment. This early influence, as Justice Brennan has pointed out, had several causes. First, ours was the first written constitution in history; second, it came from a nation conspicuous on the world scene; and third, the Framers "took it upon themselves to proselytize the Constitution abroad."

Still, freedom traveled fitfully and acceptance abroad of our philosophy of rights was sporadic and often impermanent. The early promise of our Bill of Rights as a standard to which other nations would repair bogged down after its early impact. As late as World War II, repressive monarchies and authoritarian or dictatorial regimes ruled most of the world's developed nations. And the underdeveloped world was governed largely by colonial rulers, which, even if democratic at home, were repressive abroad.

In modern times, the renewed influence of our charter of liberties came in the aftermath of World War II, as the world reacted with revulsion against the Nazi era. Soon after the founding of the United Nations, it adopted the Universal Declaration of Human Rights, which drew heavily upon our Bill of Rights. At the time, there were 46 member states in the United Nations; today, there are nearly 200. More than two-thirds of the current national constitutions are less than fifty years old. Most of the new constitutions include guarantees of fundamental rights patterned after the American Bill of Rights and the United Nations Universal Declaration. So, too, the civil and political rights guaranteed by our Bill of Rights influenced the human rights revolution that swept over Eastern Europe in the late 1980s and early 1990s. In Eastern Europe, where many nations currently are engaged in constitutional revisions, our nation's charter of rights serves as the model for human rights guarantees.

Contemplating this renewed worldwide influence of our Constitution at the Columbia Law School Bicentennial Celebration, Justice Brennan reflected:

> There must be something about the Constitution's substance that accounts for its worldwide appeal. Three distinct characteristics of American constitutionalism coalesce to distinguish our Constitution as a human rights charter. First, is the very premise on which the Constitution is based—that government springs from the People. Second, is the Constitution's enumeration of specific rights that are guaranteed against government intrusion. Third, and in my view most important, is the Constitution's implementation of a mechanism—judicial enforcement—that makes those enumerated rights meaningful. Those three human-rights elements have, to varying degrees and in various ways, infiltrated their way into the constitutional schemes of our neighbors abroad.

Elaborating on these characteristics, Justice Brennan views the second—the limitations on a government's powers—as the most "auspicious attribute" that distinguishes our charter of rights. Yet, as Justice Brennan succinctly put it, "merely to enumerate human rights on paper is not to guarantee them. The rights of the people—even if expressly enumerated—are not worth the parchment they are written on if they are easily abrogated, unenforceable or anachronistic." The required elements for effective implementation of rights, he said, are stability, enforceability, and adaptability.

The stability is "not necessarily permanence, but resistance to abrogation," stemming from an amendment process that makes it extraordinarily difficult to diminish textual rights. It is striking that permissive amendments undermined most of the constitutions in other nations. And it is a telling affirmation of Justice Brennan's observation that many emerging democracies instituting new constitutions have taken pains to burden the amendment process with attributions to our Constitution.

Enforceability and adaptability are the other two elements needed to stiffen "parchment barriers." Lack of these, as Justice Brennan has noted, brought the French Declaration of the Rights of Man into desuetude and voided the panoply of rights in the constitution once heralded by the Soviet Union.

Justice Brennan finds the primary means to safeguard the people's will, as embodied in our charter of liberties, in judicial review—one "adaptable" to modern needs and conditions. Yet these elements of judicial enforcement and adaptability lay fallow during most of the history of the Bill of Rights. Essentially, it was not until 1925 that *Gitlow v. New York* started the slow march to incorporation of at least those rights deemed "fundamental" and essential to a scheme of "ordered liberty."

It took the "adaptability" of the Court during Justice Brennan's first two decades on the Court to impart modern relevance and vitality to our guarantees of freedom of speech, religious liberty, equality, and procedural fairness. To be sure, more than one mind contributed to this expansion; but most often, it was Justice Brennan who was the architect.

The new adaptability of our Bill of Rights to modern conditions had a salutary effect not only within our nation, but beyond the water's edge. Landmark decisions of our Supreme Court gave fresh meaning to the principles of the Bill of Rights and began to be studied by courts overseas. As Justice Brennan himself once observed, there developed a "vigorous overseas trade" in Bill of Rights decisions, as American constitutional law influenced not only the drafting of rights charters abroad, but the jurisprudence implementing those charters.

For example, decisions of our Court encouraged the European Court of Human Rights in the late 1960s and 1970s to render more expansive interpretations of the European Convention's rights and freedoms. So, too, Supreme Court decisions interpreting our Bill of Rights have often been cited and followed by Australian, Canadian, English, Indian, Irish, Israeli, and other courts, particularly in areas of freedom of expression, due process, equality of treatment, and the right to privacy.

It is not surprising that it has been Justice Brennan who is the justice most quoted by foreign tribunals. We know from judges, practitioners, human rights advocates, and government officials that Justice Brennan's decisions inspired foreign courts into channels paralleling those first navigated by him. And we know also that governments that are still considering the adoption of constitutional charters of liberties, such as England and Israel, look to Justice Brennan's advocacy of "an entrenched, enforceable bill of rights" to edify and to guide them.

Emerging from this review is the simple but significant point that our Supreme Court decisions are not only of vital importance to our own liberties, but have a much further reach as well: influencing the law of liberty in other nations to expand, as in Justice Brennan's heyday, or to retract, in the mode of the Rehnquist Court.

Spurring emulation of our charter of liberties abroad also has significant benefits in development of international law. International law requires a covenant or consensus. As more nations embrace our charter of liberties and Justice Brennan's expansive application of these liberties, the support builds for their incorporation into customary law with binding international effect. That is not a small matter. Put plainly, the way we interpret our rights and freedoms matters all over the world. And Justice Brennan's opinions have mattered most—both here and abroad.

THE UNIVERSAL PRINCIPLE OF HUMAN DIGNITY

To highlight Justice Brennan's influences abroad as a judicial exemplar of our liberties is an easy task. Far more complex, subtle, and seminal is his contribution to principles of international law in a Court that has hardly been a devotee of international law.

It has been wryly noted that the Supreme Court regards United States law as the "real" international law—one that other nations should follow, but without any mutual obligation by the Court to apply international standards cases here. The criticism has plausibility. In modern times, the Court has rarely invoked, or even discussed, international standards in crafting its decisions. But the Court's aloofness from international law is understandable. Even the American Law Institute does not have a Restatement on International Law, instead covering the subject in a restatement entitled "Foreign Relations." Moreover, international law is an odd assortment of doctrine, molded by considerations of peace, diplomacy, security, national interest, and other forces. During most of the history of international law, it has functioned as a system for coordinating clashing wills, rather than as an articulation of universal values.

Still, there is one area of modern international law that does articulate universal values: human rights. And it is in this vital area that Justice Brennan is more attuned to international law and more affirming of the underlying moral philosophy of human rights than any other justice in this century. To best perceive this, some history is pertinent, even if we traverse ground familiar to many.

The "unalienable rights" embraced by Jefferson and set forth in our first ten amendments did not rise newborn in Philadelphia in 1776 or in that hot summer of the Constitutional Convention of 1787. A good bit earlier, John Locke, Montesquieu, and other seventeenth- and eighteenth-century Enlightenment philosophers, expanding on themes of Grotius and Pufendorf, developed the secular doctrine of natural rights. This doctrine postulated that all human beings were born in a state of nature, which was a state of freedom. In that state, individuals were able to determine their actions without being subjected to the will or authority of another. However, because of the hazards in that state of nature, individuals entered into a social contract to establish a body politic—a government to provide its members with law and security. But government would be obliged to safeguard the individual's natural rights of life, liberty, and property. And if government neglected this obligation, it would forfeit its validity and office. This natural rights philosophy justified the revolution against George III, who, by denying the colonists their natural rights, forfeited his right to govern them. Jefferson's "unalienable rights" are essentially Locke's natural rights. The first ten amendments incorporated these rights in our Constitution.

While natural rights philosophy became embodied in our domestic Bill of Rights, the doctrine did not flourish in international law. One impediment was the constraining demands of sovereignty; another was the daunting task of determining which rights were natural and unalienable. Moreover, competing philosophies of positivism and utilitarianism soon come to the fore. Positivism emphasized the supremacy of national law unrestrained by inherent rights, while utilitarianism permitted subjugation of the individual to the greater good. Under these philosophies, in vogue during the nineteenth century and a good part of the twentieth, there was little room for any *a priori* source of rights above the state.

Whatever the conceptual or political reasons, until World War II international law was not developed sufficiently to sort out competing philosophies. The law of nations continued to focus on state relations with little regard for the status of individual rights.

The real impetus for an international protection of human rights arose from the Nazi experience and the tragedy of the Holocaust. As World War II wound down, the world became aware of the horror wrought by a positivist system such as that in Nazi Germany in which the individual counted for nothing. It is not surprising that there should emerge a renewed search for immutable principles which would protect humanity against such brutality.

What developed and became embodied in the United Nations Charter and the Universal Declaration of Human Rights was a qualified natural law approach, marked by an attempt to identify values having a universal call. Here, the moral philosophic underpinning came from Immanuel Kant's compelling ethic. Kant's ethic maintains that the moral law needs a categorical foundation that must be *prior* to all purposes and ends. That basis is the individual capable of exercising an autonomous will. Rights then flow from the autonomy of the individual in choosing his or her ends, consistent with a similar freedom for all. In short, Kant's great imperative is that the central focus of morality is personhood, namely, the capacity to take responsibility as a free and rational agent for one's system of ends.

A natural corollary of this Kantian thesis is that the highest purpose of the state is to promote conditions favoring the free and harmonious unfolding of individuality. Kant's theory being transcendental, also *a priori* and categorical (all amount to the same thing), it overrides all arbitrary distinctions of race, creed, and custom and is universal in nature.

Stated simply, the universal normative value that modern international law has bestowed on civilization is that of the *inviolability* of the individual. Rights preserving the integrity of the person flow logically from the fundamental freedom and autonomy of the person. So does the principle of nondiscrimination that must attach to any absolute concept of autonomy. One can articulate these concepts as "human dignity," "human worth," or "unalienable rights"—all amount to the recognition of the individual as an autonomous being.

This universal value permeates Justice Brennan's constitutional philosophy. Resonating through his opinions and addresses is reverence for "human dignity." The words "human dignity" or "dignity of man" do not appear in the Constitution. But Justice Brennan regards safeguarding "human dignity" as the overall aim of our charter of liberties and as a critical test by which to judge adherence or violation of that charter.

Even before his nomination, Justice Brennan affirmed that the American system was "based upon the dignity and individuality of the individual soul." In his Cardozo Lecture (1988), Justice Brennan said, "Due process required fidelity to a more basic and more subtle principle: the essential dignity and worth of each individual." In one sentence, he articulated the basic questions to test observance of international human rights: "whether government has treated someone fairly, whether individual dignity has been honored, whether the worth of an individual has been acknowledged." In his Holmes Lecture at Harvard (1986), he repeated, "Even the vilest criminal remains a human being possessed of common human dignity." And even at his ninetieth birthday celebration at the Supreme Court, Justice Brennan pleaded for abolishment of the death penalty, affirming once again his passionate commitment to human worth.

So, too, the creed of human dignity courses through Justice Brennan's life on the Court. As Chief Justice Earl Warren observed in his moving *Harvard Law Review* tribute (1966): "His belief in the dignity of human beings—all human beings—is unbounded. . . . These beliefs are apparent in the warp and woof of all his opinions." Thus, Justice Brennan wrote in *Goldberg v. Kelly* (1970): "the Nation's basic commitment has been to foster the dignity and well-being of all persons within its borders." In *Furman v. Georgia* (1972): "Death stands condemned as fatally offensive to human dignity." In *Smith v. Foster Families* (1977): "The liberty interest in family privacy has its source . . . in intrinsic human rights." In *Owen v. City of Independence* (1980): Constitutional interpretation must be "in aid of the preservation of human liberty and human rights." There are many more such statements.

Most often Justice Brennan's hallowing of the individual, while expressed in terms of universal application, has been set in the context of domestic constitutional law. But when the opportunity was presented, he brought our domestic jurisprudence into harmony with international law, providing at the same time a deeper insight into the values underlying the international law prescriptions.

Two cases involving different rights, one in the area of capital punishment, the other regarding rights of aliens, well illustrate Justice Brennan's fusing of constitutional and international principles in furtherance of human dignity.

Stanford v. Kentucky (1989) presented the issue whether the death sentence imposed on a seventeen-year-old juvenile violated the Eighth Amendment's prohibition of cruel and unusual punishment. The standard that had been articulated by Chief Justice Warren in *Trop v. Dulles* (1958) and in earlier decisions was whether the punishment contravened the "evolving standards of decency that mark the progress of a maturing society." Now, Justice Scalia, writing for the majority, emasculated that standard, limiting it to "American conceptions of decency." These conceptions, Justice Scalia said, supported the death penalty; and, he curtly denied the relevance of the sentencing practices in other countries. Justice Scalia did not even deign to mention the international covenants and resolutions pertinent to the issue.

Justice Brennan's dissent rejected the majority's jingoism. "The choices of governments elsewhere in the world," he said, "also merit our attention as indicative whether a punishment is acceptable in a civilized society." The fact that the death penalty for juveniles was rejected by the International Covenant on Civil and Political Rights, the European Convention on Human Rights, the 1949 Geneva Conventions, by resolutions and decisions of various United Nations bodies, and generally throughout the world "provide to my mind a strong grounding" that the execution of adolescent offenders is not tolerable.

Even more, Justice Brennan took on the majority's conclusions that the death penalty accorded with current American conceptions of decency. Even if that were so, it was not enough: "A penalty must also accord with the 'dignity of man' which is the basic concept underlying the Eighth Amendment." Thus, the universal value of human dignity was the overriding concept to be protected, whether or not in accord with the current majority.

Another example further illustrates the point. In *United States v. Verdugo-Urquidez* (1990), the Rehnquist Court ruled that the Fourth Amendment did not apply to warrantless searches of an alien's residence in Mexico by U.S. law enforcement officials. The majority's rationale for that ruling was that the Fourth Amendment only protects "people," and "people" refers only to a class of persons "who are part of a national community or who have otherwise developed sufficient connection with this country to be considered part of that community."

Justice Brennan dissented. He first criticized the majority for requiring an alien to adhere to U.S. law, while not recognizing a correlative right to constitutional protection. He then alluded to the long-standing tenet of international law: "By respecting those rights of foreign nationals, we encourage other nations to respect the rights of our citizens." But Justice Brennan did not rest only on the reciprocal benefits of mutuality. He turned to a higher ground of underlying values:

Mutuality also serves to inculcate the value of law and order. . . . If the government becomes a lawbreaker, it breeds contempt. . . . For over 200 years, our country has considered itself the world's foremost protector of liberties. The privacy and sanctity of the home have been primary tenets of our moral, philosophical and judicial beliefs. . . . We exhort other nations to follow our example. How can we explain to others—and to ourselves—that those long cherished ideals are suddenly of no consequence when the door being broken belongs to a foreigner?

In this instance, as in others, Justice Brennan endorsed international human rights principles and brought them into the compass of our own Constitution.

Where, Then, Do We Stand?

It would be cheering to say that Justice Brennan's universalist vision of human rights based on individual worth and dignity is now accepted doctrine here and worldwide. But, in fact, his vision is under siege. It is beset abroad by repressive rulers who derogate human rights under the guise of national security. It is under attack by cultural relativists who claim there are no human rights absolutes, that all cultures are equally valid, and that truth is just for a time or place. It is also besieged at home by those who manipulate theories of "original intent" or pose majoritarian rationales to constrain individual rights.

In this climate, Justice Brennan's vision of individual dignity remains an affirming flame, warming the hopes and spirits of those who labor to advance human rights.

What of the Future?

The road to recognition of individual human rights has been arduous, slow, and painful, both at home and internationally. Though the course is still not secure, we have come to acknowledge that human dignity is a universal value. That alone is a heartening advance. But, as Justice Brennan said on his ninetieth birthday, we have not yet achieved a comprehensive definition of the "ideal of human dignity." As civilization progresses, so does our understanding of the rights and liberties that develop and nourish the human being. International human rights obligations, especially economic, social, and cultural rights, already encompass more rights than those now considered within our charter of liberties. Whether, and how soon, we shall enlarge our own compass of rights, through recognition of international law or through deeper under-standing of due process and equal protection, remains uncertain. But, if that will be done, then the guiding moral concept must be Justice Brennan's vision of human dignity.

For Justice Brennan, the "foundation of freedom, justice and peace in the world" lies in recognition of "the inherent dignity and of the equal and inalienable rights of all members of the human family." That vision captures the moral philosophy of a just world order.

Perspectives

Justice Brennan's Place in Legal History

DAVID H. SOUTER

Without the authority of Holmes's caution that certitude is not the test of certainty, this Festschrift volume would hold no place for me or my subject. For my allotment is to say a few words on Justice Brennan's place in history, a subject that calls for nothing but the obvious (and therefore no more than a few words and no historian to utter them). I feel, in fact, an uncommon inclination to be brief, to speak to the matter merely with a question: Is there any reason to doubt William Brennan's place in history? Of course not. No one needs shoring up on that issue.

One has only to look at the deluge of secondary evidence. In the mere six years since the Justice retired, the law reviews have produced some forty tributes, two biographies have come on the market, and Steven Wermeil is within sight of completing the authorized life after years of the scholarship the subject calls for. Now there is even this book of celebration to add to the list. Nor can all of this be discounted as just friendly effusion coming well ahead of the critical exercise of ranking by importance, for Justice Brennan had not even finished his second decade on the Court before one survey was putting him into the "near great" category, and the most recently published pronouncement on Supreme Court caliber puts him up in the top ten. All of this, admittedly, is happening a little too soon to qualify as "history," but it's enough to tell us what's really up.

The closest approach, indeed, that I can make to any qualification of our common assumption of Justice Brennan's historical significance is merely to ask an obligatory question in this age of specialization: Just where in history's domain are the Justice and his work going to be most at home? I recall some reading I happened to do in law school, not in

The author is an associate justice of the Supreme Court of the United States. He assumed Justice Brennan's seat on the Court in 1990.

a book assigned for any course, but in an antidote to the required read-ing. Samuel Eliot Morison's *Oxford History of the American People* left me with the impression, thirty years ago, that judges make a fairly mod-est splash in the general reader's history, and a recent look at the index to Morison's volume confirms the old impression. The Supreme Court has its place in the pageant, of course, with dozens of references to the institution and its individuals. But a good many of its justices turn up as much in pre-judicial incarnations as in robes (Jay, Hughes, or even Holmes, for example), and only the most careful student will likely re-call much about the Court beyond *Marbury* and *McCulloch, Dred Scott* and *Plessy,* the 1937 turnaround, and *Brown.* As for individuals, the first Marshall will stand out in most readers' minds, and so may Warren and Taney as pendant objects of current popular esteem and its opposite, but mostly it will be the notetakers who register anything about Story or Chase, or the first Harlan or Black. The reasons for this are not hard to see, being to the discredit neither of general historians nor of justices. It is actually a matter of the Court's good luck to lend itself only rarely to the dramatic narrative, and to be staffed with judges only rarely hav-ing the swagger of generals, the magnetism of great politicians, or enough popular identification to personify the force of some vast social shift. I know: Not many generals could out-swagger Holmes, Warren was not short on magnetism, and the second Marshall stood unmis-takably for the civil rights movement whose lawyer he had been. But these are the exceptions, and few enough. Readers of general history books seem not to cry out for fewer wars and more judges.

What this tells us, though, is not that history only lights on a jus-tice who happens to have been the institution's de facto founder, or in-vited a civil war, or lent the Court his name at some moment when constitutional perception shifted. Morison's *History* simply tells us not to look for the judges in competition with wars and political landslides. Judges having been chosen to live in the nation's law, not its politics or its armies, it is in legal and judicial history that a judge's achievements live in the retelling, and it is there on that particular shelf of history's books that our instinctive confidence places the figure of Justice Bren-nan. The primary evidence bears out our intuition.

Let us start with numbers. When Justice Blackmun was the Court's personal statistician, he'd usually begin his report at the end of a Friday conference with the words, "Well, Chief, the numbers tell the story." And the first signal that Justice Brennan is on his way into history is the very number, the mass, of opinions piled up over thirty-four terms. He wrote a grand total of 1,360 of them from *Putnam et ux. v. Commissioner of Internal Revenue* (1956) through *Metro Broadcasting, Inc. v. FCC* (1990), and even after subtracting per curiams, chambers opinions, and dissents from denials of certiorari, there are still nearly 1,200 left. Among them, leaving aside concurring opinions, separate opinions, and mixtures of the two, 461 for the majority win out over 425 dissents. In sheer quantity, only Justice Douglas rivals him, and no historian who looks back at the case reports of this century's second half will ever be able to resist the gravitational pull of the Brennan production.

But the numbers are only prefatory. Just as the historians of politics and war find the pleasure of their craft in spying out the subtleties lying beyond the voting totals and casualty figures, so historians of constitutional ideas look for the telling details along the way that lead to a mature doctrine, the quiet moves of shrewdness that affect the law's direction. They will revel in Brennan examples, as their precursors are finding out already. Consider what happened in *Shapiro v. Thompson* (1969), for example.

Shapiro began with a challenge to a one-year residence requirement for getting state welfare benefits. The restriction was held to violate equal protection, and the opinion by Justice Brennan stands for the rule that a classification turning on the exercise of a fundamental constitutional right (in that case, the right to travel) is invalid unless it can survive strict scrutiny, as being necessary to serve a compelling state interest. The case has puzzled commentators, who have asked what is gained by subjecting the abridgment of a fundamental right to strict scrutiny under the equal protection clause, when any abridgment of a fundamental right would be scrutinized strictly without even bringing equal protection into the analysis. There is an answer. While there may even be a doctrinal answer in so-called equal allocation cases, my guess is that *Shapiro* is important not as a source of doctrine that in theory could not have taken shape without equal protection, but for its author's use of equal protection to get a result (and a resulting doctrine) that might not in fact have occurred any other way. So *Shapiro's* history suggests.

The case was argued twice. When it was considered first, in the 1967 term, there was a majority for holding state-imposed durational residence requirements for welfare recipients constitutional, because they were authorized by Congress in a valid exercise of Article I power. The Brennan papers show that Justice Fortas planned a dissent on the grounds that the state law violated both the right to travel and the equal protection clause. Justice Brennan said he would join a Fortas opinion on travel but not on equal protection. As it turned out, the case was put down for reargument, Justice Fortas resigned, and Justice Brennan found himself not dissenting but writing for a majority, with an opinion not only turning on equal protection, but equal protection at the strictest level (whereas an old Fortas draft would have applied nothing more than rational basis scrutiny). "Since the classification here touches on the fundamental right to interstate movement," Justice Brennan wrote, "its constitutionality must be judged by the stricter standard of whether it promotes a *compelling* state interest. Under this standard, the waiting period requirement clearly violates the Equal Protection Clause."

What if the Court had not relied on equal protection? It would have had to decide on the limits of the right to travel, in order to know whether temporary denial of welfare benefits to recent interstate travelers abridged the right. But seeing the case in terms of equal protection made it easy to invoke the fundamental travel right without seeming to confront the hard job of giving it exact definition. All the Court had to do was to hold that a ground of difference (recent arrival in the state) did not count for equal protection purposes (absent a compelling state justification) if it was a fact dependent on an exercise of a fundamental right (interstate travel). And of course it did so depend; like most recent arrivals, Thompson came from another state. That was all a court had to know. Equally certain is the fact that after equal protection had done its work, the right to travel stood implicitly defined with a greater precision, but that precision was only the natural by-product of an ostensibly easier exercise than confronting travel head-on and defining its limits. The choice of equal protection as a rationale was a tactical one for a justice who knew which direction he wanted the law to travel.

Seen in this light, as an example of finesse in the process of getting others to decide, *Shapiro* does not seem quite so lonely, quite so much the analytical sport, as it appears to be in its purely doctrinal guise. For what Justice Brennan did in *Shapiro* he did again not long after in *Eisenstadt v. Baird* (1971). The challenge in *Eisenstadt* was to a Massachusetts statute forbidding dispensation of contraceptives to an unmarried person for the purpose of birth control (rather than health protection). After eliminating some conceivable justifications for the ban, the Court came to the point at which the statute could be explained only on the theory that the use of a birth control device was per se immoral. The questions directly presented were thus whether the legislative judgment of immorality, absent further harm to someone, expressed a state interest adequate to justify the prohibition, and at what level of scrutiny. So understood, the final issue in the case was one of substantive due process, which had been resolved in favor of the statute by the court of appeals.

But Justice Brennan, writing for the Court, stepped back from the due process issue. Instead of addressing it, his opinion added both a fact and a recharacterization of prior law, and turned the issue into equal protection. The fact was that the statute imposed no ban on dispensing and using a device for contraception when the recipient was married. The recharacterization came as if in passing, when the Justice observed that of course it was proper to treat the married person using a contraceptive as an individual, not just one of a pair, that the right of privacy recognized in *Griswold v. Connecticut* (1965) (dealing with advice to a married couple about contraception) was the privacy of each of two separate persons, who merely happened to be joined in holy matrimony. Once it was established that two individuals, alike in their respective interests in reproductive privacy, were differently treated under the statute, there was a simpler way to decide the case than by ruling on the constitutional status of morality per se as a ground of criminal liability. There was no need even to give the right in question a definite rank in the hierarchy of constitutional values; rational basis scrutiny would seemingly do. It is hard not to think of the mind of John Marshall, as one reads Justice Brennan drawing the Court back from facing the sufficiency of substantive morality, only to strike the fatal blow to unequal treatment.

So, *Shapiro* and *Eisenstadt* may be seen as companion pieces of Brennan equal protection. In one case, an added constitutional fact about the claimant sealed the statute's fate (the novelty of her residence followed her exercise of a fundamental right); in the other, an added proposition about a third party controlled the outcome (a married person is just an individual for purposes of reproductive privacy). But each decision was an act of tactical skill in adding facts to convert an issue into equal protection from something else. Anyone who earns his pay by appellate judging has to see Brennan the tactician the way joggers see marathoners. And down the road, historians looking for truth in the details of doctrinal growth will find plenty of Brennan details to repay their pains.

The historians will take those pains, too, for so much of our century's doctrine grew in the text of Brennan opinions. Could, a century hence, the scholars possibly overlook the author of *Baker v. Carr* (1962), for example? Before *Baker, Colegrove v. Green* (1946) typified the law that legislative districting controversies raised nonjusticiable political questions. But *Colgrove* went down in the face of Justice Brennan's opinion for the Court in *Baker,* holding that a claim of legislative malapportionment simply raised a question of "the consistency of state action with the Federal Constitution." A matter was no longer nonjusticiable just because it touched on matters of state governmental organization. *Baker* opened a door, and through it passed *Reynolds v. Sims* (1964) and *Oregon v. Mitchell* (1970), notwithstanding Justice Harlan's powerful dissenting view on the scope of the Fourteenth Amendment. The first case held claims of vote dilution cognizable under the equal protection clause, while the second in large part sustained the 1970 legislation on voting qualifications. *Baker,* indeed, opened an epoch of voting rights litigation that continues in full swing even as I write this. Its author has no hope of obscurity.

Or could history possibly ignore the justice who wrote *New York Times v. Sullivan* (1964), which famously raised the First Amendment bar to a public official's recovery of damages for defamatory falsehood bearing on his official capacity, unless he shows what has come to be called "*Times* malice," the speaker's knowledge of the falsity or his reckless disregard of it? Beyond its first-tier doctrinal position as a constitutional limit on the common law of defamation, the case (as Cass Sunstein points out) can be read as an implicitly broader statement about the relationship between state action and the common-law background. To be sure, the latter statement has yet to be worked out, and the first-tier doctrine is subject to continuing objection that the wrong party got charged with the price of the speech. All of that, however, is just to say that history will have more than one reason for interest in the *Times* case, and one of those reasons will be its significance as verbal icon: Justice Brennan's "profound national commitment to the principle that debate on public issues should be uninhibited, robust, and wide-open" may rival Justice Holmes's marketplace of ideas, from his dissent in *Abrams v. United States* (1919), as a font of speech protection.

Or would historians fail to note the author of *Penn Central Transportation Co. v. New York City* (1978), the "landmark" opinion that was itself the first landmark in half a century of the Court's jurisprudence on compensable governmental takings? Maybe it's not as famous as

Baker v. Carr and *New York Times v. Sullivan,* but *Penn Central* was the first of the Court's cases to address the limits of uncompensated restrictions on property rights since Justice Holmes said in *Pennsylvania Coal Co. v. Mahon* (1922) that "while property may be regulated to a certain extent, if regulation goes too far it will be recognized as a taking." The occasion for *Penn Central* was a landmarks preservation law, and the authority it conferred on New York City to resist construction of a fifty-three-story office building on top of Grand Central Terminal. Justice Brennan's opinion for the Court rejected the owners' challenge to the law and established a three-point analytical framework looking to economic impact, interference with distinct investment-backed expectations, and the character of the governmental action. *Penn Central* is still with us and sure to be seen as a reference point in the evolution of takings doctrine.

But there isn't time or space to go on marshaling evidence of doctrinal nobility this way, and for most of the Brennan eminences, a string cite will have to be excused: *Bivens v. Six Unknown Named Agents* (1971) (damages for constitutional violations by federal officials); *Craig v. Boren* (1976) (intermediate scrutiny in gender discrimination cases); *Davis v. Passman* (1979) (*Bivens* action for sex discrimination); *Dombrowski v. Pfister* (1965) (First Amendment overbreadth); *Fay v. Noia* (1963) (waiver standard in habeas cases); *Goldberg v. Kelly* (1970) (due process before termination of welfare benefits); *Green v. County School Board* (1968) (prompt school integration under *Brown*); *Katzenbach v. Morgan* (1966) (congressional powers under Section 5 of the Fourteenth Amendment); *Larson v. Valente* (1982) (strict scrutiny for government preferences for religious denominations); *Malloy v. Hogan* (1964) (application of Fifth Amendment privilege against self-incrimination to the states); *Metro Broadcasting, Inc. v. FCC* (1990) (intermediate scrutiny for federal affirmative action); *Missouri v. Jenkins* (1989) (Eleventh Amendment's allowance of attorney fee awards); *Monell v. Department of Social Service* (1978) (local government liability for unconstitutional customs or policies under 42 U.S.C., Section 1983); *NAACP v. Button* (1963) (First Amendment protection of litigation); *Nixon v. Administrator of General Services* (1977) (executive privilege); *Pennsylvania v. Union Gas Co.* (1989) (congressional abrogation of state sovereign immunity); *Plyler v. Doe* (1982) (equal protection of children of illegal aliens); *Roth v. United States* (1957) (exclusion of obscenity from First Amendment protection); *Shapiro v. Thompson* (1969) (strict equal protection scrutiny for statute burdening right to travel); *Sherbert v. Verner* (1963) (accommodation of religious practices under free exercise clause); *Speiser v. Randall* (1958) (state burden of proof in free speech cases); *United Steelworkers v. Weber* (1979) (Title VII's allowance of affirmative action); *Texas v. Johnson* (1989) (First Amendment protection of flag burning); *Thornburg v. Gingles* (1986) (vote dilution under Voting Rights Act); *In re Winship* (1970) (due process requirement of proof beyond a reasonable doubt in juvenile cases).

The list is even growing. Not that Justice Brennan is ghosting opinions for any of us (though if he had the chance he would; if an unsigned draft ever slides under the door, I'll have reasonable suspicion). But scholarship is turning up Brennan authorship and influence in significant opinions that bear no Brennan name. "The voice is Jacob's voice. . . ." Here are two examples.

The first, in *Brandenburg v. Ohio* (1969), has no acknowledged parentage. The opinion is by per curiam, the author for all occasions when signed work won't do, as, for instance, when the author of the first draft takes untimely leave. So it was in *Brandenburg,* as we have recently been apprised by Bernard Schwartz. The per curiam was Justice Brennan's, and it was his largely by adoption, but adoption with a twist that First Amendment history won't ignore. When *Brandenburg* first came before the Court, Justice Fortas was on the bench, and it was he who circulated a draft opinion harking back to Holmes and clear and present danger: "The constitutional guarantees of free speech and free press do not permit a state to forbid or proscribe advocacy of the use of force or of law violation except where such advocacy is directed to inciting or producing imminent lawless action and is attended by present danger that such action may in fact be provoked." One of the critics of the old clear-and-present-danger test (with its proven susceptibility to manipulation) was Justice Douglas, who poured his dissatisfaction into the draft of a concurring opinion. Before either draft got as far as the bench, however, Justice Fortas resigned and the Court's opinion was reassigned to Justice Brennan. His papers showed little tampering with the Fortas language, save on one point. Where the first draft conditioned any permissible restriction on proof that the speech would be "attended by present danger that such action may in fact be provoked," Justice Brennan changed the condition to read, "likely to incite or produce such action." The shift was subtle; Justice Douglas never threw away his concurring opinion. Nor did the change incite any response from those who joined the per curiam (so far as we can tell from the private papers available). And yet *Brandenburg* today is a First Amendment compass point, right up there with the Brennan-name opinions in that long cite string above.

Mention of Justice Douglas calls to mind another milestone that bears no Brennan name but a very substantial Brennan inheritance, *Griswold v. Connecticut* (1965). Part of the story of that case is very familiar by now, how Connecticut's birth control statute had first come up to the Court in *Poe v. Ullman* (1961) (in which Justice Brennan had agreed to dismissal for want of a substantial controversy), only to be brought back four years later in *Griswold,* which held it unconstitutional. Everybody recognizes the "emanations" and "penumbras" of the Bill of Rights in Justice Douglas's opinion for the Court, but without recent scholarship (from Bernard Schwartz and David Garrow) most of us would know nothing about Justice Brennan's important impact on the Court's final opinion.

In the first draft, Justice Douglas rested the conclusion ultimately on the right of association protected by the First Amendment, reasoning that any associational right stopping short of protecting marriage would be a "travesty." But the opinion finally released recognized a right of marital privacy flowing not only from First Amendment association, but from the Third, Fourth, and Fifth Amendments, too, with a nod to the Ninth. The change occurred after a memo to the author from Justice Brennan, urging protection of marital privacy without sole reliance on First Amendment association, and the kaleidoscope of sources in the Court's published decision was just the mixture that Justice Brennan had recommended.

Knowing the Brennan role in *Griswold* not only makes for another addition to the string cite, of course, but illuminates the path to *Roe v. Wade* (1973). We have already seen Justice Brennan's part in *Eisenstadt's* conceptual shift from *Griswold's* marital privacy to a very individual privacy right, a crucial step toward *Roe.* But now we (and doctrinal historians down the road) can see *Eisenstadt* not as the first, but as the second major Brennan accomplishment leading to the current conception of reproductive privacy. The points that set the trajectory to the modern law are both Brennan points.

Maybe the unseen Brennan hand will emerge again as more internal papers come to light for the scholars to pore over. It will be good fun if it happens, but just so much more coal to Newcastle. It would be greed to ask for any more defining doctrinal statements from Justice

Brennan than the ones we know he wrote: on prior restraint of speech, public figure defamation, association, equal protection for women, administrative due process, desegregation, voting rights, municipal constitutional liability, landmark protection, the right to travel, establishment of religion, adjudication of juvenile delinquency, reproductive privacy. I wonder who in the present century could match the Justice's list of major opinions likely to endure; if I had to judge right now, I'd say no one could, though I know that history demands a perspective I can't claim in the spring of 1996. For now, it is enough to say that if we can make any prediction of enduring influence, we can make it of William Brennan. On all the subjects in that long list, the lines of development, unknowable today, will lead back to a Brennan statement, still revered a century hence, perhaps, or perhaps taken as a point of doctrinal rebellion by some later Court; but, either way, to be accounted for. Historians surely will have to see the Justice as the father of an intellectual multitude, acting on countless lives, every day. But they will attend to him for more even than that.

Justice Brennan has proposed his own principle of unity to bind together that great multiplicity of opinions that bear his stamp. "The Essential Dignity of Man" was what he called it in the title of a 1961 speech, and the discrete holdings on voting rights, libel, "new" property rights, and gender equality have been for him only instances of what he called a "constitutional vision of human dignity," one powerful enough in his eyes to condemn even the constitutionally recognized death penalty as cruel and unusual. The conception comes from a man who was not quite a month old on the tenth anniversary of *Plessy v. Ferguson* (1896), who grew up in a nation that largely accepted the separateness that *Plessy* sanctioned, and who ultimately dedicated his tenure on the bench to attacking the human diminishment that *Plessy* implied, replacing it with a vision of worth to be recognized in every last person in the republic. He saw the enormous corpus of his work stretching across thirty-four years of federal judging as epitomized in that vision, much as history, I expect, will see the Justice himself as epitomizing the liberal judiciary of his time. He arrived in the aftermath of *Brown* and left after giving what may come to be seen as the final blessing to affirmative action in *Metro Broadcasting*. Black and Douglas and Warren were on the Court when he came to it; his retirement in 1990 anticipated Thurgood Marshall's by only one term, and Harry Blackmun's by only four. Justice Brennan's tenure was the longest of all the links between the Court's liberals of the New Deal and those of the later century, and his years on the Court's bench enfold the ascendancy of modern liberal jurisprudence, as for at least a decade his positions were the measure of its undeniable hegemony.

Does anyone seriously wonder whether the man whose friendship and affection honor those of us with the fortune to receive them will himself be honored by the consideration of history? My thoughts end as they began, with a question whose answer none of us has the power to doubt.

The Yardstick for Us All

Roberta Cooper Ramo

Most of the time, lawyers in private practice feel far removed from the United States Supreme Court. Ironically, at the same time most lawyers, whatever their area of practice, feel great pride and closeness to the Court in a very personal way. In medicine, there is no chief doctor and even the surgeon general, when we have one, holds no formal tie to providing medical care or setting research goals. No one claims to be head architect or number-one accountant. But the nine men and women of the United States Supreme Court are not just the lawyer chiefs—they are the ultimate people's court. We lawyers watch the justices, each and all, and listen with enormous fascination to news of controversial cases that break new ground or clarify old rules.

If we get the chance to be in Washington, we walk up what seem to be the 1,000 marble steps of the Supreme Court Building. We have our pictures taken in front of the building, taking special care to make the chiseled words "Equal Justice Under Law" appear over our shoulders. We feel goosebumps when we look into the courtroom that produced *Brown v. Board of Education* (1954), remembering how wrong the Court was in *Dred Scott* (1856), how brave in *Roe v. Wade* (1973), and how key to the shaping of our contemporary democracy in *Baker v. Carr* (1962).

We lawyers stand inside the Court chamber, first wondering how it would feel to argue any side of any case in the chamber that heard Abe Fortas argue *Gideon v. Wainwright* (1963) (finding a right to court-appointed lawyers in criminal cases), Thurgood Marshall argue *Brown*, and Ruth Bader Ginsburg argue *Frontiero v. Richardson* (1973) (striking a federal law that reduced benefits for female officers). Then, like eight-year-olds playing out a role in the NCAA Final Four or an Olympic downhill race, we don a black robe and fly behind the bench: Justice Ramo has a question, Justice Smith and Justice Chavez next. Finally, we

The author, who was president of the American Bar Association when she wrote this essay in 1996, is a partner at Modrall, Sperling, Roehl, Harris & Sisk in Albuquerque.

think about the men and women who do sit on that bench and we wonder about their lives. And although most of us never have the honor of meeting a justice, we feel that we know these great minds and great people.

In that same sense, although I have never had the honor of meeting Justice Brennan, I feel that I know him. Through his work, both on and off the bench, he has represented the very best that our legal system offers. Justice Brennan stands as a yardstick against which we measure ourselves as people and as brothers and sisters at the bar.

In his thirty-four years on the Court, Justice Brennan served as the people's justice and, in many ways, the lawyer's justice. His opinions and his votes joined adherence to his bedrock principles with, at the same time, a flexibility that most often crafted a majority opinion and gave us a needed framework for future cases.

There are three aspects to his years on the United States Supreme Court that ring with special resonance to lawyers. First, he never isolated himself from the rest of the profession, but continued a wide range of professional interaction. Second, he worked hard to define a middle for the majority in difficult situations, which is what most of us do for our clients whether in court or in our offices. Finally, his ability to be powerful yet feel the pain of powerlessness, to be at the height of American society yet never forget the need to protect the individual from the majority or the vast power of the government, represents what lawyers are really about. We are members of the profession, loved or loathed, who combine our independence with our oath to protect the United States Constitution as officers of the court. We are called upon every day to protect not just the powerful, but also those whom the rest of the world would throw away or run over using "the greater good" to comfort themselves from any pang of conscience. To lawyers, Justice Brennan's career on the Supreme Court embodies the model of professional passion, personal compassion, and problem solving that we strive to meet.

Justice Brennan's influence on the profession in part arose from his willingness to step outside the marble Court to speak on a regular basis to law students and lawyers. He understood that, for all of us in practice, the Court is far more than the arbiter of major cases on the law. Its justices are our models, our teachers, our gadflies, and the ultimate reminders that our justice is made one case at a time.

While it is important to their complete independence that the justices be removed to some degree from the grind of daily society, lawyers and the legal system would be far poorer in every way if there were no interaction at all with the justices. Throughout his time on the Court, Justice Brennan spoke to law students and to the profession on matters of importance to our country's legal system. Even the titles of some of his speeches seem prescient. In 1990, for example, he gave an important lecture at Washington University Law School titled "The Criminal Prosecution: Sporting Event or Quest for Truth? A Progress Report." One can only imagine how he views the advent of criminal trials as the soap operas of 1995.

After seven years on the Court, Justice Brennan returned to Harvard Law School to help celebrate the fiftieth anniversary of the Harvard Legal Aid Bureau. While his remarks sharply pointed out the need for the law school and the profession to spend more time attending to the public good, he demonstrated why, however far from his beginnings, he never forgot what it felt like to be less than adequate at some moments. With a quick story, he endeared himself to every lawyer who, in those early days of practice, had been set straight and put in her place by a judge.

> Just after I was admitted to the Bar, I was assigned to defend a young man charged with manslaughter by automobile. I obtained a character witness, an elderly retired gentleman from the boy's neighborhood. I asked him the question from the book: "Do you know young Logan's reputation in his neighborhood for truth and veracity?" The old gentleman promptly replied, "He's a good automobile driver." I had no better sense than to stick to the book and ask the same question twice more in the same words. I got only louder and irritated responses. "I've told you. He's a good automobile driver." The jury and the spectators were amused but not the trial judge. He took over and asked, "Mr. Witness, does Logan tell the truth?" The old gentlemen replied, "I've never known him to tell a lie, Your Honor." "Well Mr. Witness," said the Judge, "that's what Mr. Brennan was asking you, but you see, he's a Harvard graduate and doesn't speak English."

In 1968, Justice Brennan wrote a piece in the *American Bar Association Journal* setting out "The Responsibilities of the Legal Profession."

> We have been a legalistic society from the beginning. Lawyers were conspicuous in the vanguard of the revolutionary movement and in the draft-

ing of the Constitution, and ever since, the diversity of our people, combined with their ingrained sense of justice and moral duty, has caused the society to frame urgent social, economic and political questions in legal terms—to place great problems of social order in the hands of lawyers for their definition, and in the hands of judges for their ultimate resolution. . . . it seems to me unquestionable that the lawyer in America is uniquely situated to play a creative role in American social progress. Indeed I would make bold to suggest that the success with which he responds to the challenges of what is certainly a new era of crisis and of promise in the life of our nation may prove decisive in determining the outcome of the social experiments on which we are embarked.

Then, in his usual scholarly way, Justice Brennan devoted much of the essay to telling us that we have let the nation down and not risen to the challenges required. He set out practical ways for lawyers and the bar to meet our public responsibilities. The Justice who is so attendant to individual rights ends with this directive to lawyers about their individual responsibilities:

In the final analysis the obligation rests on the individual lawyer, whatever may currently be his position within the profession, whether he is in a large or small firm or is an individual practitioner, to devote himself, however it may be possible, to some project involving the public interest. Every lawyer should have at any given time, I think, at least one public service project to which he is in some manner actively devoting his professional ability.

Justice Brennan never hesitated to tell us as lawyers what was expected of us in our individual practices and in improving the law or legal education. Because it was so clear in his mind that the success of American society was in large part dependent upon American lawyers, he left the halls of the Court often enough to remind us that he was once a lawyer representing a driver accused of manslaughter and knew what it was like to be in practice. Always, he required greatness of each of us in our everyday lives at the bar.

Lawyers understand, perhaps better than the general public, that each justice is only one of nine and, without the ability to find at least four others in agreement, is destined to write nothing but concurring or dissenting opinions with no real power to change the law. Justice Brennan understood well that the great give-and-take of the Court was a crucial exercise in finding the middle ground, and that often the process of exchanging ideas itself changed minds and helped define the holding in a much better way.

To lawyers or judges, this give-and-take is not an academic exercise or a game, but rather the key to one of the aspects of the American justice system that makes it strong and unique. A Supreme Court decision comes from a combination of immutable first principles of each of the nine justices against which is woven the decisions of past Courts, the facts of the particular case, and the constitutional question that is raised. Justice Brennan's opinions over the years speak of, and show the importance of, finding common ground. In some areas it took him many years to find that place; in others it seemed easily won. In these days of negative and socially painful polemics based often on complete ignorance of the facts, learned discussion, listening, and then scholarly writing seem even more valuable than in those days in Philadelphia when the genius of our system was conceived.

Justice Brennan's first decade on the Court led to a tribute by Lord Parker of Waddington, then lord chief justice of England. He understood very well how our Supreme Court must work, and he wrote of Justice Brennan, who, as the son of an Irish laborer, must have especially enjoyed the source:

> Justice Brennan, as compared with Justice Holmes who became known as The Great Dissenter, has more often functioned as the balance wheel, standing in the center and working out the uneasy compromises and accommodations necessary for the Court to get on with its work. [Justice Brennan] has worked out the decisions which would command the assent of a majority when the Court seemed hopelessly split into minor fragments. It has often fallen to him, too, as in the sit-in cases, to tread the difficult line between clear-cut extremes at a time when there was no clear consensus among the Justices or in the country.

Working to find consensus when it seems impossible is what the best lawyers do in their practices and as some of our country's best citizens. When we are at the very top of our professional game, it is not as masters of the arcane or as adversaries. It is, rather, Brennan-like, listening to everyone and helping each no matter where she sits to find those principles that cannot be moved and articulate them so they can be accepted by others with equally strong views to make sure that the process continues to move forward. Recent political wars in which compromise has become a synonym for defeat have resulted in chaos, not accomplishment. Lawyers in public life who emulate Justice Brennan never give up their core beliefs, but work to fashion the compromises required to solve our deepest social problems and our simpler ones, too.

In the struggles of American life, Justice Brennan's strong sensitivity to individual human rights moves lawyers most. No matter how powerful he became, every day, in every case, Justice Brennan perceived the human beings being affected. He cared about the Bill of Rights not out of any school of politics but because he somehow always knew what it must feel like to be at the bottom of the social heap, to be at the mercy of a powerful government, to be seen as less than human because of the color of your skin, as less than intelligent because of your gender.

He reminded everyone at that dinner in honor of the Legal Aid Bureau why it was important for every single lawyer to know how it felt to be without resources. "There was also the lesson [from Legal Aid] that living law has its compassionate aspects—helping confused and worried little people over problems of rent and family and small inheritances—problems of little or no significance in the large but which can assume terrifying proportions for the people concerned."

What Justice Brennan's opinions, speeches, and writings tell lawyers in practice is that we do not deserve our licenses if we ever forget for one day that we are officers of an American justice system that must work for all of the people all of the time. Someone "loses" in every court case. What must not ever be lost is the party's faith in the integrity, caring, and fairness of the system.

Justice Brennan at the Court was the "People's Justice" and also ours. He required excellence in legal reasoning, flexibility in coming to decisions, and absolute firmness on basic constitutional principles. He is a warm human being. The model for lawyers comes not just from his writing or his powerful intellect, but from his understanding, his passion for justice, and his human touch.

Burt Neuborne, a professor of constitutional law at New York University Law School, speaking at a roundtable in the *ABA Journal* entitled "The Brennan Legacy," explained his impact in one vignette. "When [Justice Brennan] entered the room [in 1986] to deliver the second Madison Lecture, a significant proportion of the audience had tears in their eyes. This is not an emotional crowd. These are lawyers, law professors, judges, these are not people who are given to shows of emotion. . . . When he walked in, they gave a standing ovation of at least 20 minutes and people cried, because they saw in Brennan what a lot of them became lawyers for."

What impact does any single justice have on the profession? In the case of Justice Brennan, it is this: In many of our heads, many days, we lawyers wonder to ourselves, "Did I do my job this week the way Justice Brennan expects?" When most of us answer yes, that will be a great time indeed for our profession and our country.

The View from a Distant Vantage Point

BRIAN WALSH

At the very outset I must admit to not being a neutral observer where Justice Brennan is concerned. Ever since I first made his acquaintance thirty-five years ago I have been an admirer as well as enjoying a warm personal friendship with him. Our friendship commenced in about 1961, which was when I became a member of the Supreme Court of Ireland. Thereafter, on very many occasions in both the United States and Ireland, I have had the pleasure of meeting with him and conferring with him. These meetings and discussions have continued since my compulsory retirement on reaching the age of seventy-two in 1990, which was the year of his own voluntary retirement from the Supreme Court of the United States. Over the years I have also enjoyed the great pleasure of the friendship of members of Justice Brennan's family and of his dear wife, Mary. All these meetings have been for me occasions for continuing my legal education as well as occasions of great personal pleasure.

In the summer of 1968 the Institute of Judicial Administration at New York University invited me to join the faculty for the appellate judges' regular seminar (where in reality I was more of a learner than a teacher). I had for a few weeks the benefit of observing Justice Brennan and learning from him in a very distinguished gathering of members of the United States federal judiciary, including some justices of the Supreme Court and members of the supreme courts of very many states in the Union. In that rare company I had a unique opportunity of witnessing the brightness of his star and the clarity of his thought.

Justice Brennan first swam into my ken some years before I had the pleasure of meeting him. That encounter was on foreign soil. In 1957

The author, a justice on the European Court of Human Rights, was formerly senior associate justice of the Supreme Court of Ireland.

when I was at the bar I appeared before the European Commission of Human Rights in Strasbourg (still some years before the establishment of the Court of Human Rights) as counsel for the government of Ireland. There I was asked to apply my mind to the then recently pronounced opinion of Justice Brennan in the very important case of *Jencks v. United States* (1957), which required prosecutors in criminal cases to turn over written reports to the defense. I was struck by the truth and the stark simplicity of his words, "Justice requires no less." This opinion was self-explanatory, uncomplicated in its language and humane in its outlook.

These characteristics, which appear in so many of the opinions he has handed down, are what make him so attractive to foreign jurists, particularly in the field of human rights and fundamental freedoms. Ironically, it was a former chief justice of New Jersey who said, "We write opinions, we don't explain them." In my opinion it can be truly said of Justice Brennan's opinions that they did not require further explanation.

LEGAL POSITIVISM UNDERMINES EUROPEAN HUMAN RIGHTS

In order to appreciate Justice Brennan's influence outside the United States, particularly as it relates to human rights, it is important to understand the historical backdrop. The United States has gloried in the common law, which reached America from England in 1608. The United States was fortunate to escape most of the malign effects of the philosophy of legal positivism, which developed later, infecting the law in England and much further afield.

Legal positivism enshrined the precept that, in Jeremy Bentham's words, "rights are the fruit of the law and of the law alone. There are no rights without law, no rights contrary to law, no rights anterior to the law." Legal positivism was eagerly embraced by those elements which sought to use the law to undermine human rights. They suppressed the natural-law background, which held that certain rights were inalienable.

The effects are still with us. In the period between World Wars I and II, the positivist philosophy dominated the law in Germany and delivered the German judiciary, bound hand and foot, into the toils of Nazism. The consequent mechanical approach to the judicial function left the law unusable for the protection of the millions who were murdered without breaching the law. The apotheosis of the positivist position, and its consequent downfall, came in Nazi Germany.

AMERICAN REJECTION OF LEGAL POSITIVISM

In the meantime, in the United States, the common law had retained a flexibility and a vigor lost earlier elsewhere. The Declaration of Independence flatly rejected legal positivism, proclaiming that all men were created equal and that they were endowed by their creator with certain "unalienable rights," among which were life, liberty, and the pursuit of happiness. Nor could the Bill of Rights be reconciled with a positivist philosophy. America opted for freedom from the law as distinct from freedom through the law.

What a great source of pride it must be to the citizens of the United States to recall that more than 200 years ago their forefathers produced a Constitution which included guarantees of individual rights which cannot be abridged under any circumstances. The ten amendments comprising the Bill of Rights became the bedrock of the individual liberties which have been so jealously guarded in the United States for more than two centuries.

EUROPE EMBRACES THE AMERICAN EXPERIENCE

Once the democratic world came to appreciate the evils of legal positivism, it was ready to learn from the American experience. Since the end of the Second World War, the public has been concerned with the problems of individual liberty and equality; in all the democratically ruled parts of the world there was a discernible shift in social concern.

The Universal Declaration of Human Rights, proclaimed by the General Assembly of the United Nations in 1948, was the first worldwide manifestation of the desire of the peoples of the world to turn their backs on the tyrannies of the past and not to trust their lives and liberties to the tender mercies of a simple parliamentary majority in their national parliaments.

While the Universal Declaration defined in some detail certain fundamental rights, it was not intended to be a legal instrument binding on member states. However, it did have the advantage of being regarded as an authoritative guide, and did, in effect, for the first time raise the question of the individual before international tribunals.

The first concrete effort to give the individual status before an international tribunal was made by the European Convention of Human Rights and Fundamental Freedoms, which entered into force in 1953. Its preamble expressly stated that the object was to take the first steps for the collective enforcement of certain of the rights stated in the Universal Declaration by the governments of European countries which "are like minded and have a common heritage of political traditions, ideas, freedom and the rule of law." These rights were modeled upon those that the United States had developed over the course of two centuries.

Justice Brennan's Influence on Human Rights

It has been said with truth that the soul of the government of laws is the judicial function. The Supreme Court of the United States stands like a lighthouse in the democratic judicial world. It has illuminated the way and equally it has exposed the dangers.

Wheresoever in the world the United States Supreme Court is known, so also is the name of Justice Brennan. For some years during the 1980s, when I had the honour to be a vice-president and successively the president of the International Association of Judges (a Rome-based organization), I had the privilege of traveling in many countries and meeting judges from all over the world to discuss legal topics and to participate with these judges in study commissions. In every discussion touching upon liberty, or fundamental or human rights, there were invariably references to the United States Supreme Court and in particular to Justice Brennan. That was not in any way surprising given his well-known devotion to, and his widely read views about, the Bill of Rights. His many closely read opinions in this field of law taught that it was the primary task of the judiciary to protect the integrity of the individual and that the procedural aspects of the judicial process are essential safeguards for the substance of human rights.

It may be of special interest to an American reader to learn that virtually no foreign precedents are cited in Irish constitutional case law save those of the United States. This is not dictated by any sentiment but simply by the fact that there are many similarities between the Constitution of Ireland and the Constitution of the United States and, like the United States Supreme Court, the Supreme Court of Ireland is a court of a wide general jurisdiction. (Unlike most European states, Ireland chose the U.S. model instead of a special Constitutional Court. The establishment of Constitutional Courts has now become a virtual "growth industry" in Eastern Europe.) Because of this leaning toward American jurisprudence it is scarcely surprising that in Ireland the name of Justice Brennan and his pronouncements on fundamental rights are held in high esteem and not only out of pride in his ancestry.

Justice Brennan has had a profound impact also on many decisions of the European Court of Human Rights. In many cases the complainant alleged that he had been the victim of an absence of fair procedures. As a member of that court I can testify that very frequently the criteria of the United States Supreme Court, many of which were developed by Justice Brennan, are considered.

In a similar vein, his opinions and addresses have revealed to the world his great interest in making the courts accessible to as many people as possible. People in every country in the world are heartened by such an attitude on the part of such a high judicial officer. In many countries the people are all too accustomed to the type of judges who with dire warnings about "opening floodgates" expend much effort in trying to keep people out of court. It is the universal experience that for the ordinary citizen nothing is more frustrating than the feeling that nobody will hear him. Even where a court grudgingly or reluctantly hears him, he at least has the satisfaction of knowing he had his day in court, notwithstanding that the result was not the one sought.

I am happy to say that in my own country the Supreme Court has for many years always followed this course, not uninfluenced by the views of Justice Brennan. Access to justice has been raised to the level of a constitutional right. (Once, when discussing this topic with members of the German Constitutional Court, I ventured to suggest that it was, in the general interest, far better to have people in court rather than on the streets. I am happy to say the members of that court present appeared to take the same view.)

As pervasive as Justice Brennan's influence has been in these contexts, it cannot compare to his profound influence in the whole field of fundamental rights. The opinions handed down by Justice Brennan during his tenure in the U.S. Supreme Court have caused him to be regarded as akin to the personification of the Court in this field. His famous opinions have greatly strengthened the freedom of expression, the rights of criminal defendants, and the necessary equality of protection of the laws particularly in the fields of racial and sexual discrimination.

His principled views on the death penalty find an echo all over Europe. The Sixth Protocol to the European Convention of Human Rights prohibits the imposition of the death penalty in times of peace and the great majority of the member states of the Council of Europe—twenty-four states out of thirty-seven—have already ratified it, including, I am happy to say, Ireland. In practice, the death penalty no longer exists in Europe. The last execution in Ireland was in 1954.

The famous case of *New York Times v. Sullivan* (1964), in which Justice Brennan delivered the opinion of the Court, has had widespread support and agreement outside the United States. This is particularly so because in some member states of the Council of Europe the law makes the publication of defamatory falsehood relating to a public official a criminal offense, which makes the protection all the more crucial.

Article 10 of the European Convention of Human Rights permits interferences with freedom of expression only when they are prescribed by law and are necessary in a democratic society and only in specified and limited types of cases. The onus of proof is cast upon the state to establish that the restrictions are necessary in a democratic state. In interpreting the freedom of expression guaranteed in the European Convention, the European Court has turned to the *New York Times* case for guidance in the consideration of what are the necessities of a democratic society.

In one respect, the European Court has not yet fully adopted all the protections of *New York Times*. *New York Times* accords the same protection to the press whenever it writes about any conduct of a public official—regardless of whether the conduct is public or private. Unlike *New York Times v. Sullivan,* the European Court has so far drawn a distinction between defamation relating to official conduct and defamation relating to the private life of a public official, according less "press protection" when it reports on private matters.

The cases referred to were essentially criminal cases. It was not until recently that a case, *Tolstoy Miloslavsky v. The United Kingdom,* came before the Court in Strasbourg, relating to civil proceedings in defamation which could have brought into full play the effect of *New York Times v. Sullivan*. Much to the disappointment of many members of the Court the case did not squarely present the question whether a defamation suit involving the private conduct of a public official is subject to the same constraints as a suit involving the official's public conduct.

Thus, the Court in Strasbourg still awaits a civil action in which the full effect of the *New York Times* case will be considered in the light of whether or not the necessities of a democratic society can justify the equation of a defamatory falsehood relating to official or public conduct, made without actual malice or not made recklessly, with a defamatory falsehood relating to a person's private activities.

THE LIVING CONSTITUTION AND HUMAN DIGNITY

All of the opinions by Justice Brennan described above illustrate a consistent philosophical conviction. Justice Brennan has a great belief in the dignity of human beings irrespective of race or origin. He has a concept of a higher law that proclaims that man has inherent inalienable rights simply because he is man and that the law must be concerned with seeing things whole and draw its validity from its position in the entire scheme of things. He draws inspiration from the significance that the Constitution of the United States is written in the present tense and that the protection for human liberty that it proclaims means protection today. Justice Brandeis once wrote, in an unpublished dissent, that "the United States Constitution is 'a living organism.' As such it is capable of growth—of expansion and of adaptation to new conditions. . . . Because our Constitution possesses the capacity of adaptation, it has endured as the fundamental law of an ever developing people."

I believe that this concept of unenumerated rights which can still call for constitutional protection is not far from the mind of Justice Brennan. The fact that the Founding Fathers had not experienced or been confronted with the types of problems and situations which arise in modern conditions of life does not mean that they fall outside the sweep of the broad but fundamental principles enunciated by them. In Irish constitutional jurisprudence a very wide range of unenumerated rights has been recognized and given the full force of constitutional protection. In many instances these are traditional common-law rights transformed into constitutional rights. This is also partly due to the fact that the Constitution of Ireland gives a higher place to justice than it does to law and in the clauses dealing with fundamental rights there is an expressed recognition of the existence of a higher law when they speak of certain rights "being anterior to and antecedent to all positive law." In Ireland the Constitution means what the Supreme Court says it means, words which are not unfamiliar to American jurists.

I have always regarded the common law as a system of law which builds the law case by case, in decisions which reflect the ideas, the customs, and the beliefs of the people of the particular country rather than a worldwide body of law applicable to all common-law countries.

Justice Brennan's opinions demonstrated that he was always conscious of how the laws affected real people and of the fact that native common sense is an essential element in the judicial solution. This commends him to a world which has suffered so much from legal positivism and has learned that human rights are founded on the very nature of man.

It has been said that in many respects the legacy of Justice Brennan is to be found in the statutes and jury verdicts. But it has also been pointed out that his legacy will also be found in the state courts because an entire generation of judges was educated to receive Justice Brennan's ideas as an orthodoxy which they now apply.

The same may be said of his influence abroad, and particularly in countries which have had a common-law tradition. During the last forty years the opinions of Justice Brennan have been admired and carefully studied. Law teachers add a new excitement to the lives of their students by relying heavily on the opinions of Justice Brennan in the field of fundamental rights. Many judges in their own opinions have borrowed heavily from his opinions without always acknowledging their source. In most cases, particularly at the highest levels of courts, these unacknowledged borrowings reflect not a vulgar plagiarism but rather a desire to emphasize their importance by "nationalizing" them and thus ensuring that the ideas are safely engrafted onto the national jurisprudence because they appear not only to the judges but also to the public as being so fundamentally just and fair.

Justice Brennan has traveled in many countries outside the United States and judges of other countries who have had the privilege of meeting him and speaking with him are often surprised to confront a man of such vitality and who has such a pleasant smile and warm handshake and an enthusiasm to meet people. They warm instantly to him and for those who are familiar with his work there is also an instant recognition that behind his modest demeanor and engaging personality there is an outstandingly great jurist. One recalls the words of the Irish poet Oliver Goldsmith, in "The Deserted Village": "And still they gazed, and still the wonder grew, that one small head could carry all he knew." This impression has been a most potent force in the acceptance of the validity, and attractiveness, of his opinions.

I am more than happy to acknowledge borrowing from the late Justice Goldberg what he said in his tribute thirty years ago: "This kindly, warm, and thoughtful man is one of the finest human beings there are." Justice Brennan so often used a quotation from W. B. Yeats's play *Cathleen Ni Houlihan* to illustrate the aged but endless "quest for the freedom, the dignity and the rights of men":

> "Did you see an old woman going down the path?"
> "I did not," replied Patrick, "but I saw a young girl and she had the walk of a queen."

If I might borrow from and build upon the quotation, I assert that we do not see a man old in legal history but rather a man who is ninety years young. *"Felix qui potuit rerum cognoscere causas."* How appropriate is Virgil's compliment for the philosopher judge who centered his pleasure in that which was for the benefit or instruction of mankind.

Justice Brennan's Influence on His Colleagues

HARRY A. BLACKMUN

Linking the word "influence" with the Brennan name is almost to state a redundancy, for the Justice's judicial life, as these essays demonstrate so convincingly, has had a profound influence in the enunciation of governing legal principles, in the law's development and its achievement of new principles, and in making the law known and intelligible to the layperson. Small in stature, articulate, pleasant in personality, seldom showing resentment or a grudge, he was not only likable but well liked, a winning combination for outstanding judicial activity.

One might be content merely to state a skeleton biography and let it speak for itself. Thus, one might say:

> William Joseph Brennan, Jr., was born in Newark, New Jersey, April 25, 1906. He received his bachelor's degree from the University of Pennsylvania in 1928 and his law degree from Harvard in 1931. He has been the recipient of numerous honorary degrees, including those from Harvard, Yale, Princeton, Pennsylvania, Notre Dame, Columbia, and Brandeis. He was admitted to the New Jersey bar in 1931 and practiced in Newark for eighteen years. He served on New Jersey tribunals as a judge of the superior court for a year, of the appellate division for three years, and as a justice of the state's supreme court for four years. He rose to the rank of colonel with the General Staff Corps of the United States Army in World War II. He was an associate justice of the Supreme Court of the United States from October 16, 1956, until he took retirement status on July 20, 1990, a period of over thirty-three years. He served as the only Roman Catholic on the Court for thirty years.

One might say that the foregoing paragraph, or one like it, is the raw judicial biography of Mr. Justice Brennan, and that is all that need

The author is associate justice, retired, of the Supreme Court of the United States, who served on the bench with Justice Brennan for twenty years.

be said. There would be much truth in that conclusion, for it reveals his character, his staying power, and his acceptance by fellow jurists. But there is so much more.

I shall attempt to fill in some of the gaps, although the facts are known by all constitutional scholars and students and Supreme Court watchers.

Son of a New Jersey labor leader, the Justice had a childhood exposure to what I presume to call the class struggle. He was not "born" to riches of privilege or of intellectual renown or of accepted authority. He had the good fortune to be of pleasing Irish ancestry. It stood him in fine stead and gave him a valuable charm and ease of manner.

Some commentators have described Justice Brennan primarily as a "consensus builder," able to pull five justices together to a common ground of his liking. Perhaps so. If that description compels an image of a chambers-visiting, table-pounding advocate—as, in my eyes, the description seems to do—that was not my experience with Justice Brennan. Instead, my experience with him was that he stated his case—at conference and in any opinion he circulated—in quiet but firm tones, persuasively to be sure, but never in a two-fisted, belligerent, or quarrelsome manner. He was a gentleman, first and foremost, and quite content to leave the infighting and elbow-punching to others. I cannot say that he enjoyed the infighting. He watched and, I suppose, tolerated it. Yet he could be embarrassed by it, too, as was evident to me on occasion. And who is to say that his is not the far better approach?

Justice Brennan has lived in every decade of the twentieth century. He, most of all, represents this century on the Court. On January 1, 1901, when the century began, the Supreme Court consisted of Chief Justice Fuller, the first Justice Harlan, and Justices Gray, Brewer, Brown, Shiras, Edward Douglass White, Peckham, and McKenna. When Justice Brennan retired, it consisted of Chief Justice Rehnquist and Justices Brennan, Byron R. White, Thurgood Marshall, Stevens, O'Connor, Scalia, Kennedy, and myself. As we know, Justice Souter succeeded Justice Brennan.

Do these two arrays of personnel indicate a profound change of direction in the Court? I would have difficulty in drawing contrasts of liberal/conservative, or of federal/state rights, or of outstanding/ mediocre/poor ability, or of political/nonpolitical overtones and influences, or of any other meaningful measurement. It was a tribunal where the dynamics and leading influences naturally changed somewhat with every new face, but there was no change of earthquake or major proportion. The multiple membership was a steadying factor and surely was so intended. Yet through such changes as were made—Whittaker for Reed, Stewart for Burton, Byron White for Whittaker, Goldberg for Frankfurter, Fortas for Goldberg, Thurgood Marshall for Clark, Burger for Warren, I for Fortas, Powell for Black, Rehnquist for the second Harlan, Stevens for Douglas, O'Connor for Stewart, and Kennedy for Powell—Brennan was there ascending in seniority or observing adjustments in the rungs of the seniority ladder junior to him. He served with 22 justices of the 108 that have been on the Court. His is an enduring influence. That perhaps is the major key in evaluating his influence on his colleagues.

By any measure, William J. Brennan, Jr., must be classified as one of the great justices of our time and, indeed, of all those who have served on the Supreme Court of the United States. And he has exerted a profound influence upon his colleagues over the long period of his service. We are all the better because of that influence.

ROB ROGERS reprinted by permission of United Feature Syndicate, Inc.